Super Visible

SUPER
VISIBLE

THE STORY OF THE WOMEN OF MARVEL COMICS

MARGARET STOHL

WITH JEANINE SCHAEFER AND JUDITH STEPHENS

GALLERY 13 BOOKS
New York Amsterdam/Antwerp London
Toronto Sydney/Melbourne New Delhi

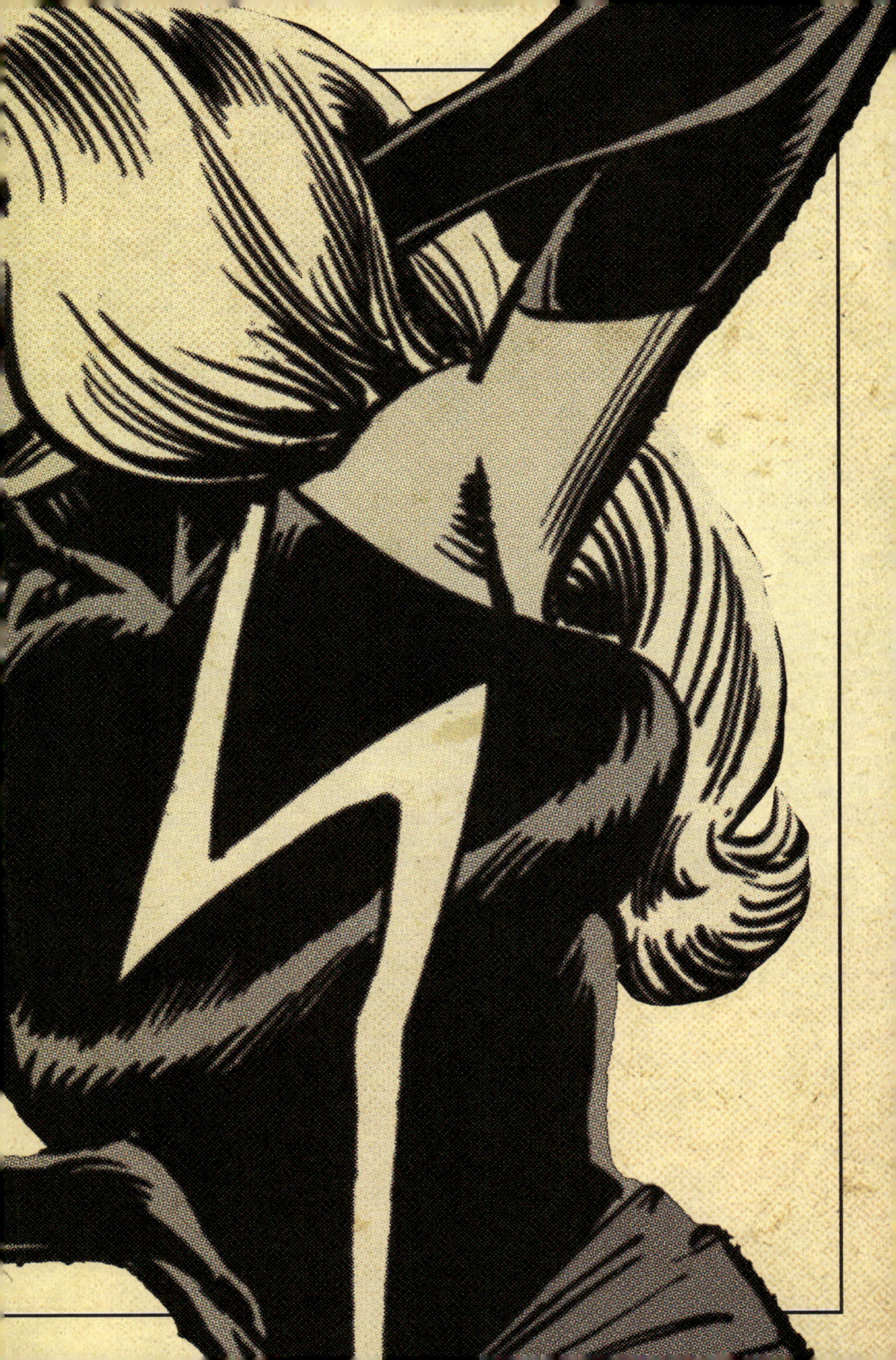

An Imprint of Simon & Schuster, LLC
1230 Avenue of the Americas
New York, NY 10020

© 2025 MARVEL
MARVEL PUBLISHING
Jeff Youngquist, VP, Production and Special Projects
Brian Overton, Manager, Special Projects
Sarah Singer, Editor, Special Projects
Jeremy West, Manager, Licensed Publishing
Sven Larsen, VP, Licensed Publishing
David Gabriel, VP, Print & Digital Publishing
C. B. Cebulski, Editor in Chief

All rights reserved, including the right to reproduce this book or portions thereof in any form whatsoever. For information, address Gallery Books Subsidiary Rights Department, 1230 Avenue of the Americas, New York, NY 10020.

First Gallery 13 hardcover edition June 2025

GALLERY 13 and colophon are trademarks of Simon & Schuster, LLC

Simon & Schuster strongly believes in freedom of expression and stands against censorship in all its forms. For more information, visit BooksBelong.com.

For information about special discounts for bulk purchases, please contact Simon & Schuster Special Sales at 1-866-506-1949 or business@simonandschuster.com.

The Simon & Schuster Speakers Bureau can bring authors to your live event. For more information or to book an event, contact the Simon & Schuster Speakers Bureau at 1-866-248-3049 or visit our website at www.simonspeakers.com.

Interior design by Laura Palese

Manufactured in the United States of America

1 3 5 7 9 10 8 6 4 2

Library of Congress Cataloging-in-Publication Data is available.

ISBN 978-1-9821-3461-7
ISBN 978-1-9821-3463-1 (ebook)

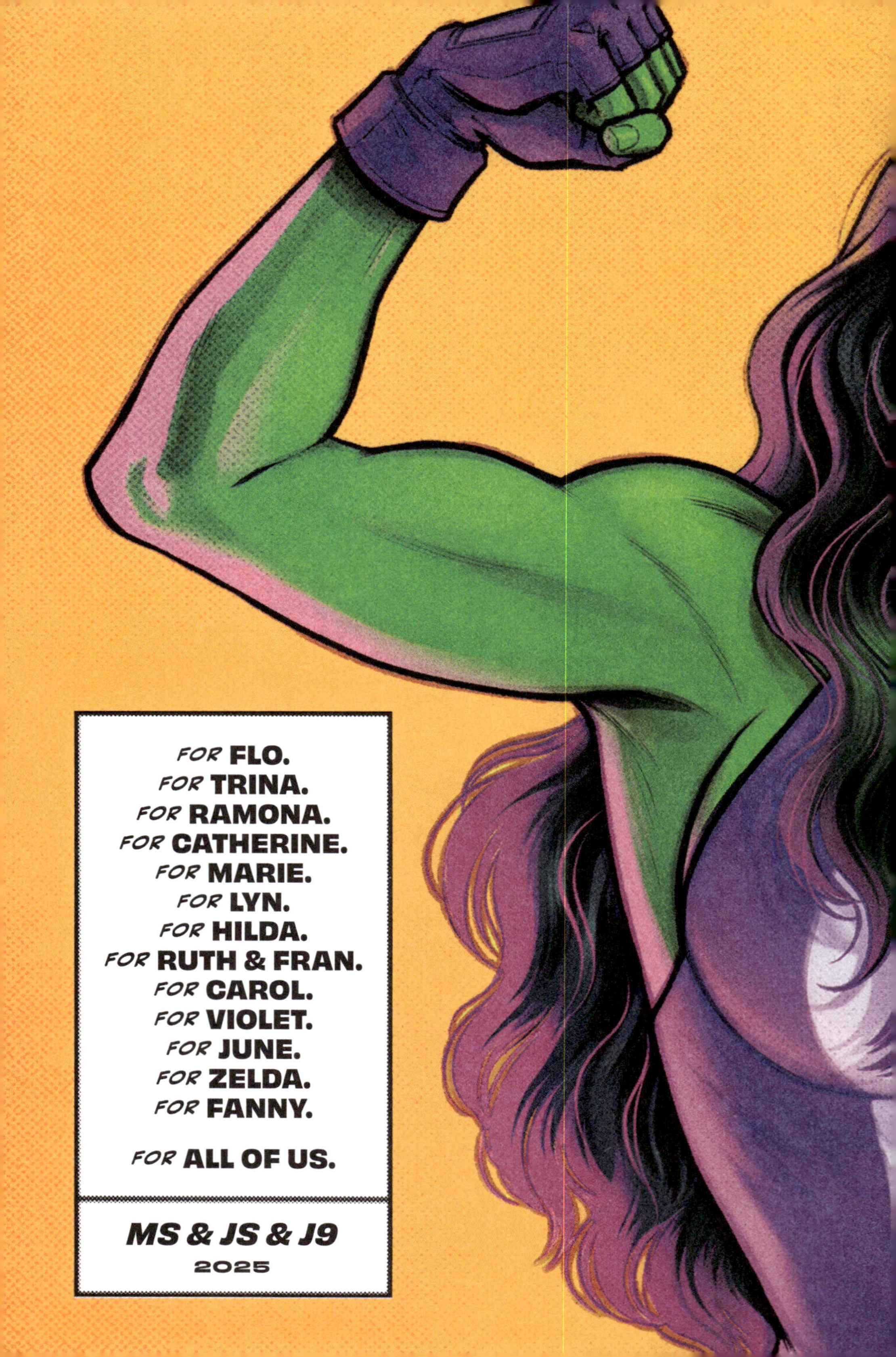

FOR **FLO.**
FOR **TRINA.**
FOR **RAMONA.**
FOR **CATHERINE.**
FOR **MARIE.**
FOR **LYN.**
FOR **HILDA.**
FOR **RUTH & FRAN.**
FOR **CAROL.**
FOR **VIOLET.**
FOR **JUNE.**
FOR **ZELDA.**
FOR **FANNY.**

FOR **ALL OF US.**

MS & JS & J9
2025

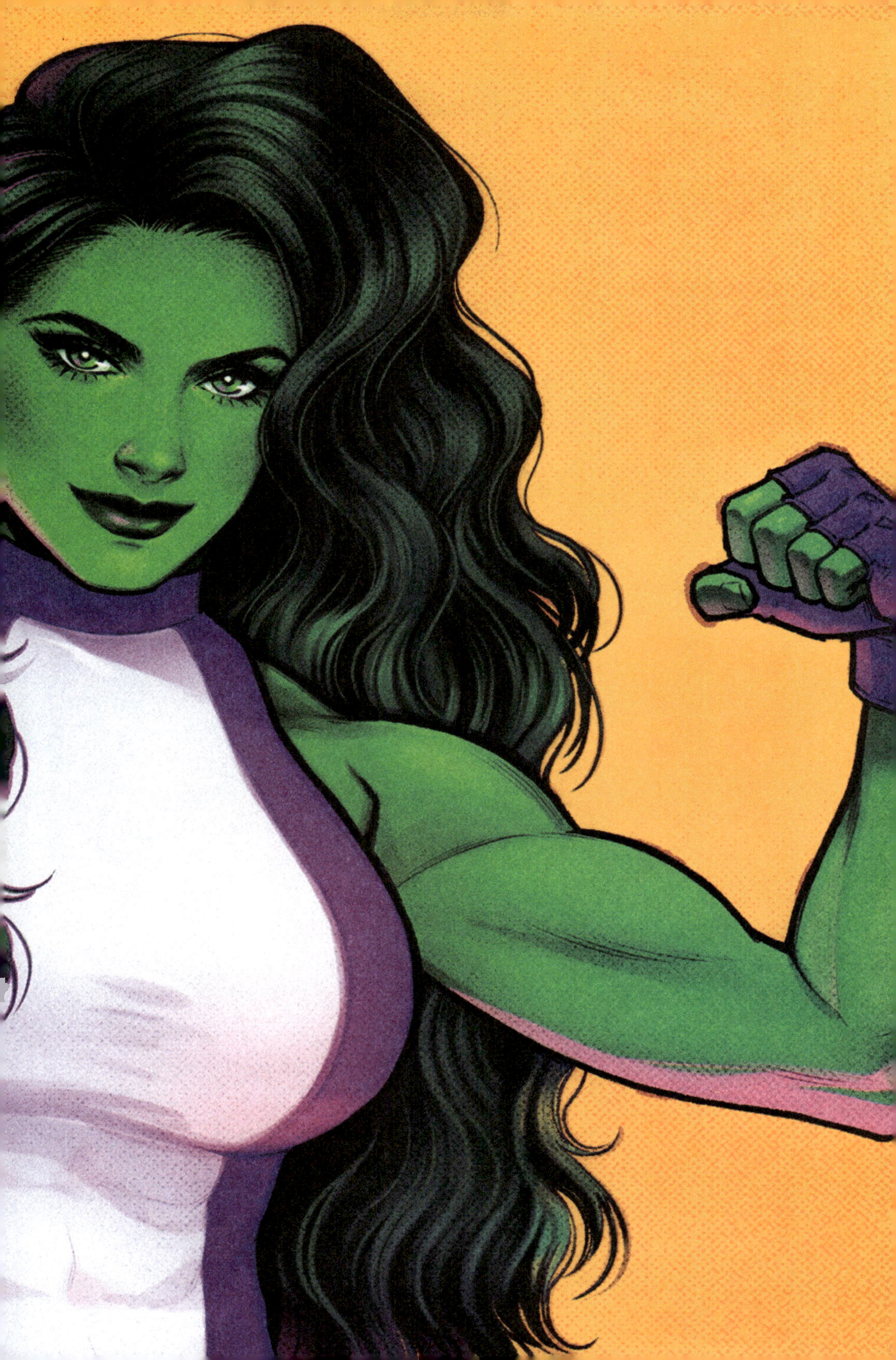

CONTENTS

400 PAGES!

PREFACE XII

CAST OF CONTRIBUTORS XIV

PROLOGUE: THE SECRET DEFINITIVE ONE STORY OF ALL WOMEN AT MARVEL, EVER XVIII

PART ONE

THE VISIBLE (SUPER) WOMAN: WOMEN IN THE FIRST TWO DECADES OF MARVEL COMICS

CHAPTER ONE
It Took a Village: Marvel Comics in the '60s, and the Women Who Ran the House of Ideas 3

CHAPTER TWO
Going Underground: The Underground Comix Scene, Marvel, and the Woman at the Center of Both 35

ORAL HISTORY: Heifers in the Bullpen 44

ORAL HISTORY: Louise Simonson 66

PART TWO

THE BEST THERE IS AT WHAT THEY DO: THE WOMEN WHO TOOK MARVEL COMICS HIGHER, FURTHER, FASTER

CHAPTER THREE
From the Astonishing to the Uncanny: The Origin of a Show That Launched a Thousand Fans and, Arguably, the Marvel Cinematic Universe **79**

ORAL HISTORY:
Margaret Loesch **98**

CHAPTER FOUR
The Carol Corps: Carol Danvers, Kelly Sue DeConnick, and the Start of a Movement **111**

ORAL HISTORY:
Kelly Thompson **138**

CHAPTER FIVE
The Billion-Dollar Club: Keeping Comics Relevant in a Sharply Contracting Market **145**

PART THREE

THE CALL IS COMING FROM INSIDE THE HOUSE: PAY ATTENTION TO THE WOMEN BEHIND THE CURTAIN

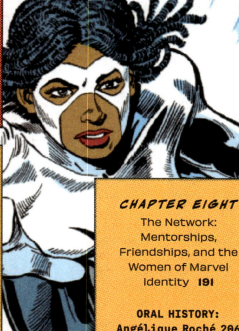

CHAPTER SIX
Meet Me in the Bathroom: How Women Find Each Other in an Industry That Prioritizes Male Spaces **159**

CHAPTER SEVEN
Draw like a Girl: Gatekeeping, and the Repositioning of Stories for a Broader Audience **171**

CHAPTER EIGHT
The Network: Mentorships, Friendships, and the Women of Marvel Identity **191**

ORAL HISTORY:
Angélique Roché **206**

PART FOUR

THE AMBASSADORS: OUTREACH, AND GIVING OURSELVES NAMES, FACES, AND VOICES

CHAPTER NINE
Pop Culture Is Culture: Identities, Found Families, and Finally Getting to Own a First-Person Point of View **221**

CHAPTER TEN
Unlimited: Comic Shops, and the Advent of Marvel Digital **233**

CHAPTER ELEVEN
Sunday Morning: Rise of the Women of Marvel Panels **263**

ORAL HISTORY:
Origins **278**

PART FIVE

THE WORLD OUTSIDE OUR WINDOWS: THE MARVEL UNIVERSE IS OUR UNIVERSE

CHAPTER TWELVE
Knights, Not Damsels: Marvel Knights, Feminist Manifestos, and Finding Catharsis Through Empowerment **297**

ORAL HISTORY:
Reign of X **312**

CHAPTER THIRTEEN
Embiggen!: Ms. Marvel, Kamala Khan, and the Advent of the Disney+ Era **333**

CHAPTER FOURTEEN
Generation M: The Next Generation of Heroes... and Readers **357**

EPILOGUE 372
ACKNOWLEDGMENTS 374
PHOTO CREDITS 377

PREFACE

This book, the story of the women of Marvel Comics—or, as I like to say, the story of Marvel Comics as told by women—has been a long time coming. There have always been women at Marvel Comics, just as there have always been women throughout the history of comics, from indie zines and early cons to mainstream super hero publications and massive tentpole film productions.

I KNOW IT'S TRUE, because I've encountered many of them, and because I am one of them. I have been lucky enough to work at Marvel since 2009—first in comics, at Marvel Entertainment, now in television, at Marvel Studios—and many of these incredible women have forever inspired and changed me. We just don't tell their stories often enough.

Who were the women of Marvel Comics who paved the way for me, personally?

There was the beloved Flo Steinberg, Stan Lee's longtime "gal Friday" and all-around partner in crime, whom I was privileged to know when she returned to the office during my time at Marvel Entertainment. There was also the legendary Marie Severin, for many years the lone female artist in the Marvel Bullpen, who could not only do everything faster and better than everyone else, but who somehow managed to find the time to sketch them hand-drawn birthday cards, too.

And there were many more: my former mentor, the gifted editor and writer MacKenzie Cadenhead, who was one of the reasons I was able to find and keep my home at Marvel. The fearless and iconic writer Kelly Sue DeConnick, who collaborated with me on the reboot of Carol Danvers as Captain Marvel. The talented and generous writer G. Willow Wilson, who co-created the character of Kamala Khan, Ms. Marvel, with me. And before anything else, there was my own mother, the inspiration for Kamala Khan's *amma*, who told me I could be anything I wanted to be, and who still comes to see the Women of Marvel panel at New York Comic Con. (Even if she heckles me from the crowd!)

The women of Marvel Comics are as heroic as any of the characters Marvel has made famous on the page or screen, and the world should know their journeys, too. To be fair, my male colleagues and friends believe the same thing—that the women you will meet in the chapters to come are not just talented *female* contributors, but talented contributors to both Marvel and the comics industry, period.

So, on that note, happy reading, friends . . . and *Embiggen*!

Sana Amanat
SPRING 2024

CAST OF CONTRIBUTORS

FROM OVER 300 HOURS OF INTERVIEWS, THE FOLLOWING PEOPLE HELPED INFORM THE TELLING OF THE STORY OF THE WOMEN OF MARVEL COMICS.

XIV / SUPER VISIBLE

ADRI COWAN Executive director of social media	**ALANNA SMITH** Editor	**ALICE PARK** Project manager for Netmarble, 2020–2022	**ALITHA E. MARTINEZ** Artist
ALLISON BAKER Carol Corps member, 2012–present	**ALISON GILL** Executive of production, Marvel UK and Marvel NYC	**AMANDA CONNER** Artist	**ANGÉLIQUE ROCHÉ** Writer, editor, and podcast host
ANN FOLEY Costume designer, Marvel's *Agents of S.H.I.E.L.D.*, 2013–2017 and *She-Hulk*, 2022	**ANNA BODEN** Director, Marvel Studios' *Captain Marvel*, 2019	**ANNIE NOCENTI** Editor and writer	**BARBARA SLATE** Writer and artist
BOBBIE CHASE Editor and group editor in chief	**BRIE LARSON** Actor, Carol Danvers, *Captain Marvel*, 2019, and *The Marvels*, 2023	**CAROLE SEULING** Writer, *Shanna the She-Devil*	**CATE SHORTLAND** Director, Marvel Studios' *Black Widow*, 2021
CHRISTIE "MAX" SCHEELE Colorist	**CHRISTINA STRAIN** Colorist and writer	**CHRISTINE DINH** Editor for Marvel.com	**DAN BUCKLEY** President of Marvel Comics and Franchise
DANAI GURIRA Actor, Okoye, Marvel's *Black Panther*, 2018, and *Black Panther: Wakanda Forever*, 2022	**DANNY LORE** Writer	**DAVID GLANZER** Chief communications and strategy officer, San Diego Comic-Con, 1994–present	**DAWN GUZZO (NÉE DAWN GEIGER)** Production manager
DEAN HALE Writer, *The Unbeatable Squirrel Girl: Squirrel Meets World*, 2017	**DEWEY CASSELL** Writer, *Marie Severin: The Mirthful Mistress of Comics*, 2012	**ELAINE LEE** Colorist, creator-owned comics	**ELIZABETH HENSTRIDGE** Actor, Jemma Simmons, Marvel's *Agents of S.H.I.E.L.D.*, 2013–2020
ELIZABETH OLSEN Actor, Wanda Maximoff, Marvel Cinematic Universe	**ELLIE PYLE** Associate editor, then executive director, audio content and story, 2010–2014, 2019–2024	**EMILY NEWCOMEN CHIERCHIO** Talent relations specialist, 2016–present	**EVANGELINE LILLY** Actor, Hope Van Dyne, Marvel's *Ant-Man*, 2015, and *Ant-Man and the Wasp*, 2018
EVE L. EWING Writer	**FRANÇOISE MOULY** Colorist	**G. WILLOW WILSON** Writer	**GAIL SIMONE** Writer
HANNAH McLEOD Narrative designer at Crystal Dynamics for *Marvel's The Avengers*	**HILDY MESNIK** Editor	**IMAN VELLANI** Actor, Kamala Khan, *Ms. Marvel* and *The Marvels*, and cowriter, *Ms. Marvel*, 2022–present	*CONTINUES*

CAST OF CONTRIBUTORS

CONTINUED

IRENE VARTANOFF Editor and colorist	**JACINDA CHEW** Senior art director for Insomniac Games, *Marvel's Spider-Man*, 2018	**JANICE CHIANG** Letterer and Bullpen artist	**JEAN THOMAS** Bullpen writer and colorist
JEANINE SCHAEFER Editor and senior talent manager	**JEN BARTEL** Artist	**JENNIFER "JEN" GRÜNWALD** Director of production and special projects	**JENNY LEE** Editor
JO DUFFY Editor	**JOE QUESADA** Artist, editor in chief, and chief creative officer	**JOHN ROMITA JR.** Artist	**JUDY STEPHENS** Producer
JULIA LEWALD Writer, *X-Men: The Animated Series*, 1993, and producer, *X-Men '97*, 2024	**JUNE BRIGMAN** Artist	**KATE HERRON** Director of season one of Marvel Studios' *Loki*, 2021	**KATHREEN KHAVARI** Voice actor
KELLY SUE DeCONNICK Writer	**KELLY THOMPSON** Writer	**LAUREN SANKOVITCH** Editor	**LEAH WILLIAMS** Writer
LIA PELOSI Assistant editor	**LINDA FITE** Bullpen and writer	**LISA KRISTEENA JOHNSON** Carol Corps member, 2012–present	**LONI CLARK** Associate product development manager for Marvel Games
LORRAINE CINK Director of creative content and author	**LOUISE "WEEZIE" SIMONSON** Editor and writer	**LYNN E. COHEN KOEHLER** Associate editor	**LYSA HAWKINS** Assistant editor
MACKENZI LEE Author, *Loki: Where Mischief Lies*, 2019, and *Gamora and Nebula: Sisters in Arms*, 2021	**MACKENZIE CADENHEAD** Editor and author	**MARC SCHWERIN** Cosplayer, *Marvel Becoming*, 2017, and "Suit Up" for *Marvel's 616*, 2020	**MARGARET LOESCH** President, Fox Kids

XVI / SUPER VISIBLE

MARGARET STOHL Writer	**MARGUERITE BENNETT** Writer	**MARY WILSHIRE** Artist	**MAURENE GOO** Writer
MEGAN BRADNER VP, development and production, Live Action Marvel TV	**MIMI GOLD** Stan Lee's assistant, Bullpen, colorist, editor, and writer	**MING-NA WEN** Actor, Melinda May, Marvel's *Agents of S.H.I.E.L.D.*, 2013–2020	**NANCI DAKESIAN** Editor, Marvel Knights
NIC STONE Author, *Shuri: A Black Panther Novel*, 2022	**PAIGE PETTORUTO** Lead game designer for Demiurge Studios, 2019–2024, and *Marvel Puzzle Quest*, 2013	**PAT REDDING SCANLON** Editor	**PATY COCKRUM** Bullpen
PREETI CHHIBBER Author	**RAFAEL RODRIGUES** Carol Corps member, 2012–present	**RAINBOW ROWELL** Author	**RENÉE WITTERSTAETTER** Editor
ROBIN GREEN Stan Lee's assistant	**ROXANE GAY** Author	**RUTH E. CARTER** Costume designer, Marvel Studios' *Black Panther*, 2018, and *Black Panther: Wakanda Forever*, 2022	**SAM MAGGS** Author
SAMIRA AHMED Writer	**SANA AMANAT** Executive of production and development at Marvel Studios	**SANDRA SAAD** Voice actor and MoCap artist for *Ms. Marvel* and *Marvel's The Avengers*, 2020	**SARAH BRUNSTAD** Editor
SHANNON BALLESTEROS Associate managing editor, 2015–2024	**SHANNON HALE** Writer, *The Unbeatable Squirrel Girl: Squirrel Meets World*, 2017	**SOPHIA DI MARTINO** Actor, Sylvie, *Loki*, 2021–2023	**STEPHANIE GRAZIANO** Head of Graz Entertainment, 1991–2011, *X-Men: The Animated Series*, 1992
STEPHANIE MASLANSKY Costume designer for Marvel's *Daredevil*, 2015, *Jessica Jones*, 2015, *Luke Cage*, 2016–2018, *The Defenders*, 2017, and *Iron Fist*, 2017–2018		**STEPHEN WACKER** Vice president, head of content for digital media	**SUE CRESPI** Production manager
SVEN LARSEN Vice president, licensed publishing	**TAMRA BONVILLAIN** Colorist	**TINI HOWARD** Writer	**TRINA ROBBINS** Comics historian and writer, 1966–2024
TRINH TRAN Executive of production and development at Marvel Studios	**VITA AYALA** Writer	**YAYA HAN** Author and cosplayer, 1999–present	**ZOE SALDAÑA** Actor, Gamora, Marvel Cinematic Universe

PROLOGUE

———

THE SECRET DEFINITIVE ONE STORY OF
ALL WOMEN AT MARVEL, EVER[1]

WHEN IT COMES TO male-dominated industries, everyone wants *The Secret History of Women*, or *The Definitive Story of Women*, as a single footnote, a side chapter within that default-male structure. As a result, it can be easy to fall into the trap of believing that there *is* one story to tell—one note to hit, one panel to stop by, on one Sunday morning—but the truth is that there isn't, because women are not a monolith. We belong to a group that is diverse within itself, with intersecting backgrounds and particular worldviews and unique origin stories, each one informing the singular path a person takes through the comics industry.

Just like it did for every guy before us.

So from the moment we began interviewing women for this book, if we couldn't (and shouldn't, and didn't want to) set out to tell *The Secret Definitive One Story of All Women at Marvel and by Extension All Comics, Ever*—what was it, exactly, that we were looking to tell?

There are women throughout the history of Marvel. Let's start there.

It's worth saying, because we are women of Marvel, ourselves, and even we had no idea how many of us there were, or how significant our impact had been, across the decades.

———

1. Or Not.

Now we do, and the answer is (a) more than you think, and (b) very.

When we began to look for contributors to this project, what began as a short list of well-known names quickly spread, by word of mouth and by personal networks, into something inconceivably larger.

Eight hundred pages of transcripts. Three hundred hours of interviews. More than 130 conversations. Five years, from the first interview to the last draft.

During the writing of this book, we lost two of the all-time greats, truly trailblazing women who made Marvel Comics what it is today: the artist Ramona Fradon, and the writer, artist, publisher, and historian Trina Robbins. Increasingly, we began to feel like we had to make sure the voices of the women we had spoken to got out there into the world, even if all we could offer was a brief glimpse into the lives of the women who shaped Marvel Comics as it is today.

Still, we wanted to capture what it felt like to work at or with Marvel Comics, as ourselves. We wanted to take a snapshot of a string of moments across time. To capture, in names and faces and interviews, in Zooms and emails and calls, in photographs and from file cabinets, the story of the Marvel Comics story, of Marvel Comics storytelling, and Marvel Comics storytellers the way we know it. The way it feels for us, and for other women and nonbinary creators. Which isn't a single story, and isn't the same story, and isn't the story a white male Marvel Comics creator might tell.

We wanted to write out the names that never made it to the front of the books. We wanted to name the women who were in the room when it happened, whatever *it* had been, and whether or not anyone knew it.

We wanted to get everything we could down on paper, before more of these women were forgotten and lost. The invisible work of women made visible. Only that.

This creation, this story of women at Marvel, is made from hundreds of complicated conversations, and meant to spark hundreds more.

We hope, if you're reading this, you'll want to continue that conversation.

Margaret Stohl, Jeanine Schaefer, and Judy Stephens
2024

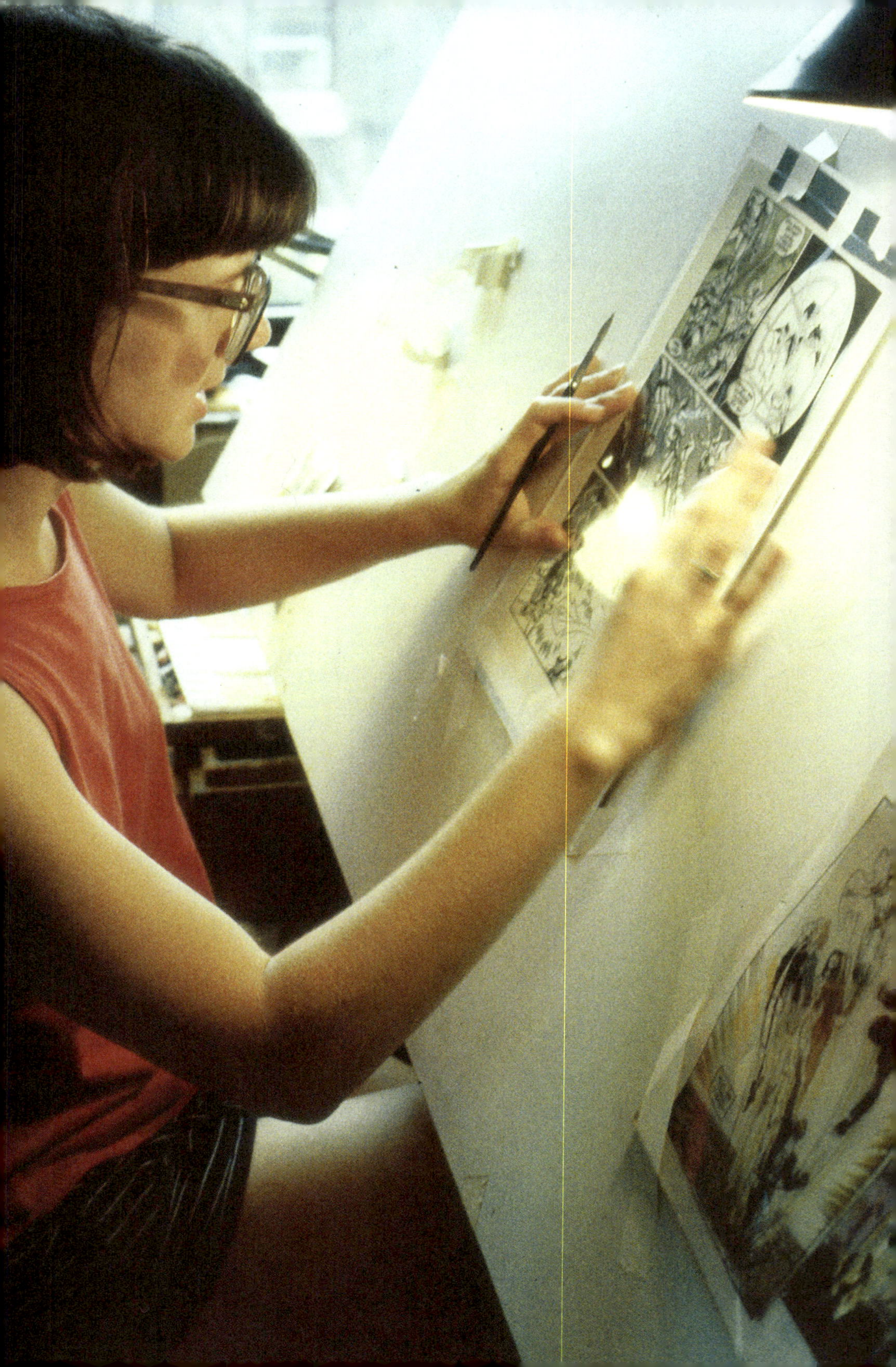

SUPER VISIBLE

"I was there, you know, I was there.
I was really there."

—CHRISTIE "MAX" SCHEELE, MARVEL COLORIST AND BULLPEN ARTIST

PART ONE

THE VISIBLE (SUPER) WOMAN

WOMEN IN THE FIRST TWO DECADES OF MARVEL COMICS

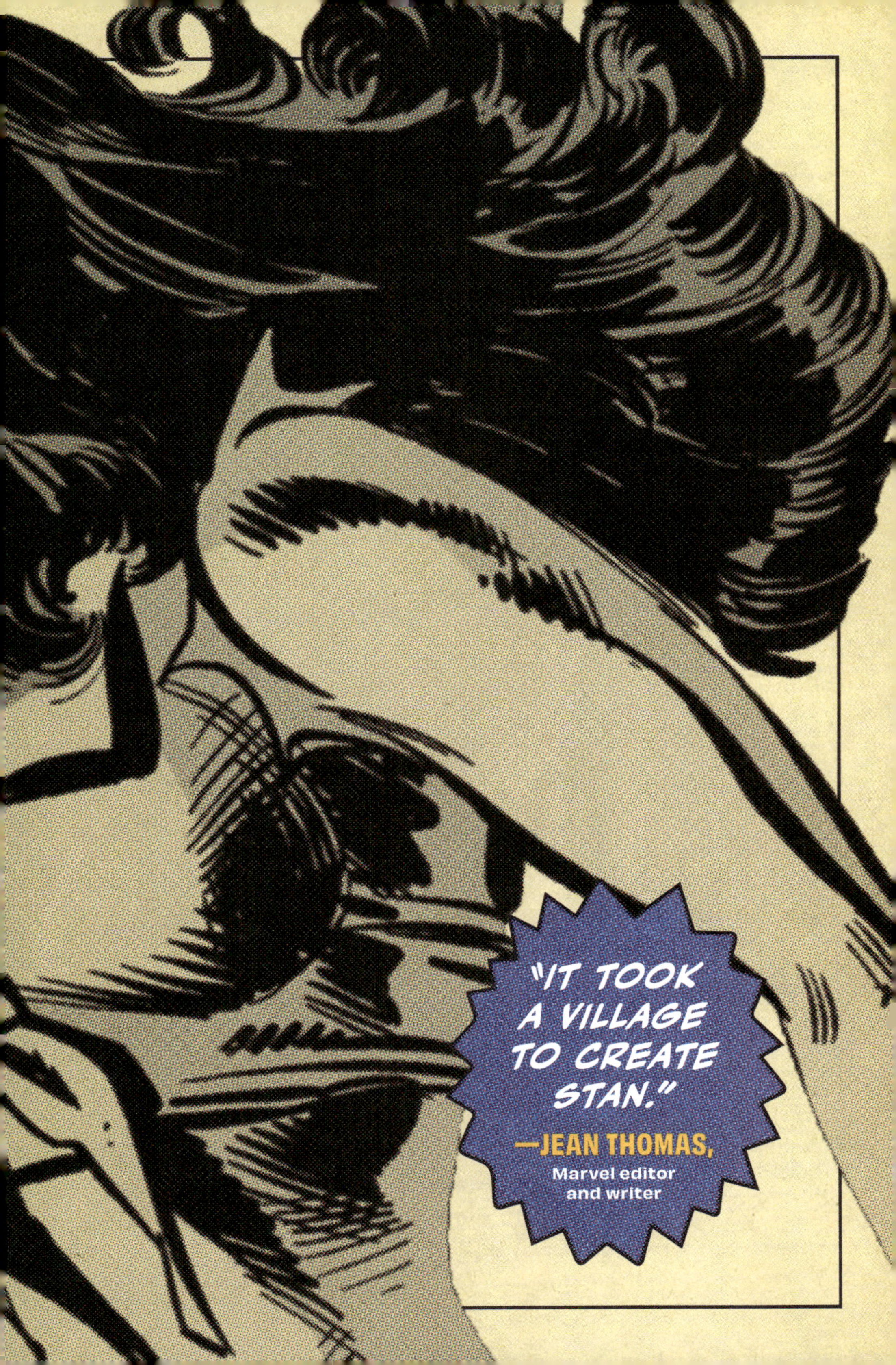
"IT TOOK A VILLAGE TO CREATE STAN."
—JEAN THOMAS,
Marvel editor and writer

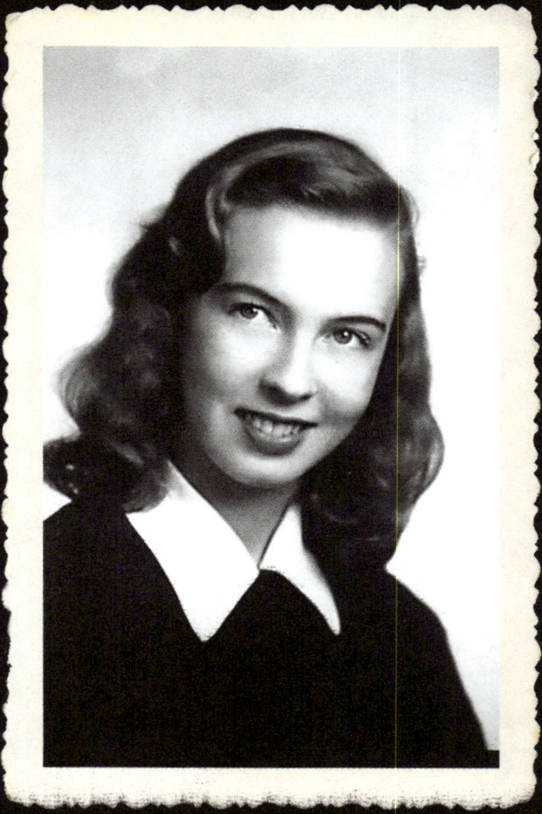

y *Walker* artist Fran Hopper.

CHAPTER ONE

IT TOOK A VILLAGE

Marvel Comics in
the '60s, and the
Women Who Ran
the House of Ideas

Depending on who you ask, Marvel Comics was founded in 1939 (as *Marvel Comics* #1, published by Timely Comics), in 1947 (as Magazine Management), in 1951 (as Atlas Comics), or in 1961, which is when the word "Marvel" was cemented by three names inextricably linked to Marvel Comics: Stan Lee, Steve Ditko, and Jack Kirby.

1961 was also the year Marvel Comics first published *Fantastic Four*, "Marvel's First Family," including Sue Storm, the Invisible Girl (now the Invisible Woman)—Marvel's first female super hero of the Silver Age.

"At the time [reading comics as a teenager], I didn't notice it. It went over my head," said Trina Robbins, a writer who worked at Marvel in the 1980s, and a comics historian who, before her passing in 2024, had written extensively about the history of women in comics. "But now, of course, more recently, I look back and I see, 'Oh my God, she's actually invisible. Typical.' And it was true, women were invisible in comics."

The last twenty years has seen the rise of "women in comics" as a concept, but it is not, as many people assume, a new invention. Visible or not, even in the early years of Marvel Comics, there have always been women in the margins keeping the larger Marvel family together. Women were present during the Silver Age; they were there in the 1940s, when a young Patricia Highsmith, known now for psychological thrillers like *The Talented Mr. Ripley* and *Strangers on a Train*, took a job at Timely Comics to pay the bills, working on her novels at night.

THE LAST TWENTY YEARS HAS SEEN THE RISE OF "WOMEN IN COMICS" AS A CONCEPT, BUT IT IS NOT, AS MANY PEOPLE ASSUME, A NEW INVENTION.

There are, of course, the Silver Age names everyone knows—Stan Lee, Steve Ditko, Jack Kirby, Joe Simon, John Romita Sr., Dave Cockrum. But there are other names, too, also critically important to the inception of the modern Marvel era—Linda Fite, Jean Thomas, Carole Seuling, Marie Severin, Paty Cockrum, and Virginia Romita.

Even earlier, there were those who built the foundation for the modern era.

Fanny Cory, creator of *Sonnysayings* and *Little Miss Muffet*, was a syndicated cartoonist in the 1890s.

Zelda "Jackie" Ormes, thought to be the first African American cartoonist in the United States, worked from 1937 to 1950, creating *Torchy Brown in Dixie to Harlem, Candy, Patty-Jo 'n' Ginger*, and *Torchy in Heartbeats*.

Hilda Terry, whose *Teena* strip ran from 1946 to 1964, was the first woman inducted into the National Cartoonists Society, in 1950.

June Tarpé Mills signed her work simply "Tarpé" so as to not reveal her gender, but was the first prominent female artist to freelance for Timely Comics, and also the first to create a character (Miss Fury) in 1941.

Ruth Atkinson co-created Patsy Walker for Timely Comics in 1944, and Millie the Model in 1945—two of Marvel's longest-running characters—both appearing in one incarnation or another to this day.

Fran Hopper was hired by Ruth Atkinson to draw additional *Patsy Walker* comics for Timely in 1945, as well as a number of other titles involving female characters: *Jane Martin, Mysta of the Moon*, and *Camilla*.

Violet "Valerie" Barclay became one of the first female employees of Timely Comics, working as an inker from 1942 to 1949.

They were there, too.

TOP: Fanny Cory, seen here at her drawing table. BOTTOM: Jackie Ormes, known as the first Black cartoonist in America.

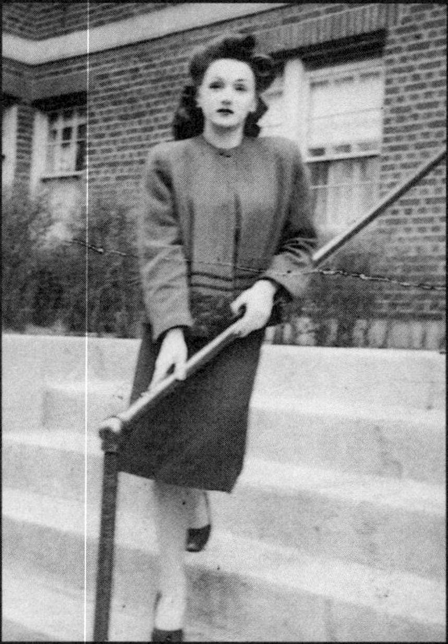

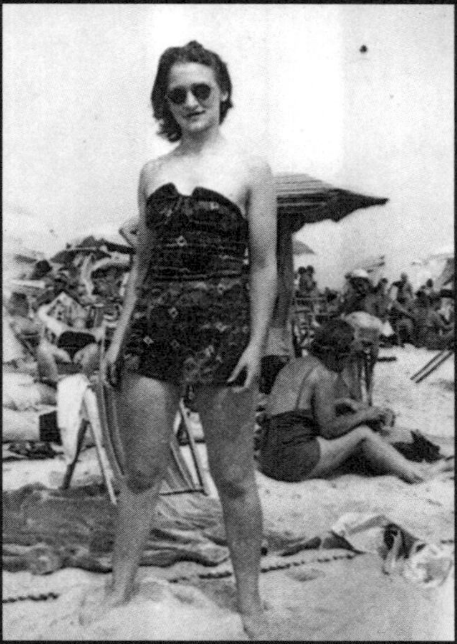

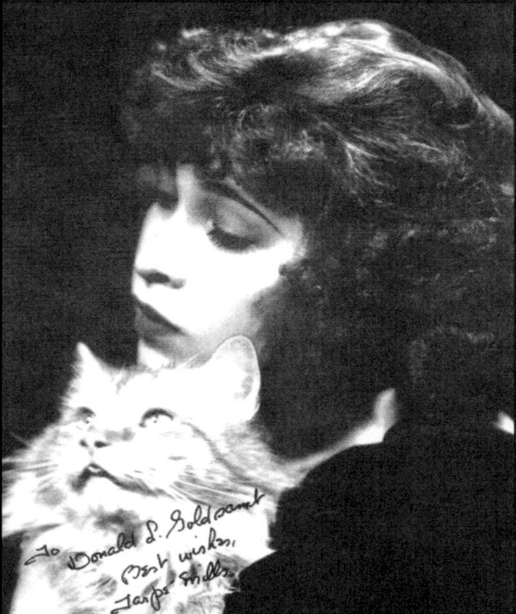
To
Donald L.
Best wishes,

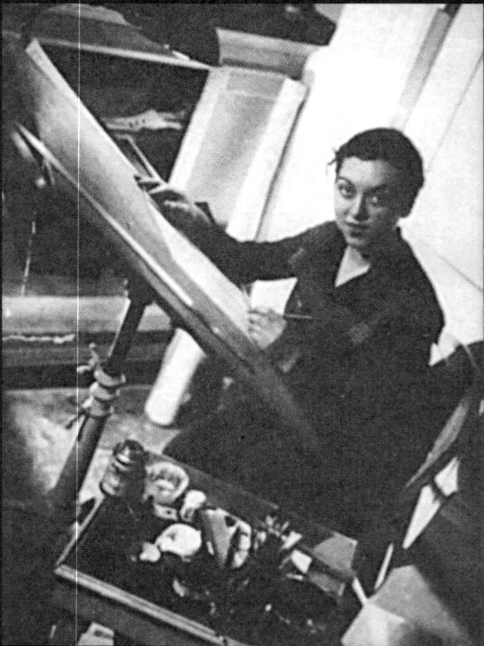

Although not as known as their male counterparts, women were very much a part of the origin of comics as we know it in America. OPPOSITE, CLOCKWISE FROM LEFT: Ruth Atkinson, Valerie "Violet" Barclay, Hilda Terry, and June Tarpé Mills. ABOVE: A self-portrait of Fanny Cory.

ONE WOMAN in particular has long been considered the beginning of the story of the women of Marvel: Flo Steinberg.

While Flo Steinberg may have not been literal family when she joined the company in 1963 after moving to New York from Boston, Stan's original "gal Friday" clearly came to be regarded as found family, whether for the legendary Marvel Bullpen, for Stan Lee himself, or for the innumerable number of women who subsequently worked at Marvel over the next fifty years.

Flo was a constant presence during Stan Lee's initial run at Marvel, from 1963 to 1968, then returned to the Bullpen in her later years as a proofreader. She had only stopped working a few weeks prior to her passing in 2017.

The feeling of the big "Marvel family" so often mentioned in the conversations we had with contributors to this retrospective recalls a time when Marvel Comics was a literal family affair.

"To put this in perspective," said Marvel writer Jean Thomas (who was at one time married to former Marvel editor in chief Roy Thomas), "the very organization was founded with Stan Lee being the cousin of a publisher, who then brought in his brother, Larry Lieber. Plus you had the Severins, brother and sister, both talented artists, and Sol Brodsky invited his daughter, Janna Parker, who became a colorist and assistant production manager. And you can't forget the Romita family."

Carole Seuling, writer of *Shanna the She-Devil* (who was married at the time to Phil Seuling, once one of the largest comic book dealers and convention organizers in the country), had a similar experience. "Returning to comics as an adult, I was reading from [Phil's] collection and realized I enjoyed the characters in Marvel comics. While I was still married to Phil, we had a lot of people from the business in the house—Jim Steranko was there a lot; Roy Thomas, I remember when he first came up from Missouri. And later, Roy would become my editor at Marvel."

But it was only wherever the stakes were lowest that women seemed to have the best access. For many women, the 1960s seemed to usher in a time of at least measured opportunity in New York professional circles. And a small industry like comics—supported by a fledgling, insular "nerd culture," where everyone already knew everyone—was an easier entry point for a career-minded wife or girlfriend than more established Madison Avenue vocations like advertising or book publishing. (And yes, *nerd culture*. People

The story of women at Marvel begins with Flo Steinberg, seen here posing with friend and fellow comic creator Trina Robbins.

IN FACT, DURING THE SIXTIES, A TWENTY-SOMETHING WOMAN HEADING TO MADISON AVENUE WAS FAR MORE LIKELY TO HAVE GROWN UP READING COMICS THAN SHE WOULD IN LATER DECADES.

talk about the 1960s like it was just Republicans and hippies. But it was actually, as more than a few of our contributors have corrected us, Republicans, hippies, and nerds.)

Within comics circles, everyone already appreciated the countercultural, niche appeal of the industry, explained Jean Thomas. Comics people already had "an appreciation for them, a respect for them, a respect for the creators, a respect and enjoyment of the creative process, which not everyone in corporate America would have."

While the balance of available jobs was highly gender-defined, and often involved (for women) some form of office support, the comics industry itself had only recently begun evolving into a male-dominated space. In fact, during the sixties, a twenty-something woman heading to Madison Avenue was far more likely to have grown up reading comics than she would in later decades. Anecdotally, most of the women interviewed from that period of Marvel Comics' history had matured reading at least the ubiquitous "funny papers" section of the daily newspapers.

Prior to the crackdown of the Comics Code Authority in the mid-fifties and the related birth of the super hero comics industry, comics had been created across the board for children in general, regardless of gender.

In other words, these women were not only determined to work, they were anything but unequipped for the job.

OPPOSITE: Smilin' Stan Lee, Mirthful Marie Severin, Jazzy Johnny Romita Sr., and the first-ever Spider-Man costume, modeled by Rascally Roy Thomas.

BECAUSE OF their office support roles—in Stan's inner circle, as his team—women ironically played a critical role in constructing what was read, heard, and seen as the voice of "Stan the Man" himself. In a time when "writing" aligned with "typing," Marvel's staff and fan community communications fell to women—because these appeared to be the least important and least creative occupations at the time. The Merry Marvel Marching Society, the "Marvel Bullpen Bulletins," the No-Prize postcards, even answering the phone when a reader tried to contact Marvel, or intercepting the overzealous fans when they turned up at the office, all fell under the purview of women employees.

In the 1960s, the Marvel Comics editorial office, located at 635 Madison Avenue, was not what fans may have expected, with Stan's corner office and the large room that was known as the Bullpen. Stan was a visionary when it came to fictionalizing the company as the House of Ideas and casting the denizens of the Bullpen as fictional players within it, but much of the direct-to-consumer fan outreach that helped shape what became the Marvel of today can be directly traced to the tireless efforts of a revolving army of women at the front desk.

Jean Thomas remembered being "dragooned into the office because they needed someone. I had just barely turned twenty, and I was asked if I would help out. Flo had left and then there was someone else at the main desk, I think Robin Green, and they just needed additional hands."

"It was awful," Linda Fite recalled with a laugh. "It was a summer job. That was the other thing: Stan said, 'You can have it as a summer job, we'll see how you work out.' Come September, they offered me a full-time job and gave me a ten-dollar-a-week raise."

"Very definitely a boys' club," said Jean Thomas. "And very definitely the kind of place where guys had no compunction about throwing things over the dividers and just 'boys being boys' kind of thing.

"But one nice thing, the ladies, including Marie Severin, a lovely person named Nancy in circulation, and a couple of the women who worked at Magazine Management—we would go out to lunch at the Woman's Exchange or Schrafft's. They had the strongest drinks. At this point, I was maybe twenty and coming from the Midwest, where the drinking age was twenty-one. So this was probably my first time not only drinking, but drinking at lunch and drinking at work. A couple of them would even wear hats and gloves to lunch. 'Oh yes, I think I'll have another,' and another was a second or third martini. And they were slamming them down, discreetly."

Mad Men, Marvel-style.

By the end of the sixties, there were more than one or two women in the office. Jean Thomas remembered the rotation of women at the front desk, like herself, Linda Fite, Mimi Gold, Carla Conway, and Robin Green.

"I mean, no man would pick up the phone in those days," Jean said.

Robin Green was hired to be Stan's assistant after Flo Steinberg, though she only worked at Marvel for seven months before heading off to a new career in Hollywood. She would go on to be the only woman on the masthead at *Rolling Stone*, even writing a ten-thousand-word cover story on Marvel and Stan Lee in 1971, peeling back the curtain for the fan community and, in the

I MEAN, NO MAN WOULD PICK UP
THE PHONE IN THOSE DAYS.

———

process, jump-starting her own writing career. (She later became an Emmy Award–winning writer and producer for *The Sopranos*.) Even in the 1970s, a Marvel credit could attract interest outside the world of comics.

But working for Stan was often less than glamorous. As previously noted, making way for fans—or more often, not, as Flo routinely stopped readers from storming the Marvel offices looking for Stan—was a big part of the job for these women. One "that sometimes involved tripping a few," Flo liked to joke.

"Because my office was facing the front door," said Linda Fite, "sometimes I would waylay people who were coming in, and sometimes I would talk to people who had their portfolio and wanted to see Stan. I'd say, 'I'm sorry, you can't see him.' But I would take a look, and if the portfolio was halfway good, I'd go in and ask—like John Romita—'There's a kid out here who's got something, you want to see him?'"

There was also the fan mail, or Stan Mail, as the girls called it.

"I know that one of the things I had to do was a passable facsimile Stan signature, a very bold S-T-A-N," recalled Jean Thomas. "Never on anybody's checks, just on postcards that went to kids."

That was how acclaimed British artist Barry Windsor-Smith got his start, too. "He had sent some sketches from England," Fite noted, "and I said, this isn't half bad. So Stan gave him the same thing he gave me: 'If you come to America, I'd like to see you. I can't offer you a job, but . . .'"

In the end, Windsor-Smith did make his way to America, and among his other work, his work on both *Conan the Barbarian* (1970) and *Weapon X* (1991) are now seminal parts of comics history, showcasing an elevated version of the form.

But not before he got his green card, which was facilitated by another woman who sat at the desk outside Stan's office—Mimi Gold.

Mimi Gold with artist Barry Windsor-Smith.

Mimi was hired as Stan's next assistant after Robin Green's departure, but with her desk right beside Roy Thomas—with Sol Brodsky and John Verpoorten on the other side of the room—she was a quick study in both the creative and production sides of how comics were made. After six months as Stan's assistant, she asked him if she could write. She was promoted to assistant editor, moved to a new desk, and became the first woman actually credited as a writer in a Marvel comic, for 1970's *Iron Man #29*.

Uncredited, women most often helped write the *Bullpen Bulletin*, a one-page newsletter that ran each month in the back of every issue. "Stan would do his little 'Stan's Soapbox,'" Fite said of the publisher's personal column. "But alongside there would be the *Bullpen Bulletin*—who was doing what, what was coming up—because Stan very wisely personalized the entire creative team. I'd copyedit the *Bulletin* and sometimes help Stan. I came up with some Latin expressions for him because I'd studied it in high school."

And so, a circled bit on Linda's résumé—the fact that she had the ability to type—soon meant she was writing in Stan's voice to fans around the world.

The seemingly lowest-stakes job directly impacted one of the most important aspects of the identity of the franchise: Stan himself.

Said Jean Thomas with a little smile, "It took a village to create Stan."

STAN'S SOAPBOX

Let's lay it right on the line. Bigotry and racism are among the deadliest social ills plaguing the world today. But, unlike a team of costumed super-villains, they can't be halted with a punch in the snoot, or a zap from a ray gun. The only way to destroy them is to expose them — to reveal them for the insidious evils they really are. The bigot is an unreasoning hater — one who hates blindly, fanatically, indiscriminately. If his hang-up is black men, he hates ALL black men. If a redhead once offended him, he hates ALL redheads. If some foreigner beat him to a job, he's down on ALL foreigners. He hates people he's never seen — people he's never known — with equal intensity — with equal venom. Now, we're not trying to say it's unreasonable for one human being to bug another. But, although anyone has the right to dislike another individual, it's totally irrational, patently insane to condemn an entire race — to despise an entire nation — to vilify an entire religion. Sooner or later, we must learn to judge each other on our own merits. Sooner or later, if man is ever to be worthy of his destiny, we must fill our hearts with tolerance. For then, and only then, will we be truly worthy of the concept that man was created in the image of God — a God who calls us ALL — His children.

Pax et Justitia,

Stan.

Stan Lee's iconic column against racism and bigotry, published during the turbulent year of 1968.

FLO STEINBERG was the godmother of Marvel Comics, one of the first two full-time members of the Marvel staff in 1963. (The other was a guy named Stan.) "She managed the [whole] damn office," said Joe Quesada, longtime editor in chief of Marvel Comics.

Flo quickly came to know the House of Ideas inside and out. She ran not only Marvel's offices, but also the growing fandom that emerged from them. Her duties included everything from assisting with production schedules and new hires, to typing and proofreading and managing office supplies—all the while keeping an eye on anything to do with the community Stan had dubbed the Merry Marvel Marching Society. She handled all the letters (which she would often answer herself, writing as Stan to younger readers) and sent paying members of the society their fan club kits. She fielded the endless calls and the steadily growing stream of readers who began showing up at the office to meet Stan and the other creators.

But "Fabulous Flo"—which was how Stan memorialized her—became a character on the page as well. One of Stan Lee's most fruitful fandom innovations was his move to fictionalize the Marvel Bullpen itself, as part of the creation of the Merry Marvel Marching Society.

Stan somehow seemed to know, even then, that the first step to creating modern myth was mythologizing its creators. The second step was to get Fabulous Flo to oversee myth maintenance, making it all possible. From the perspective of our modern era of content transparency and accountability—where directors tweet photos from the set and video game teams publish "build notes" for weekly updates—Stan and Flo were sixty years ahead of their time.

Although Flo left Marvel in 1968 (after asking for a $5 raise and being told no), she had paved the way for a growing number of female staff members in the sixties and seventies—including Marie Severin, Linda Fite, Robin Green, Jean Thomas, and Mimi Gold in the Marvel office. Carol Seuling as a writer. Françoise Mouly and many more colorists like her as freelancers.

In many ways, Flo became the start of an entire network of women who looked out for each other at the company and in the larger Marvel fandom—those who pushed to bring more women into the industry, who did everything they could to help springboard women into better opportunities, and who worked tirelessly to get comics into a broader set of hands.

Flo Steinberg taking a spin in *Incredible Hulk* and *Wolverine* artist Herb Trimpe's plane.

Linda Fite related the story of how Flo intervened when she found Linda's job application in Stan's slush pile. "When it came time to graduate, my friend and I said, 'We're going to Manhattan, man, we're going.' I'm trying to find a job, and I wrote a letter to Stan. Flo saved the letter; she gave it to me later. But it's really corny and it goes on about how I'd like to work at Marvel and 'I realize there are no heifers in the Bullpen.'" Linda shook her head. "I swear to God, I wrote that. I'm so embarrassed!"

But it worked. Flo put Linda's résumé in front of Stan, with the relevant bits about typing circled. And when Linda finally got the call, it came from Flo herself: "We can't really offer you a job at this time. But when you come to New York, he'd love to meet you."

"So I went to New York and I sort of had a job lined up at NBC and another with this woman Pat Carbine, who turned out to be one of the founders of *Ms.* magazine," Linda recalled. "But I met Stan and I went to the Bullpen and said, 'I want to work here!' and Flo needed an assistant. So I took that job, even though it paid terribly.

IT TOOK A VILLAGE / 19

THERE WAS NOBODY LIKE FLO. WHAT SHE REPRESENTED, WHO SHE WAS. JUST THE KIND OF PERSON SHE WAS.

———

"Flo was totally competent. Real smart. She was originally hired as Stan's secretary, his personal assistant, but would become so much more than that in the office," Linda went on. "She would manage the traffic of artwork and flow of the schedules. She took care of Stan."

"Really charming and very welcoming," added Françoise Mouly, one-time colorist, now art editor at the *New Yorker* (since 1993). "Just a generous kind of person."

"Your earth mother, straight out of Woodstock," Mimi Gold, a Marvel staffer at the time, recounted. "She had this flat Boston accent . . . would wear peasant dresses, and her hair wild." Marvel editor Lysa Hawkins recalled equally wild lunches with Flo in her later years, full of "really saucy stories, which made me blush."

"Just this extremely New York lady mix of hard and soft, so kind and loving, but never a pushover," said Jeanine Schaefer, editor of *X-Men* and *Wolverine*. "That was Flo. She gave me a bookmark that she said reminded her of me. I still have it pinned above my desk."

Jenny Lee, now a television and film editor and producer, was an editor during some of the most difficult and leanest years of the modern Marvel Comics era. Many women from Marvel editorial have pointed to Jenny as one of the most important mentors for women both at that time and in the years since . . . not unlike Flo herself.

"When I first started at Marvel, I was off editing books by myself, feeling invisible to the rest of editorial. But I would still filter my books through Flo's office for proofreading, so she knew what I was doing. One day, completely out of the blue, she came by my cube and said, 'Jenny, I brought you something.' And she handed me a vintage newsprint copy of *Big Apple Comix*, this indie comic she had edited in 1975. 'I just thought you might like to read it and just know that I edited it, too.' I was so thankful that I was ready to start crying, because I felt like it was her way of saying, 'I see what you're doing, and I know it's hard. Keep going.'

"There's a generation of people who grew up with Flo being this magical person, and now new generations to comics don't understand how important she was. And there are those of us who knew her and had a connection. There was nobody like Flo. What she represented, who she was. Just the kind of person she was. And she passed a literal baton to me."

Flo died in New York City on July 23, 2017, while across the country, that year's San Diego Comic-Con—the country's largest comic book convention—was in full swing. No one talked about anything else that day. The Women of Marvel panel operated as though the head of state of a small country had been lost. Those Women of Marvel Comic-Con panels had become a unique communion for women in our industry, one that passed in a sort of ecstatic blur. They were usually held on Sundays, and by the time they were over, we were completely spent and happy. That was the spirit in the room, the day that we heard Flo had died. We felt it like a calling, even a legacy.

Flo's final gift to the Women of Marvel.

"When I started, Flo just flat-out sought me out and let me know, 'I am here for you,'" said MacKenzie Cadenhead, a former Marvel editor and current middle grade author. "I've never had more hugs, kisses, and praise from another woman in any working environment than I did from her. Thanks to her, I knew how important my voice was. How important it was that I was there. She did so much for all of us."

AFTER WORLD WAR II, the popularity of super hero comics began to wane as "normal" life resumed in America, but the comic book medium had solidified itself as a vehicle for serialized storytelling.

Now, rather than looking for escapism, readers—especially women—were clamoring for stories and characters that reflected who they were and the sort of lives they were leading. Publishers responded with comics aimed at young people in general, but specifically at women.

"I divide them into the girls' comics and the romance comics," said Trina Robbins, who exhaustively documented the history of women in cartooning and comics, and was a comics writer herself, with Marvel credits spanning back to the 1980s. "The former included *Patsy Walker* and *Millie the Model*, and they all had a girl's name in the title."

These were published by Timely and were treated the way that super hero comics were considered "boy books." Soon they were long-running behemoths, with *Millie the Model* running for 207 issues starting in 1945.

In 1947, Joe Simon and Jack Kirby, already famous for their work *Captain America*, launched *Young Romance* #1 ("Designed for the more ADULT readers of comics," a banner in bold letters exclaimed, across every cover) with Crestwood Publications. Other companies and creators followed suit, including Timely, who published *My Romance* in 1948 and then *Girl Comics* in 1949—a book that Stan Lee specifically launched to bring more girls into different comics genres than romance—featuring plots that conformed more to what would be considered "genre fiction" like thriller and adventure tales.

And the romance genre itself was a gold mine: *Young Romance* regularly sold over a million copies a month, and *My Romance* ran from 1948 until 1963. Publishers tried to create main characters that they felt would resonate with the female demographic the genre targeted. And, according to those we interviewed, it worked—women readers came out in droves.

"As a preteen," said Robbins, "I thought teenagers were just the living end, as did most of my peers. [. . .] Many girls my age read these comics, and they were immensely popular."

But that success was short-lived. Over the next decade, psychiatrist Fredric Wertham would take aim at comics, penning *Seduction of the Innocent* in 1954 and putting the industry itself on trial in the United States' Senate. Empowered by conservative watchdog groups, he waged war on comics as an immoral force corrupting the youth of America by promoting "juvenile delinquency" . . . and won. The ultimate victim was the wide breadth of genres that mainstream comics publishers had developed, as well as the diversity of its audience. Opting to self-police their own industry rather than allow the government to regulate it, the Comics Magazine Association of America established the Comics Code Authority in 1954. It was a major blow to genre comics, as publishers, who couldn't afford to risk legal penalties, pulled horror, western, and romance comics from their publishing slates. Thus the stage was set for what became known as the Silver Age of comics, focusing on super heroes.

But by the early 1970s, as Marvel looked to catch second-wave feminism at its crest, an idea was percolating: Could they go one step beyond *Girl Comics* (ironically written and drawn by men) and revive the romance genre through the lens of super heroes, with women at the creative helm?

That idea manifested in three books published in late 1972. These comics—*The Claws of the Cat*, *Night Nurse*, and *Shanna the She-Devil*—were not just for women but, for the first time in the history of Marvel Comics, credited to women writers.

For the women in the Bullpen, who had historically not been given creative roles on the scripting side of things ("Those were always given to the boys," Paty Cockrum, a member of the Bullpen staff and eventual Marvel artist, recalled of the time), it was the culmination of years of asking, as Linda Fite, writer of *The Claws of the Cat*, noted.

"I just nudged," Fite said, laughing. "I was nudging and nudging. I kept bugging Roy Thomas, 'Come on, Roy, give me a shot. Give me a shot.' And then what happened was he married Jean, and now she's nudging him. So, you know, it was even better. And she started writing *Night Nurse*."

Night Nurse was the first of the three titles to be released. "I think I said it in just those terms: I want to write more," said Jean Thomas. "And they were open to coming up with a few of those books. To be honest, everything was written by someone who was a significant other or relative of a writer or editor.

"At most it was just an idea they had. I know I made up the group of friends and the hospitals they worked in. And I distinctly remember I named it Metro General, because Metropolitan was a hospital near me and *General Hospital* was a soap opera."

Linda had a similar experience on *The Claws of the Cat*. "I think Marie Severin and Wally Wood both came up with the costume, which is not a great one, but what are you gonna do? A sash? Oh, please. But everything else was left up to me, and Roy just okayed it."

In what should be commemorated as a vital piece of Marvel history but has been lost in the shuffle like much of the details about women in the early Marvel era, *The Claws of the Cat #1* was Marvel's first book credited to both a female writer and illustrator, as Marie Severin handled pencilling, with Wally Wood on inks.

A piece of history: On her wall, Linda Fite showcases the original design of the Cat, drawn by Marie Severin.

In a 2006 interview with Dewey Cassell, Marie Severin recalled Wood's inks: "I remember saying, 'My God, I drew this woman and Wally inked her like she's wrapped in Saran Wrap.' His storytelling always had lovely inking, nice blacks and everything, but I didn't have her that revealing. The boys loved his work, though."

Carole Seuling was selected for the third book, *Shanna the She-Devil*. By 1971, she and Phil Seuling were separated, and she was working as a substitute teacher. "Roy [Thomas] approached me and said he wanted a jungle queen. They then left it up to me to make up the origin story."

There's the marketplace view as to why Stan Lee took a run at this more modernized version of so-called girls comics; as Linda Fite put it, "They wanted to get in on the women's lib thing." There's a cynical version as well, voiced by a few women we spoke with, who had the unfortunately too-common experience of being trotted out and then tossed aside: that they "would introduce girl books . . . but nobody will read them because girls don't like comics, then we'll cancel them, but be able to say we tried."

But the practical view of why Stan wanted to get into the women's comics space could be as simple as this: he was a savvy businessman and saw an audience out there who wasn't being served. After all, as Irene Vartanoff—writer, editor, and colorist at Marvel in the seventies—pointed out, "If you read the house ads at the time, they would say 'boys and girls.' They expected that girls would read comics."

Looking at the lineup of interior and cover artists on these books—a Who's Who of popular creators with enduring careers—it seems the truth lies somewhere in the middle. With greats like Jim Steranko, John Romita Sr., John Buscema, Jim Starlin, and Golden Age hero Bill Everett (creator of Namor, the Sub-Mariner), there's a credible argument to be made that Marvel as a company backed these comics wholeheartedly.

And yet, *The Claws of the Cat*, *Night Nurse*, and *Shanna the She-Devil* were all canceled either by or with issue #5—not a lot of time to begin growing an audience, or at least to firmly anchor the characters in a larger franchise, a feature of the Marvel Universe integral to a book's success.

"I know the sales were, by today's standards, excellent, but they just weren't good enough for those days," said Linda Fite.

Jean Thomas agreed: "I do believe those three comics would have done much better had they been able to integrate them properly into the Marvel Universe."

Regardless, these were nine historic months, a slice of Marvel history where women successfully made their way onto the page, leaving readers with a small window into what mainstream comics for and by women could look like, and how they could reflect and foster more diverse voices.

"I'll tell you one thing that surprised me," Carole Seuling noted. "It's amazing that my character, Shanna, has had tremendous vitality over the years. I actually have the Marvel-approved Shanna figurine. I'm just shocked that she's lasted fifty years. Except for Mary Marvel, I don't think there were any women in the forties and fifties with superpowers. Jungle queens were strong, intelligent, dedicated to the natural spaces. . . . I wanted Shanna to be what every woman wants to be: powerful, independent, very smart, not afraid to assert herself, and not taking crap from men."

Said Linda Fite, "We tried like hell to sell more women's comics, but we were ahead of our time, you know?"

THE ROMANCE revival was short-lived at Marvel, but it introduced the world of comics to the artist Marie Severin. What Flo was to Stan and production, Marie was to the Bullpen and creative. If Flo had opened the door for women in the Marvel offices—and if Linda, Carole, and Jean had written us into the Marvel pages—it was Marie who literally drew women into the picture. As a penciller, inker, and colorist, she quickly established herself as a Marvel legend.

In 1964, "Mirthful Marie" joined Fabulous Flo in the fiction of Stan Lee's carefully and joyfully mythologized Marvel offices. The first full-time female staff artist in the famed Marvel Bullpen, Marie Severin earned her place in Stan's pantheon right alongside "Jolly Ol'" Jack Kirby, "Sparkling" Solly Brodsky, "Adorable" Artie Simek, and "Kid Daredevil" Wally Wood.

Marie had been a career comics colorist since 1949 at Entertaining Comics. It was at EC that Marie learned about coloring, inking, lettering, and production—and where she further established her skills as a penciller. She was also the sole woman in a group of male artists, a position she'd occupy in one room or another for most of her life.

TOP: Marie Severin, seen here inking a comic in the Bullpen, was part of the welcoming committee to fellow women in the office.

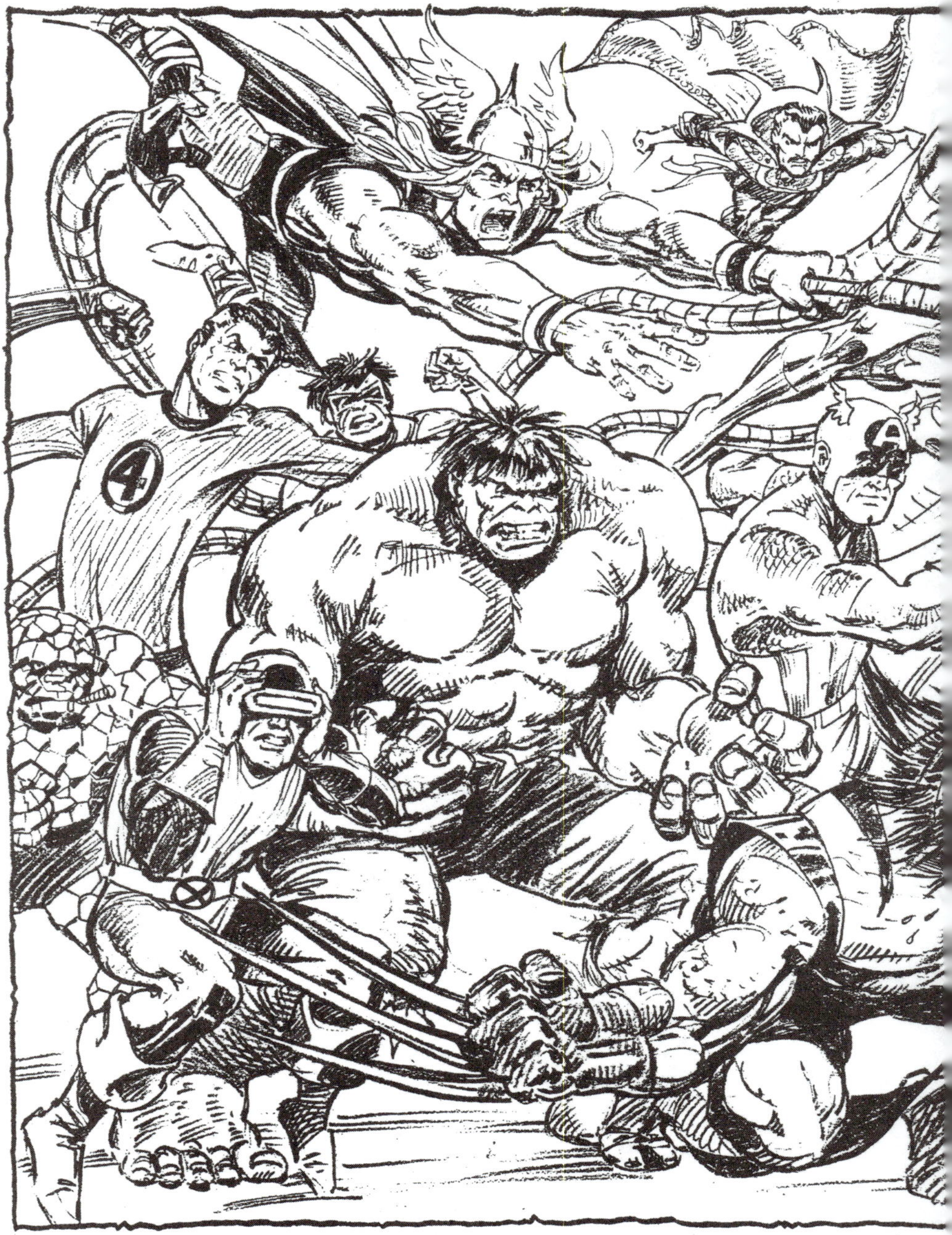

Marie Severin was known for her caricatures of fellow Marvel staff, including doodling a version of herself working at her desk in the Bullpen (PREVIOUS PAGE), and snapping a photo of the many heroes and villains she drew during her time at Marvel.

IF YOU WERE A WOMAN WHO WASN'T LOOKING TO JOIN THE SECRETARIAL POOL, BUT STILL WANTED TO WORK AT MARVEL, FREELANCING AS A COLORIST WAS ONE OF THE SUREST ROUTES INTO THE BUILDING.

"I was the only gal, but they all loved it when I colored their stuff. They didn't see my work as competition, but rather a complement to theirs. It was wonderful," Marie told her longtime friend Dewey Cassell, author of *Marie Severin: The Mirthful Mistress of Comics*. Though Marie passed in 2018, Dewey shared his personal memories and extensive biographical knowledge of her for this project.

As the comics industry stumbled in the era of the Comics Code, Marie departed EC and freelanced for Atlas Comics, briefly detouring the industry in 1957 for a job at the Federal Reserve Bank of New York. Still, Marie couldn't leave comics behind, working with her brother, John, to create one of the most distributed comics in US history, hilariously titled *The Story of Checks*.

By 1964, after John had gone back on staff at Marvel and recommended that his sister join him, Stan Lee asked Marie to come on full-time as the first female artist on staff.

"After Stan offered her the position, she was quick to jump back into comics, as she loved the art form," Dewey Cassell said. "In the 1960s, women like Marie and Flo were the absolute minority in the office. At the same time, Marie commanded respect from her peers."

It was through an assignment for *Esquire* in 1966 that publisher Martin Goodman and Stan Lee finally noticed Marie's skills as an artist, offering her the opportunity to take over from Steve Ditko on the "Doctor Strange" feature in *Strange Tales* the following year.

In her time at Marvel, Marie would go on to work on titles including *Sub-Mariner*, *The Incredible Hulk*, *Tales to Astonish*, and *Kull the Conqueror*. From 1968 to 1971, Marie became the de facto (though uncredited) art director, designing every cover that Marvel published during that time.

If you were a woman who wasn't looking to join the secretarial pool, but still wanted to work at Marvel, freelancing as a colorist was one of the surest routes into the building, and Marie Severin, aside from her personal art assignments, was known to manage and champion a small army of female colorists.

For Françoise Mouly, who'd left France for New York in 1974, an interest in comics had begun as a pragmatic way to improve her English, but ultimately led her to discover not only the underground comix scene, but also her future husband, the indie artist (and eventual Pulitzer Prize–winning graphic novelist) Art Spiegelman. Seeking out colorist assignments a few years later had been a similarly pragmatic decision, albeit an economic one.

To Françoise, Marie Severin had forever transformed the Marvel experience. "The world of comics and cartoonists was extremely small," said Françoise, "so Art knew virtually everyone and he introduced me to Flo Steinberg, who led me to Marvel. I visited the offices and offered my services as a colorist. And fortunately for me, the person in charge of that was Marie Severin. And she was just fabulous. The office [felt] unwelcoming to women, but Marie was totally at ease in her little domain, and a decent number of the colorists were women. It wasn't unusual to be a woman colorist, and she really was patient and kind and very interested in developing people to do things. To work with her and for her."

"Marie was the heart of Marvel," Dewey said.

Marie was notorious for her comical sketches of colleagues—all drawn on Marvel stationary—that showcased the looser side of her friends in the Bullpen. Most people prized the experience of being a "victim to Marie's cartoons," as Dewey described it. Even Flo loved being the recipient of one particular sketch that depicted her as being stingy with the office supplies.

Writer Jean Thomas remembered, "Marie with her portable typewriter . . . wonderful, funny, and, above all, assertive. The role model of the woman I wanted to be," despite her "wicked cartoons."

Editor Irene Vartanoff agreed: "Marie had talent dripping out of her

TOP: After finding the job via an ad in *The Village Voice*, Annie Nocenti would go on to edit Chris Claremont and write *Daredevil*. BOTTOM: Jo Duffy pauses in mid-review of a comic to pose for the camera of the Bullpen's Eliot Brown.

fingers. She was [also] irrepressible. . . . She put Post-it notes inside each toilet stall that said 'Happy Birthday.'"

Creator and editor Annie Nocenti admitted, "I was scared of her. She was so sardonic, funny, and deadpan. Kind of like you never knew if she was happy or not, if she was angry or not. But she was wonderful. And, you know, I just completely fell in love with her." Annie paused. "Marie really should have made it to art director."

Why didn't she? "Sexism." Annie shrugged. That was comics in the 1960s.

Ultimately, it seemed to be Marie's incredible talent, along with her "only girl in the room" resilience, that set her career apart.

Also of note: In 1977, Marie designed the costume for Spider-Woman, as well as the *Howard the Duck* villain, Doctor Bong. In 1978, she provided the art for the Spider-Man and the Hulk . . . toilet paper.

Marie remained a part of the special projects division, designing toy maquettes (small three-dimensional statues or models) and film/TV tie-in products until her retirement in the mid-1990s. And though "she didn't gossip," as Irene Vartanoff noted, Marie would let trusted friends glimpse the sly wit underneath the irrepressibly positive exterior. "I called her up one time and told her that an old enemy of hers had died. And she said, 'Ah, someone finally killed her!' Most people don't know that about her," Irene said.

Editor Jo Duffy also recalled Marie's wisdom, her sharp view into what made people tick, and how to navigate the tricky landscape of comics development. "Holy moly . . . she gave me an insight that has probably saved my life time and time and time again. I had always assumed people who did bad things were bad people. One day, she drew me aside and said, 'Don't assume they're all bad. Some of them are stupid, which is worse. If somebody is bad but they're smart, you can figure out what they're thinking. If they're stupid, they're a loose cannon, and liable to take everyone down with them. So never make an enemy of someone like that. And if you do, never believe you can predict what they will or won't do.' Some of the smartest advice I've ever gotten in my life. And I thank heaven and Marie for it often."

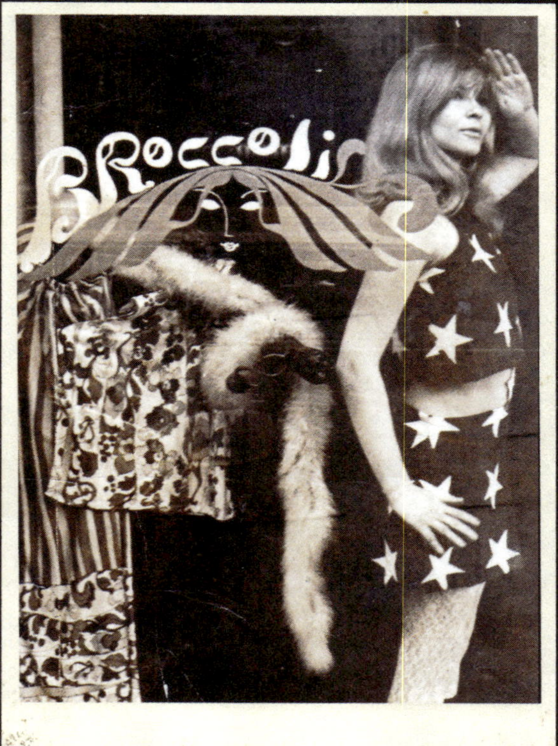

CHAPTER TWO

GOING UNDERGROUND

The Underground
Comix Scene, Marvel,
and the Woman at the
Center of Both

In the 1970s, as other comics companies remained shuttered or were still recovering from the damage done by the Senate hearings of the fifties, Marvel Comics was booming its way into what is now called the Bronze Age.

"Marvel had just expanded, and they were desperate for people who knew the business, because nobody had time to tell them what a comic book was," said Irene Vartanoff, who started her comics career at Marvel in 1974 as then editor in chief Roy Thomas's assistant. "So anybody who knew anything about comics we would invite in. And often these people would flame out really fast. But regardless, Roy had an assistant. There was a lot of correspondence, with people sending in letters and art [samples] that had to be replied to. There was proofreading the reprint comics, and we had a ton of those. Technically, I was the reprint editor for the entirety of my Marvel career."

At this point, the Bullpen looked nothing like what the average Marvel fan might expect today. The number of women in production seemed to be climbing the corporate ladder higher every day, but only to a point. "There was, unfortunately, no encouragement given to the women who tried to do creative work at Marvel when I was there," lamented Irene.

Paty Cockrum concurred: "A woman at Marvel could be a letterer, a colorist, or even an editor, but writing and pencilling . . . the real creative and superstar roles were reserved for the men."

Paty Cockrum designing and
assembling an *Amazing Spider-Man*
title page. Behind her are the flat
files used to store original art.

At the time, coloring was considered a technical skill and not an artistic one, viewed in much the same way as typing or answering phones. Which meant, as Irene recalled: "If you were female, they'd push you toward coloring."

But Marie Severin didn't see it that way. As a champion of coloring as its own art form, Marie always pushed herself to find new ways of using color to tell a story. Believing that learning to color had made her a better artist and better collaborator, Marie invited countless other women into the Marvel colorists' Bullpen, not only giving them their start in comics, but mentoring them along the way.

In the 1970s, Marie's army of colorists included Irene Vartanoff, Françoise Mouly, Jean Thomas, Michele Wolfman, Glynis Oliver, Petra Goldberg, and Mimi Gold.

"I didn't have any art background to justify doing it," said Irene, laughing. "But Marie Severin, who is such a generous soul, did her best to teach me how to do it. And then I got my sister, Ellen, coloring. She had gone to art college, and did quite a bit of work for Marvel."

It was at once freeing and limiting, something that many women in comics and other male-dominated fields still grapple with. As Paty said, "Yes, I colored comics, like other women in the office, though I really never asked to draw any comics. When I started at Marvel, I was told that my art was not suitable for super hero comics. I suppose it was true to a degree. . . . My art is highly illustrative and more fantasy-oriented."

Most of Marie's army left Marvel to go on to other creative careers. It is not entirely surprising, given the limited creative parameters of what they were tasked with doing at companies like Marvel and DC. Others, like Irene, left because they refused to sign Marvel's Loyalty Oath, which was essentially the first work-for-hire contract, transferring all art ownership to the company. Often, women left for better compensation.

So how did the steady trickle of women pushing their way out from behind the secretary's desk, into the Bullpen, and then into creative roles finally trigger the dam-breaking influx of women into the Marvel offices?

The answer came from the West Coast.

THE 1970s was the start of a new age for super hero comics, but there was a vacuum left by the closing of other major companies who did genre works, like EC and Crestwood Publications.

Their creators (and audience) were left looking for a new outlet, one that wasn't being served by the publishing industry in New York.

"Around 1968—I was living in New York at the time—but I had taken a month off to visit friends in California," recalled historian Trina Robbins. "When I got off the plane in San Francisco, I was met by a few friends who just handed me a copy of *Zap #1*, and my mind was blown. I realized that you could actually do comics that were not super hero–based."

Created by Robert Crumb and released in 1968, *Zap Comix* was part of the burgeoning counterculture comics scene that became known as underground comix. Underground comix were usually small press or self-published, so they weren't distributed through the same channels as the super hero books. Instead, they were found mostly in head shops or niche bookstores, in small runs and entirely independent of corporately run comics. This meant that the Comics Code Authority didn't apply to them, leaving creators free to explore what they wanted, how they wanted.

Unfortunately, the West Coast underground comix scene was just as male-dominated as the mainstream comics industry, three thousand miles to the east. Many artists, seeing the popularity of Robert Crumb's *Zap Comix* and his satirical take on the perception of artists, tried to emulate his mix of self- and societal loathing; they often ended up perpetuating the misogyny that permeated much of the content culture of the time—and in the process, alienating many of the women who had come West seeking a new creative vehicle.

Said Trina Robbins in Roger Sabin's *Comics, Comix & Graphic Novels: A History of Comic Art*, "It's weird to me how willing people are to overlook the hideous darkness in Crumb's work. . . . What the hell is funny about rape and murder?"

But not unlike what was happening in the Marvel Bullpen, anyone who wasn't a (straight, cis) man started gravitating toward each other, and the independence of the scene gave creators the freedom to forge leadership roles for themselves, to create their own comics, and ultimately, to forge their own career paths. If the "mainstream" underground comix scene centered itself

40 / SUPER VISIBLE

WE DISCOVERED THERE WERE SOME AMAZING WOMEN CARTOONISTS, AND THEIR FIRST WORK APPEARED IN *WIMMEN'S COMIX*. AND WE WERE OPEN TO ANY GENRES. THE PERSON SIMPLY HAD TO BE A WOMAN.

---

on the politics and issues of "traditional" maleness, other corners of this world were more interested in themes like feminism and queer issues.

Which is how, in 1970, Trina and co-creator Barbara "Willy" Mendes found themselves publishing the first all-women written and drawn comics anthology, *It Ain't Me Babe Comix*. Two years later, Trina cofounded the Wimmen's Comix Collective, which published yearly all-women anthologies for the next twenty years.

"For *It Ain't Me Babe*, I had to find the women and suggest that they draw comics," Trina said. "And then when we did *Wimmen's Comix*, we had grown, with ten women, including me, in just those two years. Every month, we would meet and just sit on the floor surrounded by photocopies of comics and decide what we wanted and what we didn't want. We discovered there were some amazing women cartoonists, and their first work appeared in *Wimmen's Comix*. And we were open to any genres. The person simply had to be a woman."

It is sometimes argued that the reason there have historically been relatively few women making comics is that the women who want to make them are equally few. That said, reaching out to involve underrepresented artists, nurturing their talents, and putting them into a position to be seen is a vital part of ensuring not only immediate success but also long-term growth for the industry. It did not often happen.

"Two weeks before the first issue with *Wimmen's Comix* in 1972," Trina said, "a comic book [named for female genitalia] was coming out of Southern California, published by Joyce Farmer and Lyn Chevli. They did it completely independent of us, and vice versa. And then we found out that we were both doing the same kinds of books, and all met at the underground convention in 1973. We were proving we could do underground comix, and helping it become a better place for women."

In 1967, the year before Trina got her hands on *Zap Comix*, *The Free Press*, an alternative weekly in New York, flew her to the city to write a story about Marvel and Stan Lee, where she and Flo hit it off. When Flo left Marvel, Trina convinced her to come out West and experience the underground comix scene. Before long, Flo started working at the San Francisco Comic Book Company, quickly getting a crash course in telling the kinds of stories she had long wanted to see in the medium.

Flo returned to New York in 1975, taking everything she'd learned and combining it with her super hero connections, enlisting creators like Denny O'Neil (best known as *the* Batman group editor), Herb Trimpe (seminal artist on *The Incredible Hulk*), Wally Wood, and Marvel editor in chief Archie Goodwin to publish *Big Apple Comix*.

Flo's vision of blending comics genres, and giving work-for-hire writers and artists the freedom to explore politically and culturally relevant topics, made *Big Apple Comix* a boundary-defying landmark work, now considered to be the bridge between the male-dominated underground comix scene of the 1960s and '70s and the thriving and diverse indie comics scene of the '80s, which matured into what we know as modern indie comics.

Flo's *Big Apple Comix* also likely impacted what was just around the corner—a blurring of the lines, especially at Marvel, about how to interpret the Comics Code Authority, and about what kinds of themes could and should be tackled by the mainstream comics industry. It also reinforced to women already trying to break into comics that any obstacles that had been established in the past were, as expressed by more than one woman, bull.

"It never occurred to me that I couldn't do it," said Trina emphatically. "Never. I was not thinking, 'I'm a girl and those are guys,' even though it was true, I was a girl, and they were all guys. But I didn't think in those terms. I just thought . . . 'This is so cool.'"

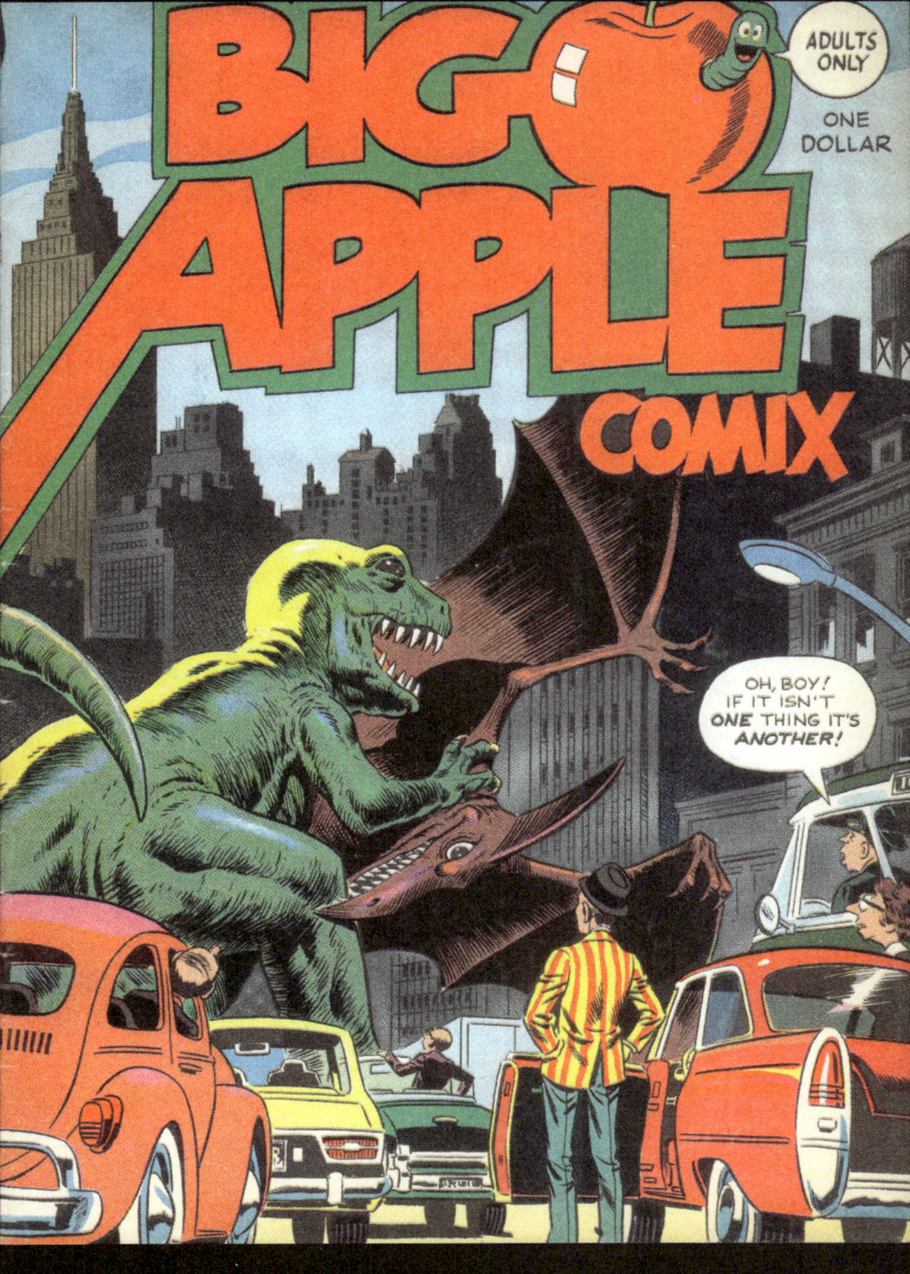
BIG APPLE
COMIX
ADULTS ONLY
ONE DOLLAR
OH, BOY! IF IT ISN'T ONE THING IT'S ANOTHER!

ORAL HISTORY

HEIFERS IN THE BULLPEN

The 1980s were a time of political conservatism and economic turmoil in America. President Jimmy Carter's warning of a "crisis of confidence" came to pass as social discontent bubbled just under the slick neon surface of the Reagan era. That turbulence brought about what is still considered the "Modern Age" of comics, with books like *Watchmen*; *X-Men: God Loves, Man Kills*; and *Daredevil: The Death of Elektra*.

At Marvel, the Modern Age was marked by the emergence of women with huge personalities, now finally in positions to make a huge impact: Louise "Weezie" Simonson, Annie Nocenti, and Jo Duffy, all of whom rose to prominence on books that weren't supposed to be "for girls"—*X-Men*, *Power Man and Iron Fist*, and *Daredevil*.

Inside the Bullpen, the old guard was changing.

OPPOSITE: Hired in 1980, Mary Wilshire was one of the earliest credited female artists, for her work on *New Mutants* and *Firestar*.

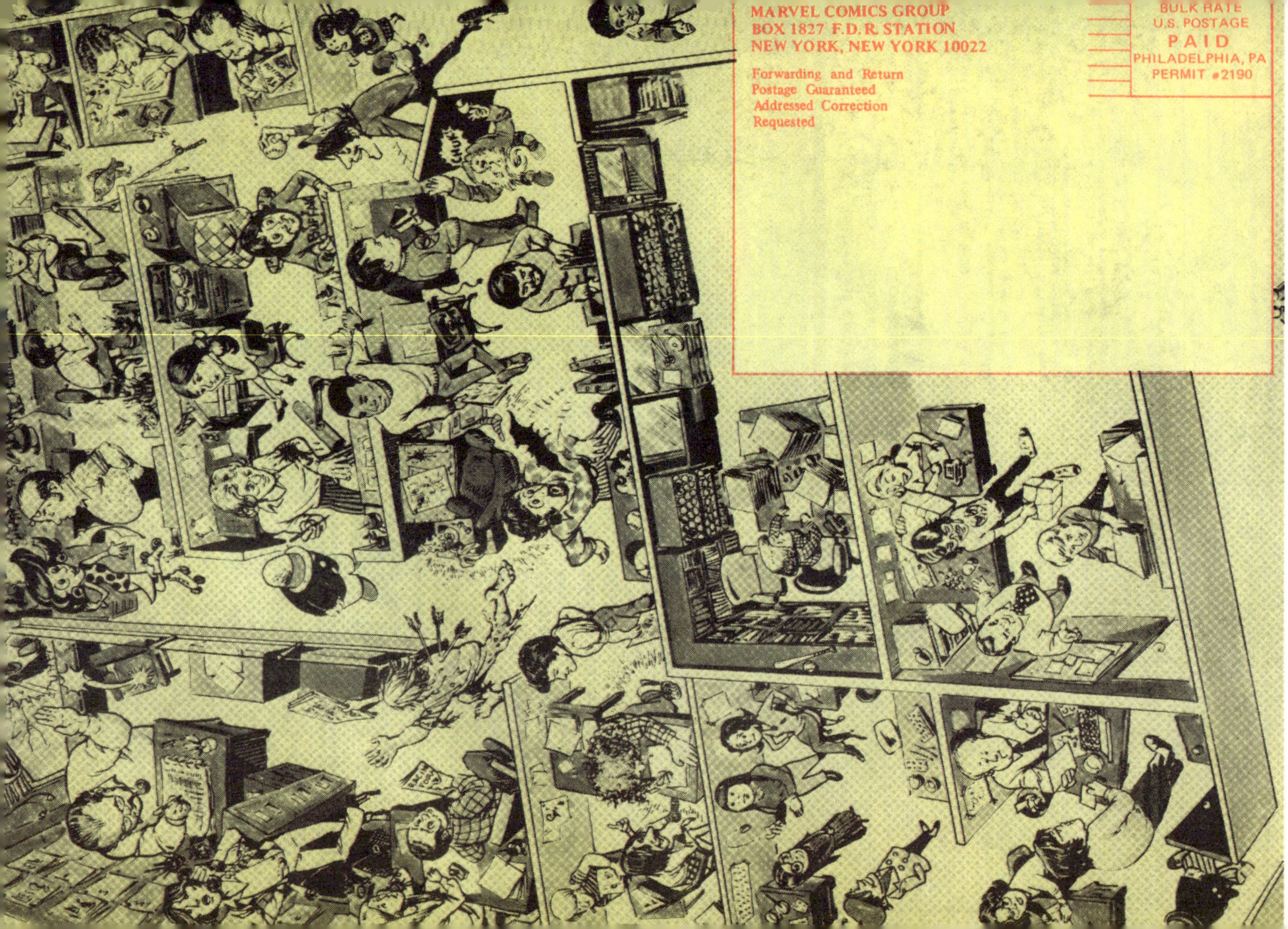
CHUK!
BUFFALO
MARVEL COMICS GROUP
BOX 1827 F.D.R. STATION
NEW YORK, NEW YORK 10022
Forwarding and Return
Postage Guaranteed
Addressed Correction
Requested
BULK RATE
U.S. POSTAGE
PAID
PHILADELPHIA, PA
PERMIT #2190

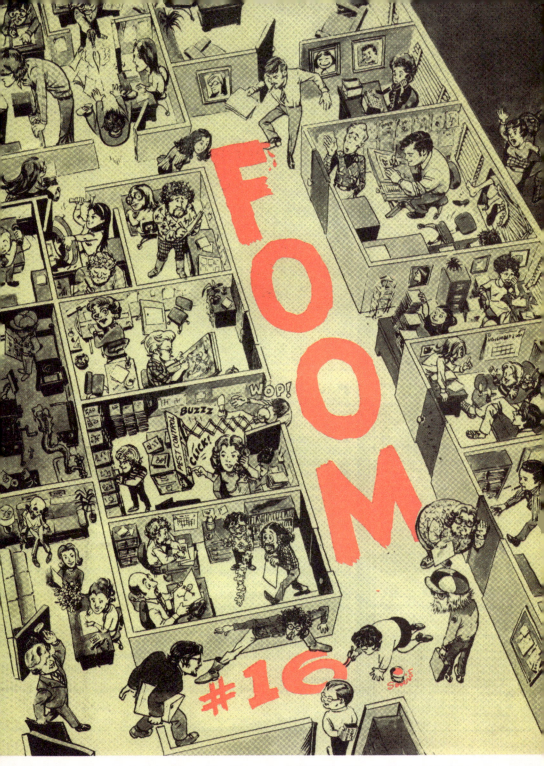

In this drawing for the cover of *FOOM* #16, 1976, Marie Severin gives readers a bird's-eye view of the Marvel offices.

PATY COCKRUM: In late 1974, a per diem position opened up in the Bullpen. Duffy Vohland and Tony Isabella, who I was friends with from fan letters and working there at the time, suggested my name. And Stan approved their suggestion.

A One-Bedroom Operation

JO DUFFY: I started as an editorial assistant, and by the summer of 1977, I was already an assistant editor. At that time, there was only one designated editor—the editor in chief, Jim Shooter by then—and every other editor, regardless of what they did, was on paper an assistant editor. There I was, suddenly working in a room with Ralph Macchio, Roger Stern, and Irene Vartanoff, with Paty and Dave Cockrum, and the Romitas right down the hall, and a little farther down was Marie Severin in the Bullpen with a bunch of great guys. Marie was in a class of her own with her talent. Also, Mary MacPherran was doing most of the administrative work at the time.

That was basically all the women I remember from then, as Marvel was a teeny, tiny little operation that could fit in a Manhattan one-bedroom apartment.

Daily Commute from the Catskills

PATY COCKRUM: Even though I was living in the Catskills, I jumped at the job. I convinced my sister-in-law to babysit my children, and I'd commute down to the city each day.

Pat Redding Scanlon would join the editorial team as Larry Hama's assistant, along with working as an inker and a colorist.

Flat as a Ken Doll

JO DUFFY: Paty is amazing, an absolute dynamo, a complete ball of fire. She's unbelievably funny and incredibly tough. She was a pagan before paganism was remotely fashionable, and she used to want to take Halloween as a religious holiday. And she was crazy about the comics. She was partisan about them.

She was the first person I know of who not only advocated for The Vision and Scarlet Witch to get together, but absolutely insisted that they would be able to have children. And she once took a drawing of Daredevil into Stan's office and said, "Look at this, he's as flat as a Ken doll. Come on, you!"

JOE QUESADA: Oh my God. Paty's a trip. She knows where the bodies are buried.

Moxie

PATY COCKRUM: It was six hours of travel a day, round-trip. A train to New Jersey, then the PATH to Manhattan, and finally a walk to 57th Street and Madison Avenue. There was actually an office pool going on how long I would last. [*Laughs.*] But I proved my "moxie"— Stan liked it, and a few months later I was brought on full-time. Eventually, I left my husband and moved down to the city.

JANICE CHIANG: We discovered this organization, created by a group of anti-war activists, including Larry Hama—the Basement Workshop in New York City's Chinatown. It was an arts organization exploring Asian American identity. At that point, I needed work. My sister asked Larry, "Can you help Janice out? She's looking for a job," and then Larry offered to teach me how to letter. I had a background in fine arts, thanks to our father teaching us Chinese calligraphy. Because of Larry, I started at Neal Adams's studio, learning from Larry and Ralph Reese.

In 1975, Neal was kind enough to give me an introduction into the Marvel Bullpen and Danny Crespi. Danny became my mentor, and I joined the staff learning production and lettering skills. My first big story featured the Black Panther, in *Jungle Action* #16. I ended up staying at Marvel for only a short time, as the curiosity and pursuit of understanding what it was to be Asian American became my driving force.

Against the Grain

JO DUFFY: I worked very closely with Paty, and a lot with Virginia Romita. She wasn't hands-on with the books, but was incredibly vital. After John Verpoorten died suddenly and so young, Virginia took over the role of production manager, and seeing that the pages got from point A to point B in a timely fashion so that we made our shipping dates. Virginia is a little lady, always beautifully dressed, soft-spoken, polite. But she absolutely knew where everything was, what wasn't where it should be, who had promised who what would be where when and whether or not they were keeping that promise. Equally important, Virginia processed the pay vouchers, and was in charge of making sure the checks got to the right people. Virginia not only got all the books out on time, but saw to it that everybody also got paid on time, even if her doing so went against the grain with some of the people who were literally, physically cutting the checks.

Bullpen Sweet Bullpen

JOHN ROMITA JR.: My mom, Virginia, started working for my father, just helping to clean out his office and straighten his files. And suddenly things became very efficient. And she was asked to work in the office on a larger scale and did very well. And then she just kept on rolling into higher positions. She said all she did was work in the office the way she did at home. She kept the house organized and didn't know any different than the way she was. And that's basically it.

JOE QUESADA: [The Bullpen was called] Romita's Raiders, which was run by Virginia. I will go out on a limb and say it wasn't named after John. They were named after Virginia.

JOHN ROMITA JR.: The women at Marvel admired her for her strength. So she affected a lot of people, including a lot of men, too, because of the way she handled herself and the fact that she was their boss. She said to handle yourself professionally with a club—you can't argue with that.

DAWN GUZZO: Our relationship was a good cop/bad cop type of thing. Virginia is a small lady, but boy, when she said something, people jumped. She'd go in and out of the editor's office, and I'd follow to make sure that nobody was offended or crying.

ANNIE NOCENTI: I once shared an office with Virginia Romita. One of the first things she said to me was, you don't smoke, do you? And I was a pack-a-day Lucky Strike girl. I lied and said no, I don't smoke, I quit. It was like it had to become the truth because I didn't want to bug Virginia. I mean, she was not somebody you would stand up to. And she, you know, was really tough, and kept all the Marvel books on time. I don't think we would have produced as much as we did in the eighties without Virginia Romita. She was instrumental. She'd darken your door and just stand there, and you'd have to answer for why your books were so late.

The Virginia Schedule

DAWN GUZZO: The "Virginia Schedule" stayed in effect for years—decades as far as I was told. I don't know if it's still in effect now, but the Virginia Schedule meant stay on it or lose it.

LIA PELOSI: She was a really smart, tough person and usually right, whether you liked it or not. She was very protective of her people. And I learned a lot from her that, as I became a manager and moved on, there's something to be said for the way she would not hold back on her people if she found some of them lacking in something. But she would also be the first person to protect them from incoming editors saying where are my pages or being a jerk, which happens sometimes. She would be the first person to stand in front of that.

Seen here during her time as Editor in Chief Jim Shooter's assistant, Linda Florio Grant would go on to be an editor, working on *Daredevil*, *Alpha Flight*, and *Ghost Rider*.

ORAL HISTORY

HEIFERS IN THE BULLPEN / 53

Stan Likes My Work

JO DUFFY: When I came in, they thought the comics industry was over. There were jobs to be had, but there was no money with which to be paid for them. The only reason anyone was getting into comics was for love of the medium. There was no chance of getting rich and famous. As a result, there was a tremendous amount of artistic freedom. Some of it was simple chaos, but some of it was freedom. And we got to do a great deal.

It was an interesting time, with the women's rights movement, and entering a field where many of the men thought my proper role was as a girlfriend or wife rather than as a colleague. In retrospect, some of them had a little difference of opinion with me on that subject. But I was so dazzled by "I'm in comics, I'm writing super heroes, Stan likes my work" (which he did), that it never even occurred to me the people who talked back and told me feminism was trash absolutely meant it.

TRINA ROBBINS: One reason I did *Meet Misty* was because still in the eighties people were saying, "Well, girls don't read comics." I knew that I, along with my girlfriends and girls all over America, had read comics. And I knew that that was bull. I thought I would try to bring back the kind of comics I'd read as a kid, and that attempt was *Meet Misty*.

What Makes You Think You Can Do This?

JO DUFFY: Looking back, it never occurred to me that I didn't belong there. One time, Will Eisner asked me, "What makes you think you can do this?" And I said, "Because I'm doing it! I like it, and I'm good at it!" It was the only time I spent with Will, and there he was, studying me as an anomaly. It was really funny. He was a lovely man and a phenomenal creator, but he just couldn't get his brain around the fact that I, a woman, wanted to do this and could. And yet there was nothing wrong with me.

A Lot of Together

IRENE VARTANOFF: Well, let me tell you: Tony Isabella is really short. One day, the guys put him into a large, corrugated box and delivered it to Sol Brodsky's office and said, "We don't want him. He's too short."

Another time, Archie Goodwin, who was, in many respects, a very dignified man, decided to see if he could get all the way around the editorial Bullpen room from desk to desk, so he did, leaping from one desk to another.

Now, there were no cubicles. So at its maximum, we had six to eight desks. Stan had a nice corner office. It was a nice office. Then the next office was most of the editors. Roy, when I got there, had [an office carved out of the editorial office].

That was, for me, the honeymoon period with Marvel. And it was entertaining—there were a lot of silly things because there were a lot of guys.

For the first year or so, it was fun . . . Then it became work. We were working the whole time—I mean, people didn't want to leave. We'd get there early and we'd stay late and we'd laugh at the people who left at five o'clock and then we'd play softball together in Central Park.

We went to lunch together. There was a *lot* of together.

BOBBIE CHASE: When we would pull all-nighters, the president's office upstairs had a suite with a bathroom, so we could go take a shower and then keep working.

JO DUFFY: Anytime anything the least bit noteworthy occurred, Marie or Dave Cockrum would sit down to do a caricature of it. We had a volleyball team and a softball team. I was not a great athlete, very clumsy, but I loved to play. Inevitably, one day after a big game I came into the office with a big old shiner, and by the next day, there was an illustration that Marie had drawn with me sitting at my desk, looking like a wounded cartoon character.

Rise of the Male Sensibility

TRINA ROBBINS: The artists had to compete in a different way. There was a tenderness to Mary Wilshire and June Brigman, lines that showed they drew with enormous heart and tenderness, which I don't even know if that's something we should be saying, you know, because it sounds gendered, but they did. But this was a time where artists like Todd McFarlane were coming in with this specific style of extremely muscled, powerful male figures, which ended up taking over the industry to a certain degree in the nineties. And I think that the rise of the male sensibility in comics did some damage.

One at a Time

BOBBIE CHASE: When I started, it did feel like you could only have one woman in the Marvel Universe line-editing at a time. First it was Louise Simonson, and when she left, [they] made room for Annie [Nocenti], and then I became editor. It was more of a coincidence, as they weren't actually doing that, but it did feel like it at the time.

ELAINE LEE: I was too outside of that world, and I think that was true of a lot of women. I know those who were colorists, had husbands or boyfriends who were comic book artists or whatever, and that's what happened back then. But there were not a lot of women mentors. In fact, I was sort of intimidated by the women who actually worked in the offices because I thought, "What secret do they have that I do not have access to?" And I told Louise that a few years ago, when a bunch of women from the biz got together for lunch. And I know they were intimidating to me because I had no idea how they got there, what magical process they went through.

Trying to Write Like a Man

ANNIE NOCENTI: Maybe I learned that from Weezie, as she didn't want to become typecast by writing female characters, to fall into the tendency to have a female write a female. When I look back on my career at Marvel, I think I was trying to write like a man. I wrote *Punisher*, *Wolverine*, *Daredevil*, *Ghost Rider*. . . . But the most powerful thing is to not fight. And it is what's behind the fist that becomes even more important. Why are you punching someone?

Maybe the super hero narrative was just waiting for creators like Kelly Sue DeConnick, Sana Amanat, and G. Willow Wilson. Those three women wrote real female super hero narratives.

In the eighties, I was trying to compete with the male writers because there were so few women in the field. The last thing I was going to do would be a female-empowered narrative, because it wouldn't have flown.

Or maybe it would have . . . but we'll never know now.

Creator's Rights

JO DUFFY: A couple of things happened in the eighties, which were good and bad. First there was the direct market, with Jim Galton and Phil Seuling from the seventies, working together to create a new system of distribution for fans to purchase comics. And by the eighties, it was catching on and went from being a niche to highly lucrative.

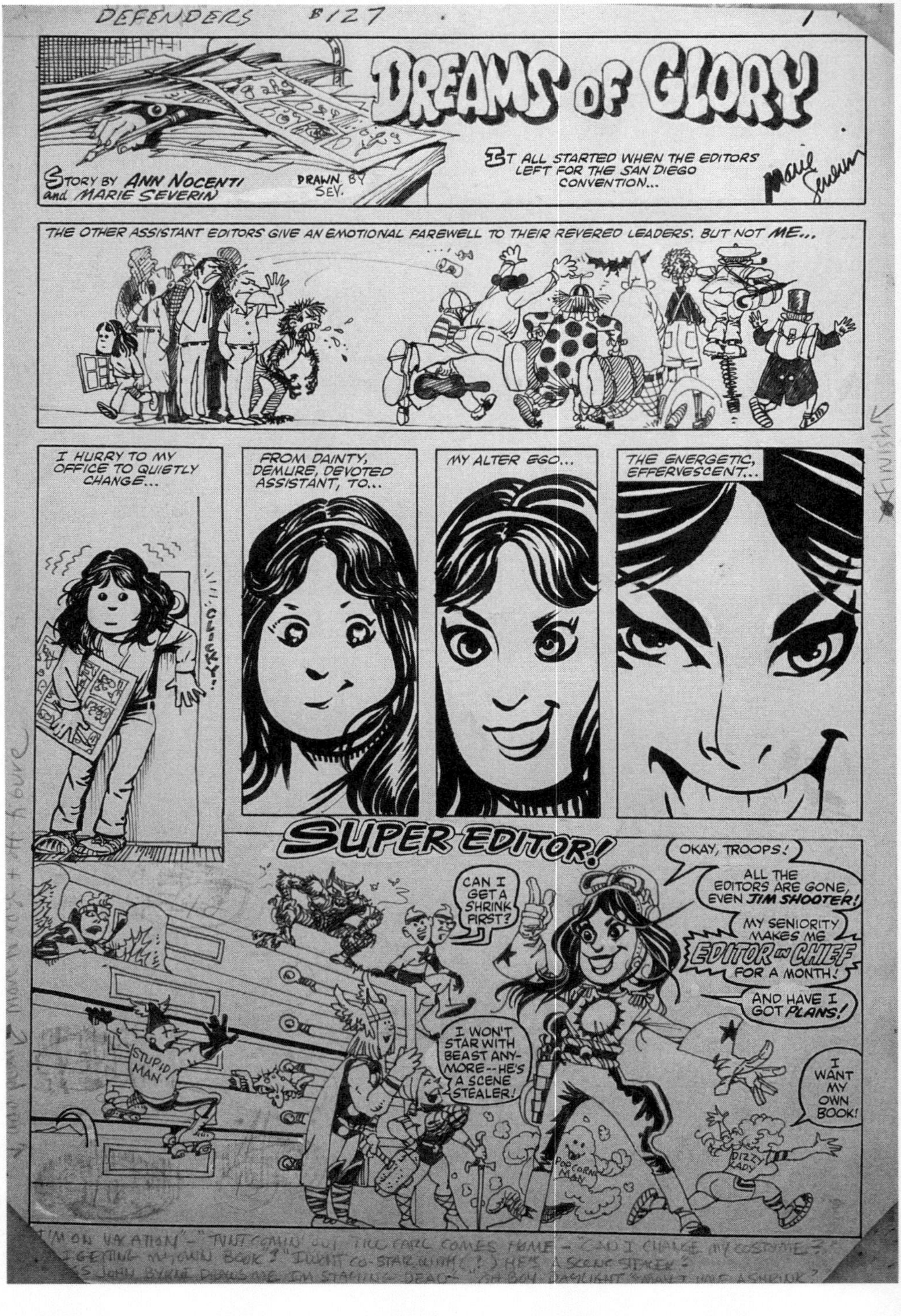
DEFENDERS #127
DREAMS OF GLORY
STORY BY ANN NOCENTI and MARIE SEVERIN
DRAWN BY SEV.
IT ALL STARTED WHEN THE EDITORS LEFT FOR THE SAN DIEGO CONVENTION...
Marie Severin
THE OTHER ASSISTANT EDITORS GIVE AN EMOTIONAL FAREWELL TO THEIR REVERED LEADERS. BUT NOT ME...
I HURRY TO MY OFFICE TO QUIETLY CHANGE...
CLICKY!
FROM DAINTY, DEMURE, DEVOTED ASSISTANT, TO...
MY ALTER EGO...
THE ENERGETIC, EFFERVESCENT...
SUPER EDITOR!
OKAY, TROOPS!
ALL THE EDITORS ARE GONE, EVEN JIM SHOOTER!
MY SENIORITY MAKES ME EDITOR IN CHIEF FOR A MONTH!
AND HAVE I GOT PLANS!
CAN I GET A SHRINK FIRST?
I WON'T STAR WITH BEAST ANYMORE--HE'S A SCENE STEALER!
I WANT MY OWN BOOK!
STUPID MAN
POPCORN MAN
DIZZY LADY
FINISH

ORAL HISTORY

And next was the creator's rights movement, with Neal Adams and Archie Goodwin being two of the main tentpoles, campaigning for creators to get their fair share. This led to the Epic line at Marvel, and "incentives."

Finally, Marvel was returning all of the original artwork to the creators after publication.

These all came together to create a wonderful resurgence, bringing in a lot more people, and suddenly the industry wasn't dying anymore—it was burgeoning.

ANNIE NOCENTI: The more you get into this, it'll be like Russian nesting dolls. We all mentored each other. Marie Severin mentored me. Weezie mentored me. I went on to hire Cynthia Martin, Mary Wilshire. . . . So it's all passed on, the females pass it on to the next females.

JANICE CHIANG: In 1980, after my son was born, I returned to Marvel and lettering. On my first story back, I was shocked there was a woman editor, Louise Simonson—"Oh my God, this is wonderful! A woman!"

She became my mentor. One of the first issues she gave me was a Conan story drawn by John Buscema, who is basically a Renaissance artist. I asked her, "You trust me to touch this?"

That first job I lettered with a pencil. [*Laughs.*] And then I came back with ink. It took me two hours [to do] a page. But eventually I got up to speed again.

I'm told when people look at my lettering, they know it's me. They don't even have to see a credit. That's one of my greatest achievements as a woman comics letterer—that I have a style distinct enough to say it's mine.

OPPOSITE: You could never say that Marvel in the '80s didn't have fun, as shown by this comic featuring Annie Nocenti as her own hero, drawn by Marie Severin for *The Defenders* #127.

Suit Up, You're Drawing *Spider-Man*

PATY COCKRUM: After I left the staff, I did an issue of *The Amazing Spider-Man*. I think it was issue #264. One day I had stopped by to drop off a few pages of Dave [Cockrum]'s art and was walking down the hall when Christopher Priest pulled me into his office and said, "Paty . . . you are going to save my life!" He was the editor of *Spider-Man* at the time, and basically begged me to draw an issue, as the rest of his artists were sick with the flu. I kept saying things like "I have about six projects on my board at home for merchandising . . . I don't do super heroes . . ."

But he wouldn't take no for an answer, so I ended up going home with this one-page script, and had a week to turn in twenty-one pages of art. Two weeks later, after turning in the pencils the week earlier and being sent home to ink it, I turned in my first and only *Spider-Man* comic. It wasn't the worst *Spider-Man* issue ever done, nor the best, but it was definitely the fastest.

PAT REDDING: I was working on underground comix and also doing some work for Marvel. I would ink their backgrounds, panel borders, or whatever they needed help with. I got to ink some of John Buscema's artwork on *Conan* and that was really pretty awesome. Also I got to know Larry [Hama] better, through inking his pages, as they were so beautiful. That was really a privilege.

BOBBIE CHASE: There was a point where I wasn't necessarily working on great books, just the ones people didn't want. I was told, "If you want to get ahead, you have to create it yourself." That's where the horror line came from, which became Marvel Edge in 1995.

Writing Me as a Character

RENÉE WITTERSTAETTER: I had a lot of books I enjoyed, but *She-Hulk* was one of the most fun to work on because I never knew what John Byrne was going to do or come up with, but it was always hilarious. At one point, he started writing me in as a character, but he didn't tell me he was doing that. He would write me having this big, palatial office overlooking New York, with assistants bringing me coffee on a tray. [*Laughs.*] At that time, my office was what we called the Dungeon, which I shared with Marie Javins. We were on a different floor than the rest of the office, with no windows, and people would sometimes forget that we were even there. Marie and I even had a pet rat in the office for a while that nobody knew about. We had a great time.

I, Claudius

IRENE VARTANOFF: In the early 1970s, PBS had that series *I, Claudius*. And the maneuvering—my sister always used to say, "Oh, Marvel. It's *I, Claudius* time." And luckily, nobody murdered anybody.

TOP: Bonded by their love of comics, Flo Steinberg and Trina Robbins were lifelong friends, seen here with Steve Leialoha. BOTTOM: The first and only group editor in chief, Bobbie Chase, seen here working in her office.

TOP: Dawn Geiger (right) poses with her mentors Flo Steinberg (left) and Virginia Romita (center). BOTTOM: Dawn would take over the mantle of production manager when Virginia Romita retired. Seen here with Dahlia Aponte, Virginia's assistant.

CLOCKWISE FROM TOP LEFT: Two iconic women in comics, Annie Nocenti and Virginia Romita, pose for the camera; editorial staff wait to sign a birthday card at Marie Severin's desk; Marvel alumni have stayed friends after their time working in comics, with Pat Scanlon and Janice Chiang posing together at a recent comics event.

ORAL HISTORY

LOUISE SIMONSON

Formerly the editor in chief of Warren Publishing, Louise "Weezie" Simonson joined the Marvel editorial staff in 1980. During her time at the House of Ideas, she helped build the X-Men universe—one of her first Bullpen assignments was editing Chris Claremont—and simultaneously helped build the profile of the women of Marvel in general.

Working alongside fellow editors like Jo Duffy and Annie Nocenti, Louise was also able to open the door for new female talent, including artist June Brigman, her collaborator on the *Power Pack* ongoing series. "I didn't hire them because they were women," Weezie said. "I hired them because they were people who were good at what they did."

Judy Stephens, a Marvel producer and co-creator of the *Women of Marvel* podcast, spoke to Louise via the *Women of Marvel* podcast on April 19, 2021. This is the excerpted transcript of their conversation.

JUDY: How did you get started in comics?

LOUISE: Well, I got started at Warren Publishing, which was a black-and-white horror book publisher back in the day. They did *Creepy*, *Eerie*, and *Vampirella*. And a war book called *Blazing Combat*, written by Archie Goodwin. I don't even like war books, but I really liked that one.

And so that kind of got me reading Archie's stuff. And then I became familiar with the other Warren material. But it never occurred to me to work there.

I was an advertising promoter for a New York magazine publisher. And I had a friend who worked at Warren and she said, "There's an opening for a job there and it pays better and you can do it."

And I thought, "Okay, I might as well apply, right?" So the job is in production. Which is pay stubs and mechanicals and that kind of thing. I was hired, and it did pay a little bit more than my last job.

I started off doing art corrections and pay stubs and mechanicals. I was not, I have to say, a great production person. But it was a very small company and what they needed was a pair of hands.

And they'd say, "Oh gosh, can somebody do a letters column?"

And I'd say, "I could do that."

Can somebody do this? *I can do that.*

So there were a lot of other things I thought I could do. I just wasn't great at the production part.

Probably a month or two into it, they created an assistant editor position for me, which they hadn't had before, and they moved me over into editorial.

And then after that, I loved it. It was small and intimate and fun. But you know, once I was at the editorial end, it was even more fun.

And so that was how I got into comics. Maybe three or four years later, editor Bill DuBay left. And I insisted on having the editor in chief job there, as it was a very small fishbowl. But I loved doing that part.

And then a couple of years later, Jim Shooter over at Marvel asked me if I would come and edit there.

It was a very small world back then, comics. To work there, you really had to live there. I had a lot of friends in the comic book industry—at Marvel and at DC. When I was still at Warren, I'd had a couple of calls from Jenette Kahn to come work at DC, but I loved my little slot at Warren. It was very, very freeing. I could do almost anything I wanted.

But I kind of wanted a bigger pond. So I was happy to move over to Marvel at that point. And also I knew Jim, and I knew the people, because I played volleyball with them.

JUDY: What was it like transitioning to super heroes?

LOUISE: I was given, at first, the licensed projects, which seems to be what the new editor always gets handed. And then two Chris Claremont books. I got handed *Man-Thing*. And then a couple of months later, I got *X-Men*.

Chris would come into my office and show me pages. And one of the pages he showed me was where Phoenix flares and takes out a planet with living people on it, living asparagus people or broccoli people or whatever they were. And I said, "You can't do that. You can't have Phoenix just kill all these people." And Chris said, "Oh, it's okay, Shooter has seen it. Shooter has approved it." Well, what do I know? I'm just learning the rules here. Maybe that's all right.

And then several months later, when Shooter did see it—either again or for the first time, depending on whose story you're hearing—he completely freaked out and declared, "Okay then, Phoenix has to die."

And he pulled Jim Salicrup off the book and plonked me right in the middle of the death-of-Phoenix story. So that's how I ended up taking over the X-Men.

I was very happy to have been given the X-Men. I think at the time they were considered kind of a second-level book, even though they sold very well. They weren't *real*, real Marvel.

JUDY: The eighties was this period of newly created characters. You worked with June Brigman on *Power Pack*, and June told the story about how she came to New York City and visited the office. You asked her: "Can you draw children?" And she said yes . . . and then the Power Pack was born. That's kind of amazing!

LOUISE: Yeah, it was such a weird idea, that you got to give Jim Shooter a lot of credit for actually going for it.

He had been wanting his editors to do freelance work as well. Not because we needed the money, because the pay was decent, but because he wanted us to see what it was like on the other side of the desk.

I thought maybe I could write stories, and I could color. But I also knew that we had writers and colorists who earned their living by doing this, and I already had a job. And it didn't seem fair to take any of their work.

But I got bored. So I said, "Well, maybe I can write something." And I went to him and I said, "Well, I have this idea—there are four little kids who are super heroes."

And Shooter sort of rolled his eyes. And he said, "Write up something, maybe we'll get a miniseries out of it," with not a lot of hope in his voice. So I wrote up a plot. And June came to me with these wonderful drawings. I went into Shooter's office and handed it all off to him . . . and a couple of days later, he came back, having loved it.

Now we had a series—not a miniseries, but a monthly series. And the first issue is double-sized and it's due in a couple of months. And June has never drawn a comic book, and I had never written a twenty-two-page comic before.

So Jim Shooter was taking a chance on the both of us.

June Brigman was Louise Simonson's partner on *Power Pack* and would go on to become an influential art professor at multiple art colleges.

That's how I started writing at Marvel, and I was delighted to work with June. Her drawings were so wonderful. The kids in Power Pack were more themselves from the drawings than just from my writing, you know. The attitudes, their physical attitudes were so perfect. That was great. I was very lucky.

JUDY: During your time, there weren't many women, but you had the opportunity to work with some tremendous ones.

LOUISE: Back in the olden days, in the eighties, there were fewer women in the office, but they were prime.

I loved Virginia Romita, the head of production. She would make sure everybody got their books turned in on time, more or less. I just thought she was the best.

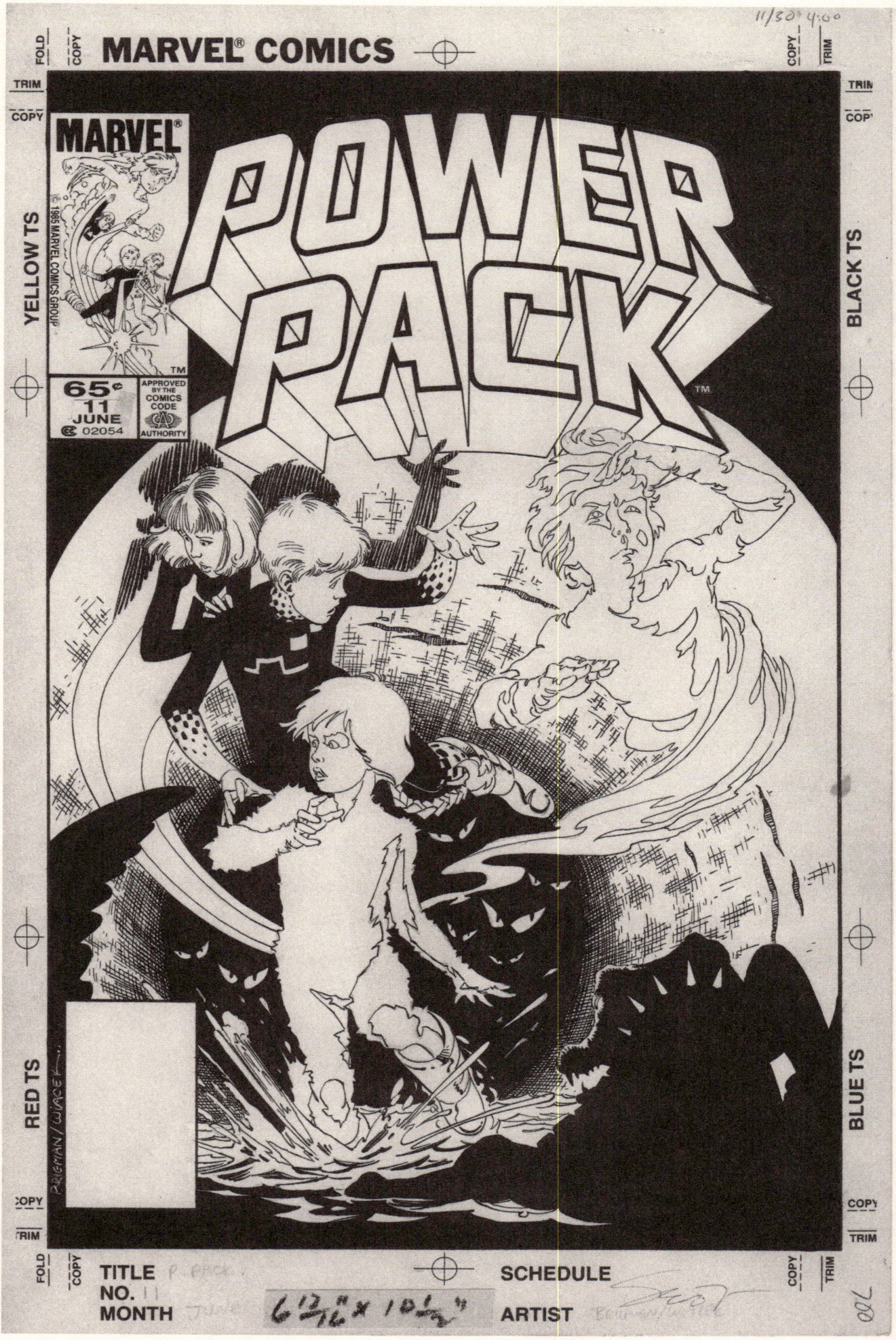
MARVEL® COMICS
MARVEL®
POWER PACK
65¢
11
JUNE
02054
APPROVED BY THE COMICS CODE AUTHORITY
© 1985 MARVEL COMICS GROUP
TRIM
COPY
FOLD
YELLOW TS
BLACK TS
RED TS
BLUE TS
TITLE
NO.
MONTH
SCHEDULE
ARTIST

OPPOSITE: Original cover of *Power Pack* #11, featuring handwritten notes and logo placement.

ORAL HISTORY

I loved it when she would come down to my office and we would talk, mostly, as I got my books in on time. So we didn't have a lot of conflict.

Every week we would have what was called the Virginia meeting. We'd go up to the conference room and each editor would explain why a particular book was late on the schedule. And there were always doughnuts or bagels and coffee. It was almost like a party for me, because my books were mostly on time, so I was good.

I loved working with Pam, who was upstairs in the financing end of Marvel, and Millie Sheriff, who made sure you got your checks.

JUDY: You've continued to work in comics as an editor since leaving Marvel. But how has it been to see some type of equality in comics?

LOUISE: It's the way the world ought to be. The fact that there are more women doing comics now reflects that there are more women reading comics. And I think a lot of that had to do with the X-Men books. I know the animated show got a lot of women interested in Marvel Comics. A lot of the women I've talked to who are now doing comics became interested because of that cartoon. And it was kind of a feedback loop, where more women became interested in doing them. And the more women who did comics, the more of a female audience started reading them more.

Another thing, speaking of women in comics, is all the colorists and the letterers, like Janice Cohen.

LOUISE SIMONSON / 73

What was odd was that I didn't think, "Oh, how few women there are in the business." I mean, every once in a while I noticed that I was the only woman in the room. But it didn't really bother me particularly. And I didn't hire women because of gender, but they were people who were good at what they did. Like Christie Scheele and Glynis Oliver and Mary Wilshire.

JUDY: It's interesting because in the foreword for the *Women of Marvel* anthology, you wrote that you didn't necessarily ever want to write female-led titles.

LOUISE: Because they would be canceled. They would last six months and then they were gone. And I didn't want to be put into that situation—a lot of women who came in and wanted to write comics, if one of the editors were feeling benevolent, they would slot a woman onto a series that was just doomed, because comics were bought by guys, who only wanted to read about guys.

I refused to be part of that. I was really happy to work on the X-Men, and then the New Mutants, first as an editor, and then later as a writer. Working on group stories allowed for more complex stories, and I enjoyed doing them. But I didn't want to be put into the "female only" category, which was a thing that happened at that time. If you were a woman, you would be asked to do one issue, or maybe a short story with Spider-Woman in it or something. And I didn't want to do that.

And you have to realize that comics are a lot of work. When you pick a comic up, you just think about a cool story, and not the hours and hours of some artist, or several artists often, mostly sitting at a drawing board for ten hours a day.

It's not an easy way to make a living. It's a fun way of making a living, if you love doing it. It's not for the faint of heart. But I love it.

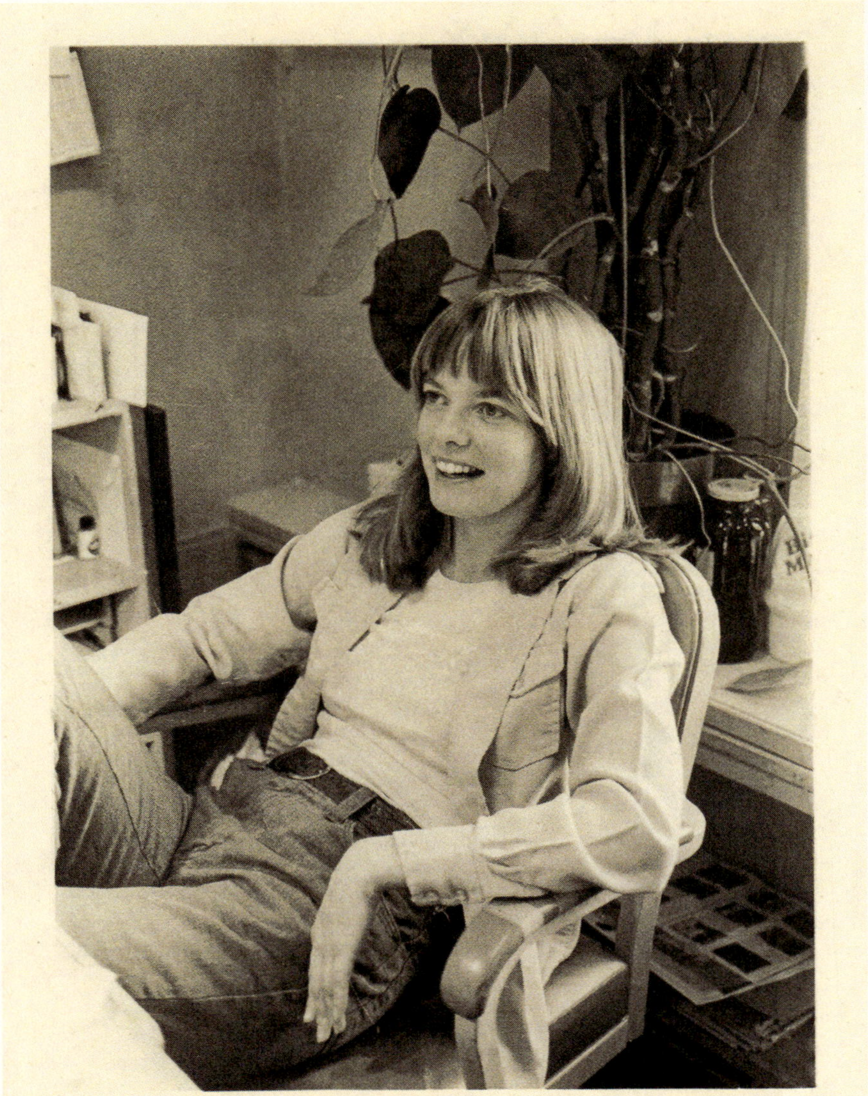

PART TWO

THE BEST THERE IS

AT WHAT THEY DO

THE WOMEN
WHO TOOK MARVEL COMICS
HIGHER, FURTHER, FASTER

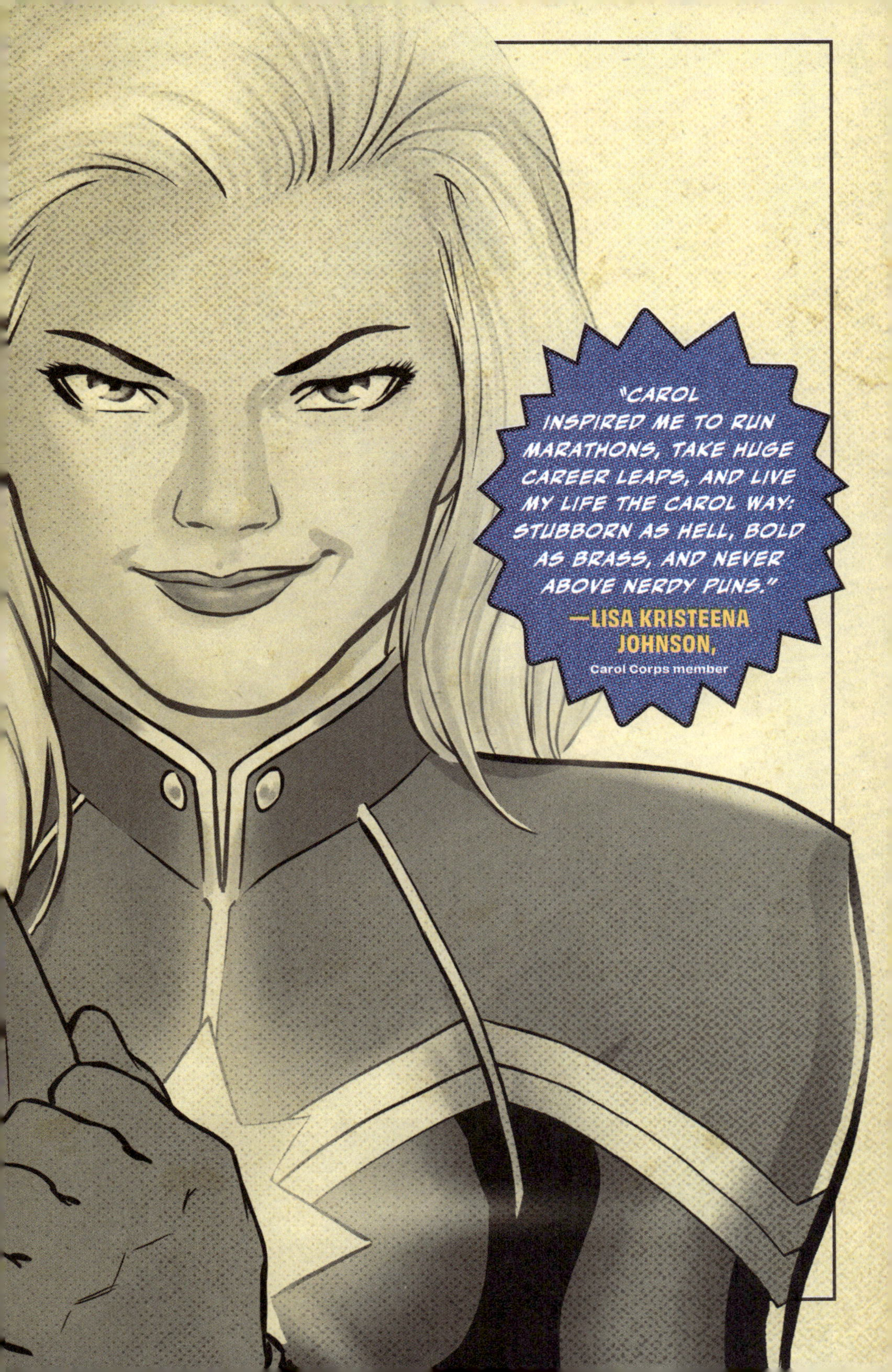
"CAROL INSPIRED ME TO RUN MARATHONS, TAKE HUGE CAREER LEAPS, AND LIVE MY LIFE THE CAROL WAY: STUBBORN AS HELL, BOLD AS BRASS, AND NEVER ABOVE NERDY PUNS."
—LISA KRISTEENA JOHNSON,
Carol Corps member

Giant-Size X-Men #1, 1975,
cover art by Dave Cockrum.

CHAPTER THREE

FROM THE ASTONISHING TO THE UNCANNY

The Origin of a Show
That Launched a Thousand
Fans and, Arguably, the
Marvel Cinematic Universe

X-Men: The Animated Series, which premiered on October 31, 1992, is one of the most well-known—and well-loved—Marvel expressions in pop culture. Here's what most people don't know: there were five women without whom it never would have happened.

First published in 1963, *The Uncanny X-Men* was conceived as a group of misfits and outcasts with powers that manifested at puberty, "sworn to protect a world that hates and fears them." Stan Lee had consistently resisted Marvel taking anything that could be considered a political stance, but in October 1968, after a reader wrote in to ask him to be more specific, Stan opened the floodgates in his "Soapbox" column. "From now on," he wrote, "whenever we have something to get off our chest, we'll assume we have a magniloquent mandate to sock it to ya, and let the chips fall where they may."

For the next month, he spent the entirety of "Stan's Soapbox" decrying hatred, bigotry, and racism, calling the last two "among the deadliest social ills of the world today," and the issues at the time grappled with Vietnam, civil rights, and the idea of "morality"—as when the Silver Surfer met the Fantastic Four and he was so moved by their empathy and humanity that, even though he knew he would be punished, he turned on his master, Galactus, saving the Earth from destruction.

By 1970, as more Marvel comics took up the issues of the day, *X-Men*'s sales began to decline and the ongoing comics series was canceled.

In 1975, American and global politics entered a new state of crisis following the Watergate scandal and the fall of Saigon, along with the continual pressure of the Cold War. In May of that year, with a then-relatively-unknown writer named Chris Claremont, Marvel relaunched the X-Men with a new, more diverse cast, expanding the mutant universe to feature characters from Japan, Ireland, Germany, Kenya, Russia, and an Apache reservation in Arizona.

If the brief for *X-Men* had always been to give a voice to the marginalized, it made sense for the team to plant a global flag at a time when American xenophobia took aim at the specter of "the Other." It was also the first appearance for characters who would go on to be tentpole members of the X-Men, both on the page and in pop culture, including Ororo Munroe, aka Storm, a Black woman with the power to control the weather.

Chris Claremont is inarguably the architect behind the rebirth of the X-Men, and the template by which modern X-Men comics are still made. He also had a knack for empowering female super heroes and writing characters women wanted to read. ("He had strong female role models when he was raised," Annie Nocenti, Claremont's editor on *The Uncanny X-Men*, said.)

Claremont's ability to perfectly balance levity and despair, small moments of quiet and literal universe-ending crisis, all set against the backdrop of the political and social turbulence of the real world of its readers—and starring stand-ins for a marginalized audience hungry for representation—rocketed *The Uncanny X-Men* to the stratosphere as both a critical hit and a bestseller.

Rainbow Rowell, an internationally bestselling novelist, as well as a writer of Marvel's *Runaways* and *She-Hulk*, was an avid *X-Men* reader growing up. "The thing about those comics was they had tons of women in them. And because they had tons of women in them, they could be different kinds of women, right? So Storm was a different sort of woman than Jean Grey was or that Kitty Pryde was or that Emma Frost was.

"Chris Claremont wrote so many women. And he also wrote very character-driven stories, where the characters were more important maybe than the plot. And I find that to be, as a woman . . . I do find that to be my way in."

Dan Buckley, current president of Marvel Comics and Franchise, witnessed firsthand how the success of the X-Men not only translated into company-wide success, but into an on-ramp for an audience Marvel had long been trying to crack: women and girls. As Dan pointed out, "Yeah, [X-Men] was written from the male point of view, with the exception of a strong female editorial voice in one of our key editorial talents at the time."

That key editorial talent was, of course, Louise Simonson.

Louise is a creative force in her own right; in addition to the books she wrote, Louise co-created the iconic X-Men characters Apocalypse and Cable, both of whom feature in seminal storylines in the comics and films.

She was always able to "get what [she wanted] from the writers and artists and have them leave the office with their tails wagging, not realizing they had to redo everything!" Annie, who was hired as Jim Shooter's assistant in 1984 but was quickly poached by Louise to be her assistant editor, said in 2013 during a joint interview with Louise at Comic Book Resources.

When we asked Annie about Louise, she said, "I can't talk about my career without talking about Louise Simonson, because she trained me. Weezie taught me how to get out of the way. How to put a good team together and get out of the way. Don't be dictatorial or hands-on, just gently herd and nudge creators along the way. If you put a good team together, you don't have to do much. And Weezie also taught me how to work with Chris Claremont, which was to just take him to lunch a lot and listen to his endless ideas and pick the best ones."

Claremont's ideas, many of which were conceived with Louise as his editor, provided the blueprint for the X-Men storylines that would go on to be made into a massive film franchise, and he gave new, more complex life to characters that are now household names. Their collaboration would span four years and some of the most revered and iconic X-Men storylines ever, including "The Dark Phoenix Saga," "Days of Future Past," and the one-shot "Gold Rush," which introduced Magneto's past as a Jewish Holocaust survivor.

It was also at Louise's suggestion that Claremont expanded on his "Mutant Massacre" storyline; together, they ran it across all existing X-book titles, affecting the creative trajectory of the entire line. That collaboration would be the first of what would become a time-honored and always-anticipated tradition in the Marvel office: the X-Men Crossover Event.

"We used to say that Weezie's superpower was that she had the power to cloud men's minds," Annie said in 2013.

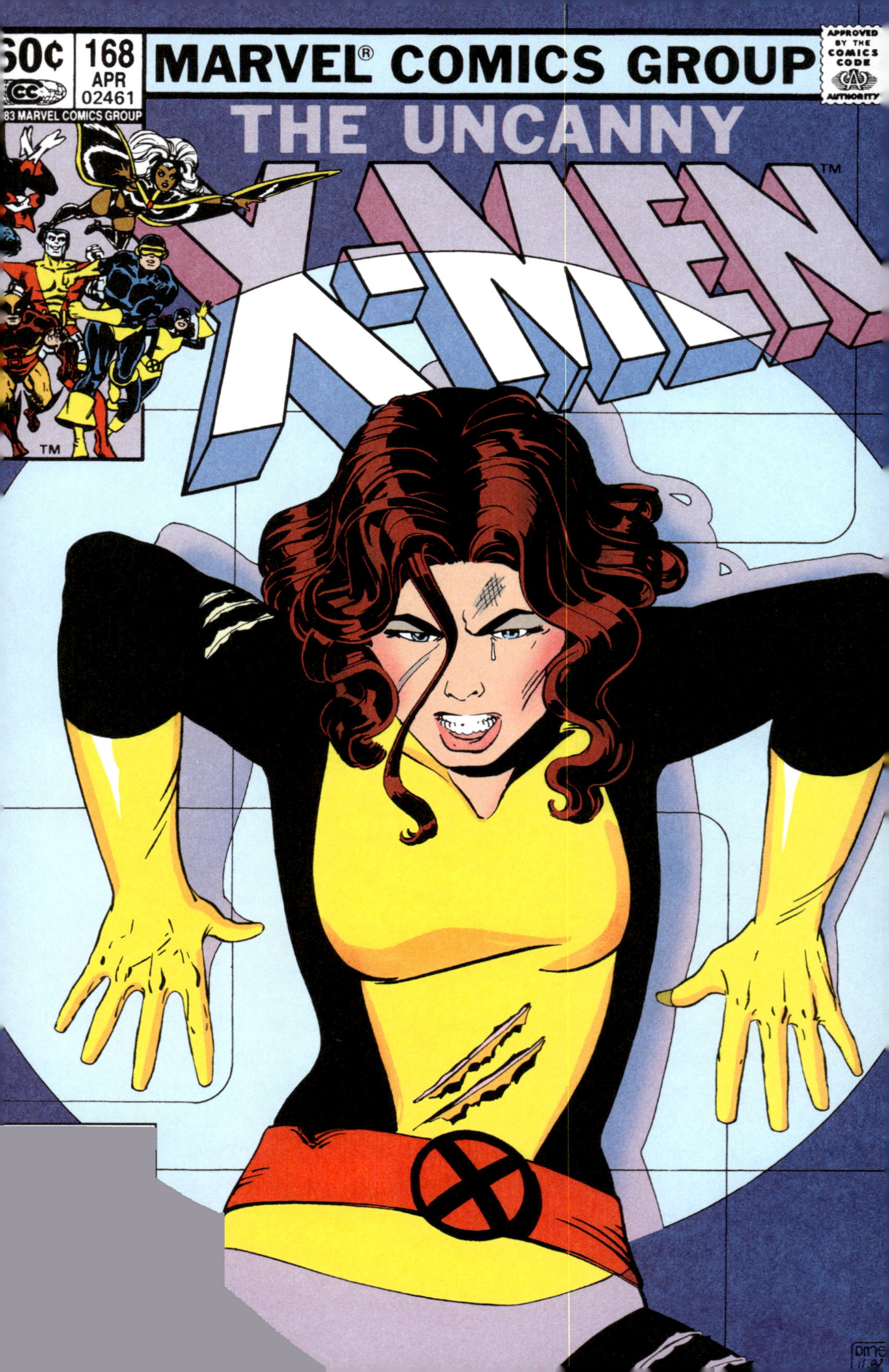
60¢
168
APR
02461
MARVEL® COMICS GROUP
APPROVED BY THE COMICS CODE AUTHORITY
83 MARVEL COMICS GROUP
THE UNCANNY
X-MEN™
TM

X-Men as a franchise became known for its centering of its female characters' stories, and it allowed them to be fully rounded heroes and villains, due in large part to Chris Claremont's historic run in the '80s. ABOVE: *X-Men* #135, 1980, cover art by John Byrne. OPPOSITE: *Uncanny X-Men* #168, 1983, cover art by Paul Smith.

ANOTHER WOMAN who had kept a close eye on Claremont's X-Men books was Margaret Loesch. The one-time president of Marvel Animation, Margaret was running Fox Kids in the 1990s, where she started toying around with the idea to develop a show that would directly adapt material from Claremont's seventeen-year run.

That show would be called *X-Men: The Animated Series*.

"Margaret does not get enough credit for her influence here at Marvel," said Dan Buckley. "Incredibly bright woman. She was such an influence behind the X-Men animated series."

The show was pivotally important for changing the broader culture's perspective of Marvel. Even in the interviews for this book, more women mentioned the animated series as their on-ramp to Marvel than anything else. (Sarah Singer, editor of special projects at Marvel Entertainment—and an editor on this book—made sure to mention in the editorial notes that they were introduced to Marvel this way.)

"I know the X-Men animated show got a lot of women interested in Marvel Comics," said Louise Simonson. "A lot of the women I've talked to, who are now making comics, became interested because of the cartoon. I think that it was kind of a feedback loop."

"*X-Men: The Animated Series* was my very first introduction to the X-Men, who have obviously become a huge part of my life and my career," *X-Men* writer Tini Howard said. "From the music, to the costumes, to the fact that my own dream was to be discovered at the mall, it was the first super hero media I saw that I felt like I connected with. Any team that could have a disaster like Jubes probably had room for someone like me, too."

"Oh, Jubilee is my favorite," said Jeanine Schaefer, editor of *X-Men* and *Wolverine and Jubilee*. Jubilation Lee, the fireworks-powered teenage mall rat created by Chris Claremont and Jim Lee was used as the audience's POV character when the show was introduced and would go on to become Wolverine's sidekick in the comics. "She caught me at exactly the right time—we were almost the exact same age—when I was desperate to see girls like me as the heroes in the shows I liked, instead of having to see myself in the boys. It's funny how all it takes is to be able to see someone even remotely like yourself doing the thing, to think that you can also do the thing."

"In my opinion, Margaret is the reason we're having this conversation

X-Men: The Animated Series would not have happened if not for Margaret Loesch (left), seen here with Marvel chairman Stan Lee (center) and then-head of Marvel Entertainment Jim Galton (right).

now, and the reason Marvel is where it is right now," said Julia Lewald, a staff writer for *X-Men: The Animated Series*. Fast-talking, funny, and passionate, Julia gave a mini oral history of the origin story of the series.

JULIA: We need to start with Margaret Loesch, who deserves all the credit in the world, who is the nicest person. She doesn't get enough credit. There you go. I said it.

Fox Kids was brand-new back then. You had ABC, NBC, CBS, and if you didn't sell a show to one of those three major networks, odds are you weren't going to get a show on the air. There was a whole syndicated market, too, but that was a different kind of beast. There weren't the five hundred channels now available to put a product out there. And Eric [Lewald, Julia's husband and writing partner] worked with the folks at Fox Kids.

Eric was hired to do a different show for Fox Kids. And the day before the meeting on that, he gets a phone call saying, "We're switching you. Come in tomorrow morning, you are going to be the story editor for *X-Men*, the comic book TV show. Okay?" He hangs up the phone and turns to me and says, "That's a comic book, right?" And I said, "Yeah, that, yeah. That's a comic book."

"Right," we both go. "Oh."

Next day, he shows up at the meeting and they're in the room. You know, Haim Saban, Stan Lee, all the folks from Marvel are there to begin the process of developing the show for TV.

This is February '92. And it became an immediate crash course in that universe. The Marvel comics, the X-Men comics were hugely popular. They were crazy big in the comic book realm. I'm drawing that distinction just because, at that time, there were folks who were into comic books and folks who weren't. And there wasn't a lot of crossover. There wasn't a lot of opportunity.

The distribution of comic books had shifted away from casually seeing them in the drugstore, the grocery store with your parents, to having to seek them out, say, in a comic book shop. And that kind of changed the pattern of people discovering, or being turned on to, casually, the comic books. If you'd asked ten people on the street back in 1992, "Name me five super heroes," you would probably get "Batman, Superman, Wonder Woman, yeah, Spider-Man, does the Hulk count?" Those might have been the five names that would come up, casually.

It's hard to believe now, but it wouldn't have been easy to find people who could name you three of the X-Men at this time.

The alchemy came together and allowed for some pretty remarkable storytelling, especially for what many people were quick to dismiss as a Saturday morning cartoon. But the fact that we're still talking about it thirty years later, I think, speaks to what kind of stories we were allowed to tell.

And to the fearless determination by Margaret Loesch to be honest and true to the X-Men characters, whom she loved.

Margaret had been at Marvel for a number of years and had tried to sell an X-Men series, even produced the one-off prior to the *X-Men* to try and convince one of the major networks or one of the major syndicators, "This is a show that has to be made."

That didn't work, but then within a couple of years, she was the president of Fox Kids. And one of her first edicts was "I'm going to do a Batman series and we're going to do an X-Men series." And that's how we now have *Batman: The Animated Series* and *X-Men*.

And I'm going to tell you this: I love that the president in *X-Men: The Animated Series* is a woman. That's one of those things that you blink and you miss it, but it's like, she's a *woman*. She's the only one we've had so far in the Marvel Universe as a president, and as a woman.

THERE WAS no promise to the writers about anything beyond the first thirteen episodes, Julia noted. "In fact," she admitted, "the betting money said it was going to fail."

But Margaret Loesch wasn't going to let that happen. Just a few years earlier, as the president and CEO of Marvel Productions, she had already tried to get an X-Men animated series off the ground, producing *Pryde of the X-Men*, a thirty-minute episode that was to function as a pilot. Reviews were, to put it kindly, mixed.

"They had some higher-ups above them that were forcing things on them," Julia recalled about the internal struggles of the production. "Like 'Hey, you know, what's a popular movie this year? *Crocodile Dundee*. You give Wolverine an Australian accent because kids like Australians.' They were not in a position to say, 'No, that's not right.'"

Now, in her position as president of Fox Kids, Margaret was going to make sure it *was* right, and she assembled a team that she knew could do it.

"We always had faith that it would be a success," said Stephanie Graziano, whose Graziano Productions oversaw production for the series. "That's one of the reasons why you put all you've got into it. It's to ensure that there are more. If they had said, 'We're really interested in more, but we're not going to pay you,' I think the team would still do it. It was that kind of situation."

Stephanie was the production head on *G.I. Joe* for many years, before being recruited by Margaret to help develop *X-Men* into a series—and to do it right. Having worked for most of her career on "boy-specific shows," Stephanie jumped at the chance.

"Stan used to say, 'I wanted to create characters for all kids,'" Stephanie said of her love of the X-Men. "In that universe, every person can find themselves in a Marvel character. And those characters stay with us as you evolve as a kid to an adult. And I think that's why so many adults still love the show. The traits those characters have don't leave you as you grow up.

"One thing that was really important in this series was consistently keeping an eye on the heart in the show. Keeping an eye on the fact that there was always heart in the characters, in the situations."

It was the one nonnegotiable term that Margaret had.

"Okay, it's a Saturday morning cartoon, but Margaret Loesch gave us the marching orders, 'You do not write down to kids. You treat this like it's a

Stephanie Graziano, seen here with her husband, Jim, was recruited by Margaret Loesch to join the team on *X-Men*.

half-hour live-action drama. You make these stories as sharp as you can. You write the toughest stuff that you can.'

"None of us had gotten that kind of edict on an animated series before. Margaret was the one who challenged us all to find the most important stories that we could tell."

And so they did. The team didn't shy away from the political, social, and cultural issues that were integral to Claremont's and Simonson's vision for the book, instead tackling head-on topics like religion, war, the AIDS epidemic, and civil rights. They also structured the show radically differently than other children's stand-alone cartoons of the time, doing up to five-part storylines with cliff-hangers each week.

"The tricky part of the process was the broadcast-standards side," Stephanie said. "And Avery Coburn, our representative at Fox, was amazing. She had a really hard job because of the broadcast standards for kids' television. We were constantly negotiating, from Wolverine's claws to the fight scenes.

"We eventually got a rhythm going between the directors of the series and the broadcast-standards team that allowed us to do some groundbreaking things for kids' TV. Which was one more piece of the integrity of the comics."

The one social issue the show wasn't able to tear into explicitly was gender and sexuality, but that didn't stop queer, nonbinary, and trans viewers from seeing the clear parallels.

"I loved the show," says Leah Williams, current *X-Factor* writer. "The show was definitely a formative part of my queer experience, and I hold it in such dear regard, both the original *X-Men: The Animated Series* and also *X-Men: Evolution* and the cartoons that came after, too. Because once you fall in love with the character, you are going to follow them in whatever else they appear in."

Julia Lewald saw it, too. "The fact that *X-Men* dealt with people who developed mutant abilities at some point in their life; again, especially during adolescence and puberty, it makes so much sense that that would speak to anyone who is dealing with questions of their own sexuality, especially in the nineties, when we still weren't comfortable having that conversation.

"I could not be more proud of anything I might have been involved with than providing a person some degree of comfort and hope."

It was no accident that the show most beloved by the majority of the women we had interviewed was shaped in development and production by three senior female contributors. On a comic book series supported by a female editor and assistant editor.

If Chris Claremont was conjuring an *X-Men: The Animated Series* dream, he didn't get there without Weezie and Annie, Margaret, Julia, and Stephanie. Or, for that matter, without Jean Grey, Storm, Rogue, or Jubilee.

"Chris built the platform to have a lot of strong female characters," Dan Buckley said. "Clearly, the most powerful characters on those teams are women, especially from a raw-power standpoint between Jean Grey, Storm, Rogue. And then you throw in Jubilee to kind of be your POV character on that show. You had the platform to make it inviting, and having those female executives involved obviously helped a great deal."

"There was never a moment where a woman had to be less than her powers or a man himself was portrayed as being less than his own powers, because a woman could do something else," Julia Lewald said.

"I really feel fortunate to have had strong women role models in my life," said Stephanie, "and they have always given me the sense that there were no boundaries. I went on to hold multiple executive roles at different companies and founded my own company, and I credit the exposure to women like her.

"Margaret was, still is, graceful. The way she interacts with people—she listens, she's very even-tempered and really open. I'm forever grateful for what I've learned from her."

But excelling at content development is one thing; distribution, especially in the highly regulated world of children's animation, is an entirely different expertise.

To that end, the initial plan had been for both animated series—*X-Men* and *Batman*—to be released concurrently in a blockbuster fall debut on Fox Kids. In the era before streaming content, "these [were] the days when September was your magic sweet spot for new shows rolling out, annually," as Julia recalled.

But when *X-Men: The Animated Series* editors got the cells back from the team overseas (because these were also still the days of hand-painted cell animation), ready to cut a print, there was a problem.

"The first four episodes had come back and they were basically unviewable," Julia said. "There were so many errors, there was so much awfulness, so much off-model. . . . They were not airable."

There was a suggestion of fixing what they could in the best-produced episodes, and then airing them out of order, but Margaret nixed that idea immediately. Airing them in order was crucial, as the storyline built on itself over time, rather than rolling out as a series of self-contained episodes—what comics calls "one-shots"—that was the norm for most children's programming of the era.

So when it came to potential solutions, the first issue was money. "It was really a struggle," Stephanie remembered. "The network wasn't willing to spend more than what a regular limited animation show was."

Julia agreed. "And as I understand it, it came from the folks at Marvel, who were getting a licensing fee, and who realized that what had come back was so problematic that it was going to shoot itself in the foot before it even got a chance to get better and find an audience. And Margaret was desperately tap-dancing here, trying to figure out what to do with what she had."

The creative team of *X-Men: The Animated Series* faithfully replicated the original costumes, seen here in an original animation cel.

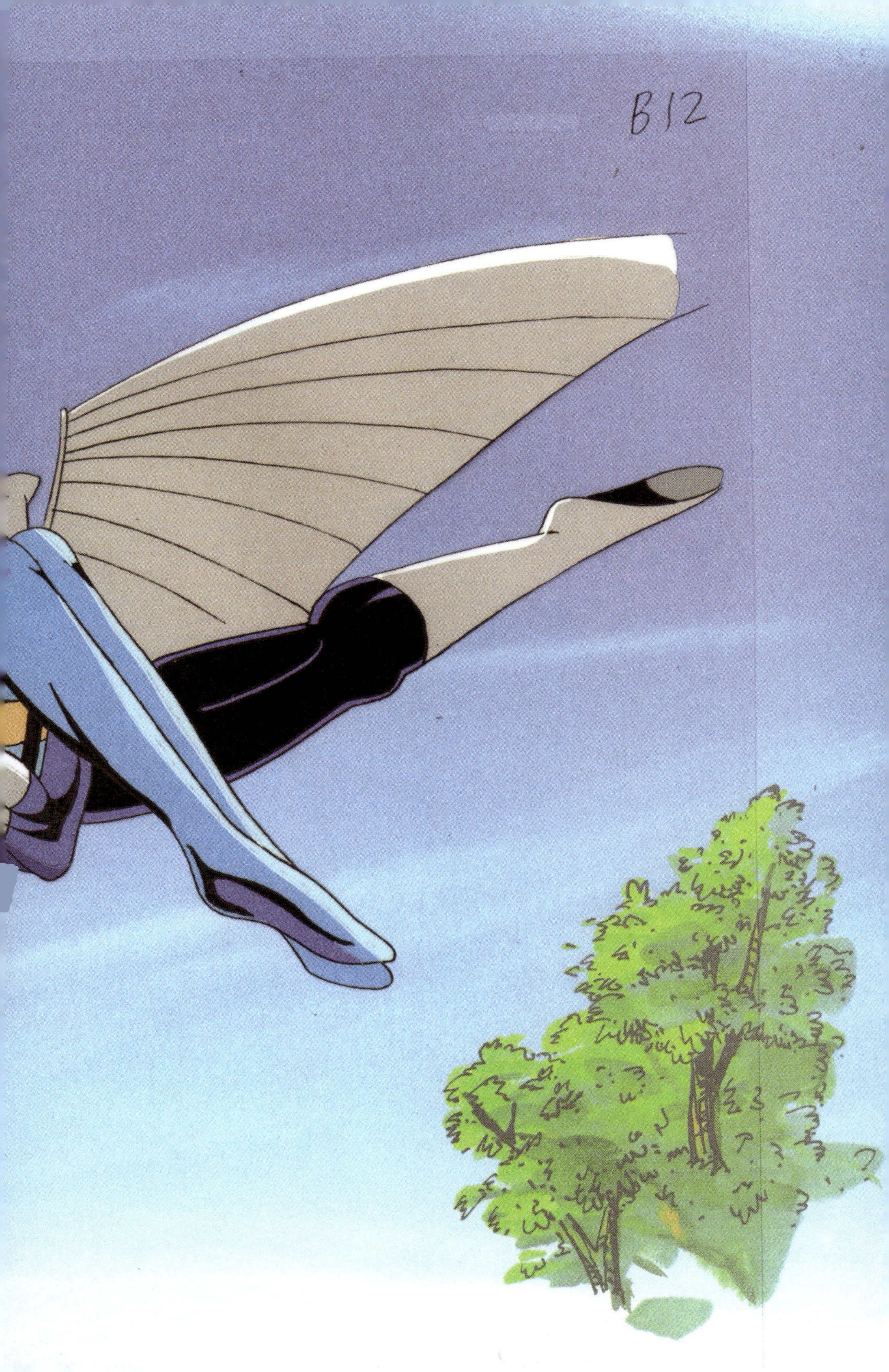
B12

TOP: Storm in her iconic white uniform, designed by Jim Lee. BOTTOM: Lady Deathstrike was one of the many multilayered villains the X-Men interacted with in *X-Men: The Animated Series*.

The second issue was time—the September deadline was rapidly approaching.

"Margaret decided to have it on Halloween night," recalled Julia. "I thought, 'Kids are going to be out trick-or-treating, this is not going to work.' But Halloween night, 1992, on prime time, she had a kids' sneak peek for the new show, *X-Men*. . . ." Julia grinned. "And the ratings were *through the roof*!"

Now that Margaret had bought them time to redo the rest of the episodes, and with things finally running smoothly, *X-Men: The Animated Series* moved to its regular time slot on Saturday morning, and within a matter of weeks, Fox Kids was the number one Saturday morning network, beating ABC, NBC, and CBS combined, according to Julia.

Margaret Loesch had staked her career on defending a high-quality approach to Chris Claremont's character-driven vision of the X-Men to both Fox and Marvel alike; when the show succeeded, Avi Arad replaced her with himself, but not before Margaret went to Lauren Shuler Donner and preached to her the previously overlooked value of Marvel as a four-quadrant franchise—arguably laying the groundwork for the Marvel Cinematic Universe of today.

"*X-Men: The Animated Series* helped set the seeds for mass-market reach for Marvel," Dan Buckley said. "That seeding continued slowly but successfully over the next several years, starting with *Blade*, the X-Men movies, and then there was *Spider-Man* [2002] that moved Marvel to another level. *Spider-Man* really opened everything up on *all* levels."

"*X-Men* was the bridge, the gateway, whatever you want to call it, for the creation of an audience that was there, then, for the empire that exploded," Julia said. "It's *X-Men* the comic books, but *X-Men: The Animated Series* is the thing that introduced it to a different medium.

"The books were huge, but without Margaret Loesch, without the success that was *X-Men: The Animated Series*, there would not have been the film franchises that then begat *Iron Man* and the whole Marvel Cinematic Universe. I'll take that to the grave."

Oral History

MARGARET LOESCH

As the president of Fox Kids in the nineties, Margaret had seen the future of Marvel, or at least what it could be, and pushed for shows like *X-Men: The Animated Series* to be created and broadcast for a new, young audience of soon-to-be superfans. In doing so, Margaret changed the world—or at least, the biggest franchise in the world—and paved the way for bringing Marvel characters like the X-Men to the big screen.

The Show Everybody Still Talks About

Over the years, the comments I get the most from people—everyday people, people not only your age but younger and older—about *X-Men: The Animated Series* are that the storytelling was so strong.

Which we knew at the time. I mean, we were very proud of it.

It had been a long struggle to get it done. I've done so many different types of shows, but that's the show that everybody still talks about.

Wrong

I get a lot of pride when I look online and they'll have it in the ranking of the top animated shows ever made.

They didn't think any girls would watch it.

Wrong.

Friday Nights with Batman

I grew up really being a fan of Wonder Woman, Batman, and Superman. And on TV there was, of course, a Superman series with George Reeves, which I watched as a kid and really enjoyed. And then when I was in college, we had such a cult following, that on Friday nights, we'd all gather in the main room of the dormitory and watch the [1960s] *Batman* series together with our dates. Then we'd laugh and talk about it and couldn't wait till next week, so Batman is seared in my memory.

And I loved animation as a child, especially as, when we went to the movies, they would have a Warner Bros. or MGM cartoon on before the movie. And interestingly enough, we would find out what the cartoon was before we'd agree to go to see a movie. We picked our movies by what the shorts were.

That was my introduction to animation, and they were funny as hell. As I grew older and went to school, I had an interest in it, but I never considered working in animation. I ended up pursuing another area of education, though I found my way there anyway.

Respect the Talent

I started in television in January of 1971, as a clerk typist at ABC. I had moved to California from New Orleans, and needed to find a job. I was staying with friends, and the father suggested I try the [TV] networks. So I did.

I didn't pass a typing test, but they let me start anyway.

I was at ABC for four and a half years. Then I got a chance to go to NBC and children's television. One of the ABC executives was moving to NBC, and asked me if I'd like to come work for him. . . .

And that was the beginning of my career in "children's programming," which was not all animation, but a lot of it.

There I am, having been in the business for less than five years, and all of a sudden I'm sitting in the offices with Friz Freleng, Tex Avery, William Hanna, Joseph Barbera, Walter Lantz, and Stan Lee.

Stan was in New York at the time, but he'd come out to LA to pitch shows. I was in heaven. I decided, probably one of the most important decisions of my career, to stay in the children's and animation television arena, instead of heading to movies and prime-time television.

I liked the people. They were all so much fun. I had been a fan and I knew the characters. That was the beginning of my career.

After ABC and NBC, I went to Hanna-Barbera. Joe Barbera and Bill Hanna invited me to come work for them, and join as an executive producer and the executive in charge of development.

After I had worked for them for five years, Marvel recruited me to run their new animation division, which they had acquired from a merger with DePatie-Freleng. That was a very tough decision because I loved Hanna-Barbera. I had been able to produce many shows that I was able to oversee the development of, such as *The Smurfs* and *Super Friends*.

Marvel was the real change in my career because I became president and CEO, and there were no women in those kinds of jobs at that time. I feel I was incredibly lucky. And I really think that I was chosen because I was known to be a fan of the talent. I respected the talent, I appreciated them.

And I don't think I was a typical executive or suit because I was a fan.

At Marvel, as luck would have it, Stan had decided to leave New York and move to the West Coast and really focus on the television and motion picture business to try and get it off the ground. And the rest, as they say, is history.

Then after Marvel, I went to Fox, and then to the Jim Henson Company, and built the Hallmark Channel. And then the last part of my journey, the Hub, which was a Hasbro and Discovery joint venture.

That's my career in a nutshell.

Stan, I Think We Can Sell That Show

Before I joined Marvel Productions, Stan used to come to Hanna-Barbera to pitch shows to us. We did end up buying from Stan *The Thing*. We put that out—it wasn't very successful. I don't know why we took [him] out of the group of Fantastic Four. I have no idea.

So I was familiar with some of the Marvel properties because Stan would come and pitch them. But when I joined Marvel Productions, I decided to do a crash course and really learn the characters. Because, after all, I was CEO of the company, and I needed to sell more Marvel shows and keep the company healthy and in production.

I traveled to New York numerous times to meet with the editorial and writer teams to tap into the world that they were building.

They mentioned the X-Men, and after talking to Stan, who told me about the origins of the story, I became very intrigued with it. And I said, "Stan, I think we can sell that show." I went back to the earliest comics, I read all that I could, and I leaned on the teams in NYC for the stories. And I thought, "This is really special, this is really something else." They were these older teens with foibles, problems, and, most important, humanity.

We developed and started pitching the show, but the only thing that people were interested in was Spider-Man. Stan and I literally could not give away the [other] properties. I had one of the buyers—who was a good friend—say to me, "Margaret, comic book stories do not make good television. They just don't translate to television."

And I said, "Why not?"

"It's all thought balloons. Overly flourished. Too wordy, and too dramatic, and too dark and too sinister."

And I said, "But they're good stories. And they're interesting characters."

"No, they're not. It just won't translate. And besides, the only people who would watch it are the readers of comic books. And the readers of comic books are eighteen-year-old nerdy boys."

That's what was said to me. I was with Marvel for six years. We were certainly successful during my tenure in Marvel, especially with the work we did for Hasbro—we produced *G.I. Joe*, *My Little Pony*, and *Transformers*. But our biggest success was *Muppet Babies*.

Please Don't Sell Any Marvel Shows

After I went to Fox, I said to Stan, "Please don't try to sell any Marvel shows, because I'm going to start this network and we're going to buy them from you. We're going to do the show exactly as you and I envisioned it. We're going to do *Spider-Man* exactly as you and I envisioned it." And that's what happened.

My boss was the president of the Fox prime-time network, and he was extremely concerned about *X-Men*. I got pressure from the minute I said we were going to do it until the minute it became a hit.

I was being hounded because they thought it was too dramatic, too violent, too serious, took itself too seriously, too everything, you name it. And I kept saying, "It's going to be a wonderful show."

The writing was so stellar. We made such an effort thanks to Julia, Eric [Lewald], and the whole team of people that worked on it. They just did a wonderful job, because everyone believed in it. I knew it was going to be a hit. And I delayed the start date so they'd have more time to do it. Once it came out, it shot us to number one.

The show was so different from anything anybody had seen. One of the biggest supporters of the show was our broadcast-standards executive. She was such a fan and believer, too, that she worked with us so that we didn't lose the drama and suspense.

All the things that people thought were the reasons it was going to fail were the reasons it succeeded. And that story has been repeated throughout my career. Whatever is different is hard to get done.

That's the story of *X-Men*. And it was really gratifying.

Characters Are Destiny

We spent a long time talking about that with the writers and our executive, Sidney Iwanter. We picked the characters for their personalities and their powers, as we wanted to complement the powers. And we wanted a really eclectic group of characters, and of course, to have several women. We weren't going to repeat what had become tradition in the industry of just having one token woman. I don't even know if that was tradition, but it was my perception that it was.

We didn't have the time and money to spend a lot on animation, but the writing was so strong that it made all the difference in the world. The other thing that made many people nervous was the multi-parters. They just thought that was a really bad idea. And I never could understand why they thought it was a bad idea. They think kids are not going to come back for the next episode? Of course they are. Just like we will. But it was too novel. And forget two-parters—we did three- and four- and five-parters. So many things that we did have become standard.

Fight for Me

My biggest talent is recognizing and then supporting the talent around me. I learned it intuitively, but it was articulated by someone I had a lot of regard for.

When we were doing *Muppet Babies*, I asked Jim Henson one night, when he was telling me about an issue that he had, "Well, okay, Jim, what would you like me to do?" He said, "I want you to do what you've always done. I want you to fight for me, fight for my vision. I can't do it. You have to do it for me."

He was the first person to ever articulate that. And that's what I'd always been doing, was fighting for the people that had the talent, and then I always felt that my job was to protect them and allow them to flourish.

Still an Outsider

I've always felt that I was exceedingly fortunate to have met the caliber of people like Jim Henson, Joe Barbera, Bill Hanna, and all these people who have seemed to have great affection and respect for me.

I don't know that I totally understood it. I know that I had a respect for them and they knew that. Why they felt that way toward me, I don't really know.

I was such an outsider—I still feel like an outsider. I've been in the business for over fifty years and I still feel like an outsider. Maybe that was good.

The people who, quote, mentored me, even though that word was never used, in looking back, they certainly had a lot to do with my success because of their support of me.

I Didn't Ruin You

I'm constantly amazed by the number of people who reach out to me to tell me how much I, in a good way, impacted their youth. And it's not just *X-Men*, which was certainly one of the highlights, but the other shows—*Batman*, *The Smurfs*, *Muppet Babies*, *Bobby's World*, *Life with Louie*—where we dealt with some real issues.

I was told many times, including on TV by Katie Couric to my face, that I was ruining a generation of children with the shows that we were doing. Particularly after *Power Rangers*, but *X-Men* and *Batman* were included in that because they were dark, dramatic, and, quote, violent.

But the first time a young adult male contacted me about how much the shows that I'd done had meant to him, my first thing I said to him on the telephone was "Oh my God. And I didn't ruin you."

I wasn't being funny.

I was so, so pleased that this young man who's a fan and now an artist was so inspired.

I felt that what we were doing was providing a safe place for kids to see all kinds of entertainment with all kinds of emotional aspects and different stories to really make their lives, make their imagination bigger.

Because that's what television did for me in my earliest days. So I never take for granted when people thank me and tell me how much the shows have meant to them. Especially with kids, young people that were challenged or had issues, and I felt, "Okay, we've done it. We've provided a safe haven."

By safe haven, I mean a world in which they can get enveloped in and feel emotion, but it's not going to hurt them. They're in their living room watching TV.

Feeling Like a Child

I think someone asked me once, how was it that I have been so successful with so many hits? And I think I hadn't forgotten how I felt when I was a child watching TV. Or when I read a comic, how it transported me, how it made me feel better, how it helped me forget all my troubles. I remember as a kid the feeling of excitement, joy, dread, suspense, and laughter. The glorious ride I was taken on, which is what I wanted to continue to bring to the shows I worked on. Did they have that quality? Was there a creator who was passionate that I could work with? And was there that element of imaginativeness or fantasy that would carry us away from our everyday life?

Even as an adult, I could hang on to that idea, as I was looking for that feeling in the shows that I was picking. And boy, did *X-Men* have it; from the very first comic I read, I thought, "My God, my kids will love this. This is amazing."

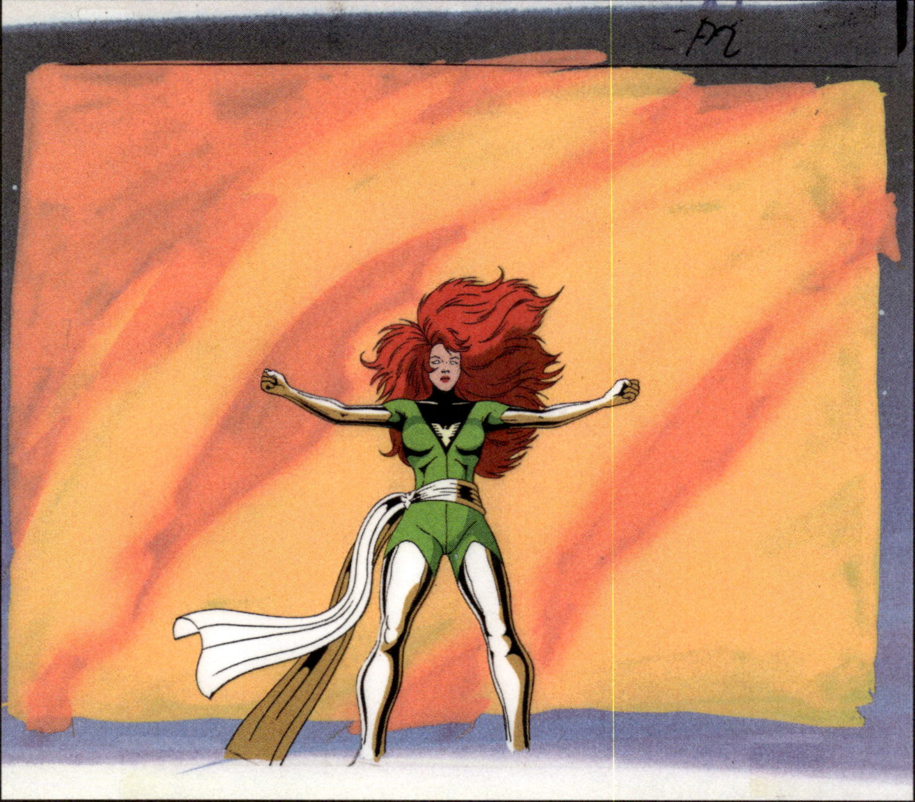

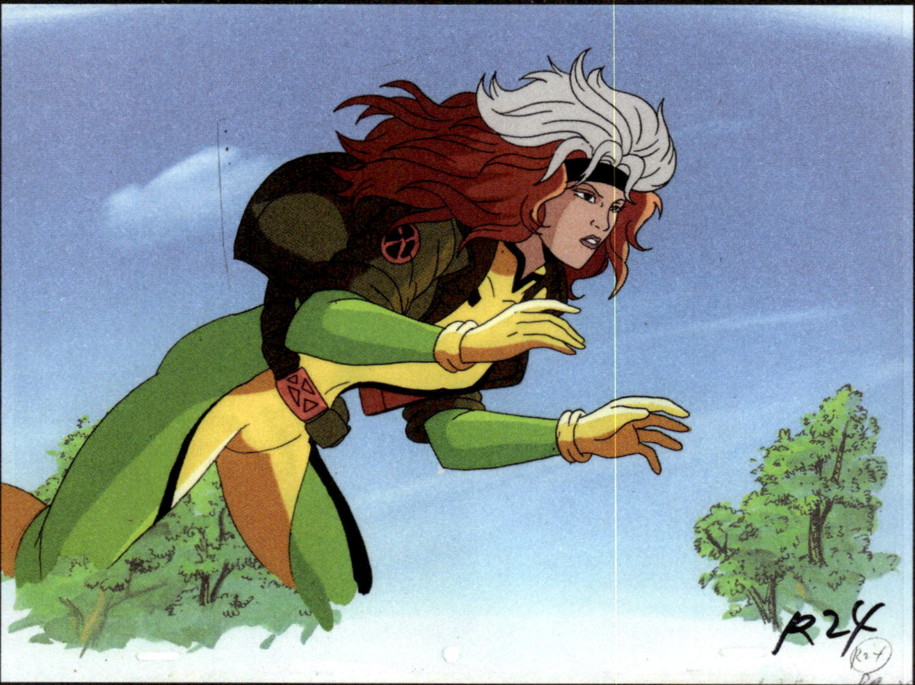
R24

OPPOSITE: Iconic moments from *X-Men: The Animated Series* featuring Jean Grey and Rogue. TOP: Years after their work together brought *X-Men: The Animated Series* to life, Margaret Loesch and Stephanie Graziano are still friends. BOTTOM: Ambassadors of the story of the creation of *X-Men: The Animated Series*, Eric and Julia Lewald.

DeConnick poses with three Marvel cosplayers.

CHAPTER FOUR

THE CAROL CORPS

Carol Danvers,
Kelly Sue DeConnick, and
the Start of a Movement

For the next twenty years, *X-Men* and its ever-expanding universe of books, television shows, and movies would be the mainstream comics door that opened the widest, deliberately inviting in women, Black, Brown, and queer fans across the world. But in 2012, when Marvel canceled the acclaimed *X-23* comics series due to sales, Dan Buckley, president of Marvel Comics and Franchise, realized "our comic book line no longer had a book with a female lead." In ending the series by Marjorie Liu, the first-ever woman to win an Eisner for Best Writer, there was now a clear gender gap in the Marvel publishing plan.

Since the start of the Women of Marvel Initiative in 2010, the company had explicitly defined the hiring of women, and the creation of books for women, as a priority. But there were still no women in higher decision-making positions; the weekly leadership team meetings were solely male. Dan and the Marvel team knew they had to make a change. "We looked outside to recruit female editors, but it became clear to me that we were better off trying to hire and train."

"When we started the Women of Marvel Initiative, the girls on the editorial staff—me, Sana Amanat, Lauren Sankovitch, and Rachel Pinnelas—talked really frankly about how every March we hired a bunch of women and then the other eleven months of the year it was business as usual, just like what happens with Black creators in February or queer creators during June," said Jeanine Schaefer, lead editor on *Girl Comics*. "We wanted this time to be different. Change never happens as fast as you want, and looking back, I wish I had done more. There were days where it was really disheartening, but we tried to stick together and stick with our allies and keep pushing."

This was an industry-wide issue, to be sure. For the last twenty years, the success of comics and comic shops had been measured in single-issue periodicals largely made by and targeted to straight white men. Why, then, would a marginalized creator who could write or draw even think about wanting to work in comics? The atmosphere sometimes felt less than welcoming.

Gail Simone had made a name for herself writing a blog about what felt like a deliberate dearth of women in comics called *Women in Refrigerators*, named for a moment in an issue of *Green Lantern* in which the male hero's girlfriend is killed and her body is shoved in a refrigerator. This "fridging," so to speak, wasn't a part of the woman's story. Rather, it was meant as a vehicle for the male hero's motivation, sending the message to readers that women in comics were expendable.

Gail went on to write seminal runs of *Birds of Prey* and *Wonder Woman* at DC, and *Deadpool* at Marvel. "When I started," she said, "there were so few women writing super hero comics at the time. I mean, it was down to almost none. A lot of the previous generation had left, and the ones to follow hadn't shown up yet. So thinking back, the few that were doing it were a bit of a closed group, with a few exceptions. I understand, but it was kind of lonely at the time."

"Especially at comic conventions," Judy Stephens said. "I would go to shows and sometimes be the only woman representing Marvel."

Thanks to the internet and social media, and, of course, the box office powerhouse of the Marvel Cinematic Universe led by *The Avengers* in 2012, access to working in comics was evolving.

"One of the biggest light bulb moments we had was shortly after the first *Avengers* film," Dan Buckley recalled. "The film was such a success, but when fans went out to purchase merch, it was very hard to find any for Black Widow. There was a hesitancy from licensees to make female character merch, but I—*we*—were seeing that a new generation of young women and girls had grown up with super heroes. Through the cartoons and films, the idea of super heroes, geeks, had become a lived experience for everyone, not specific to gender anymore."

The next generation of (millennial) women had grown up with nerd culture, and loved it. Loved the characters. Loved the stories. And they wanted to be a part of that process.

Starting as an assistant editor at Marvel in 1985, Bobbie Chase held almost every position possible in Marvel editorial, including, from 1994 to 1995, editor in chief, the only woman thus far to ever do so.

"In terms of making comics, it's always been about finding the audience and then delivering what that audience wants. And it's so important having a story about a woman that you can read," said Bobbie Chase, editor in chief of the Marvel Edge imprint (under which banner *Daredevil*, *Punisher*, *Ghost Rider*, *Incredible Hulk*, and *Doctor Strange, Sorcerer Supreme* were published) in 1994, and later the vice president of talent development at DC Comics.

"I believe that everyone wants a book they can read that looks like them or that feels like them or has the same experience as them," she continued. "Each new book or new story does make a difference; we're climbing a rock and each time we put in a chisel, from Batgirl at DC to Captain Marvel at Marvel, it all fits together eventually. For so long, the attitude had been that not many women want to be in comics, because of the toxic atmosphere, but we've been changing that."

What they needed was a catalyst, and in 2012 they got it, in the form of three stars aligning: Kelly Sue DeConnick, Captain Marvel, and the Carol Corps.

"KELLY SUE has that incredible quote that I've always wished was my own," said Kelly Thompson, who took over duties as writer of the *Captain Marvel* ongoing comics series as of January 2019, after a two-year run by author Margaret Stohl. "Something like 'Captain America gets up because it's the right thing to do, but Carol Danvers gets up because [****] you.'"

Kelly Sue DeConnick was born in Ohio, and at first was known to friends and family simply as Kelly. She would later add the "Sue" to her credited name when she started working in comics so that, as she said, "when someone sees a book with my name on it, they know it was written by a woman. I want a little girl who sees that to know that that's something she can do."

Kelly Sue spent her childhood growing up across military bases, as her dad was in the air force. She discovered comics when they were living in Germany, as she didn't have access to American TV. And there was a history in the military of reading comics, swapping with fellow GIs and collecting one's favorites. On the base, comics were readily accessible, even for an eight-year-old girl.

Comics would continue to be a part of her life, but it was Kelly Sue's passion for acting that would lead her on her first career path. Kelly Sue returned to the States for college, earning a BA in drama from the University of Texas at Austin in 1993.

After graduating, she would hold many jobs as she started on the acting path. But along the way, she would rediscover comics, specifically *Planetary*. "I thought *Planetary* was just astonishingly good. It was a comic that transcended genre, and did so by embracing genre." So she went looking for people, a place where she could talk about this comic that she loved.

Through those early comics message boards, she would begin to make connections. "So, it's—what?—the late 1990s, early 2000s and one of the things I do for fun—in my ten minutes of downtime or whatever—is I'm a fan on a comic book posting forum, and a community starts to spring up from there," she recalled.

Before the proliferation of social media as an everyday tool for connection, and as the internet became increasingly accessible, more and more women were finding groups where they could explore interests that maybe weren't available to them in their hometowns. They were also finding each other.

A military "brat," Kelly Sue DeConnick, here as a baby with her parents, drew on her own personal experiences to craft her run on *Captain Marvel*.

CAPTAIN AMERICA GETS UP BECAUSE IT'S THE RIGHT THING TO DO, BUT CAROL DANVERS GETS UP BECAUSE [****] YOU.

"I remember it very fondly," said Kelly Sue. "But I don't know how accurately? I've talked to other folks—especially other women—who were there at the same time [I was] who don't remember it fondly at all. And so I don't know how much I can trust my own perception."

She continued. "I remember it being funny and people being supportive of one another. Maybe I remember it so fondly because there are so many people who remain an important part of my life that I met there? My cohort, as I said. And, I mean, my husband! That's where I met my husband."

Her husband, the comics writer Matt Fraction, began his own career in comics at the same time as Kelly Sue; the forum encouraged both to create and pitch their own books.

"Everybody in this community is talking about making their own comics and I'm competitive, right? So, oh okay, I'll play. 'Anything you can do, I can do better,' or whatever. I consciously decided to do it, and I went for it, but I never meant for it to be my vocation. Does that make sense? I meant to be an actor right up until the day I was already a writer."

A writer, and an incredibly hard worker. Kelly Sue would dip her toe into the industry by editing and adapting English translations of manga for Tokyopop and Viz (she estimates she wrote more than eleven thousand pages of manga). From there, she would cut her teeth writing licensed comics for IDW Publishing.

In 2010, her work would be passed along to Marvel editor Alejandro Arbona.

As part of the Women of Marvel Initiative, along with an anthology, crossover events, and a reinvigoration of the Women of Marvel panel, Marvel planned for a slate of one-shots featuring female characters to address the dearth of female-led titles.

Encouraged to pitch, Kelly Sue insisted on submitting blind. Her now-husband was writing *The Uncanny X-Men*, and making inroads as a Marvel comics writer was difficult enough without the added potential accusation of nepotism.

Kelly Sue's pitch was accepted, and that book became *Rescue*, a one-shot that would give Pepper Potts, Tony Stark's personal assistant, a super hero life of her own. Kelly Sue and Alejandro would collaborate again on the critically acclaimed Spider-Man series *Osborn* (on which she would be paired up with her future comics partner, artist Emma Ríos).

What followed is a story that you might have heard before, canonized on many panels and in many interviews, in the retelling in the offices when other writers and editors would wonder if they could also capture lightning in a bottle.

But before we get to that, let's talk about Carol Danvers and the history you may not know.

CAROL DANVERS, aka Captain Marvel, née Ms. Marvel, might be a name known across the world today, but her first appearance in 1968's *Marvel Super-Heroes* #3 via her civilian form, and then later in January 1977 as Ms. Marvel in her eponymous book, went off with an unheard bang.

She was a spin-off of a character who goes all the way back to the 1940s, the male version of Captain Marvel, also known as Mar-Vell, who was reconceptualized in the 1960s as a (Kree) alien who was sent to Earth as a spy, but fell in love with the people of his adopted planet.

His series had a cult following, especially after being written by fan favorite Jim Starlin, but it never took off in the way Marvel Comics would have hoped. "Marvel didn't seem to quite know what to do with him," said comics historian Don Markstein, "but they did put his comic out every other

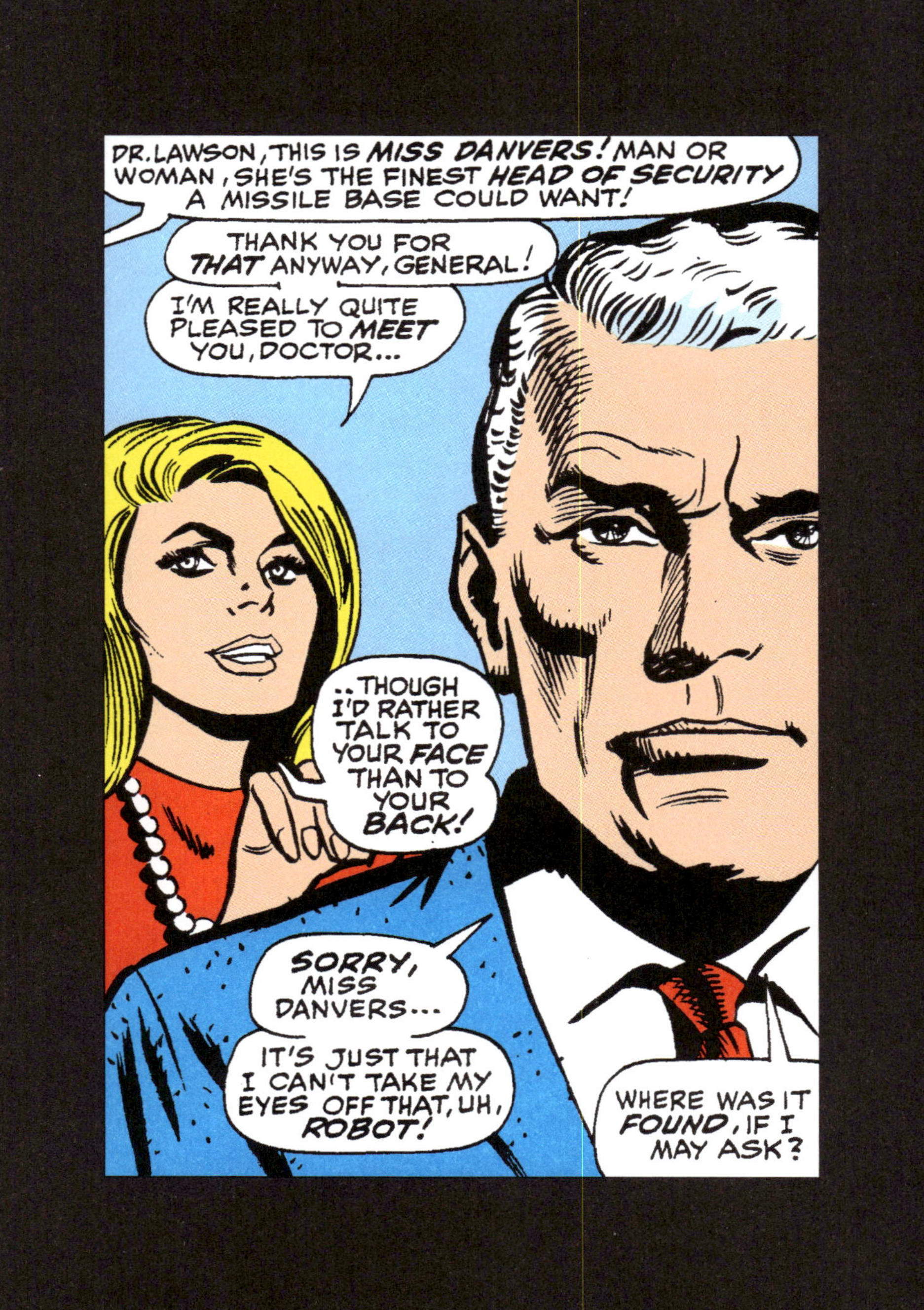
DR. LAWSON, THIS IS MISS DANVERS! MAN OR WOMAN, SHE'S THE FINEST HEAD OF SECURITY A MISSILE BASE COULD WANT!
THANK YOU FOR THAT ANYWAY, GENERAL!
I'M REALLY QUITE PLEASED TO MEET YOU, DOCTOR...
..THOUGH I'D RATHER TALK TO YOUR FACE THAN TO YOUR BACK!
SORRY, MISS DANVERS...
IT'S JUST THAT I CAN'T TAKE MY EYES OFF THAT, UH, ROBOT!
WHERE WAS IT FOUND, IF I MAY ASK?

month through most of the 1970s, if only to maintain their trademark on his name."

At the same time, Stan Lee was kicking around the idea of creating derivative female characters as a way to sell comics to more women (legend says there was a proto-version of She-Hulk on the board at the time), and who better to do it with than a character for whom they could extend their ability to retain a stamp on the Marvel name? "Gerry Conway has spoken about this on panels we've done together," said writer Margaret Stohl, who wrote *Captain Marvel* from 2017 to 2018, as well as *The Life of Captain Marvel*. "He said Stan wanted a Wonder Woman of his own, so Gerry drafted in Mar-Vell's blond NASA sidekick, a secretary-type character named Carol Danvers, though her official position was in 'security.'"

Soon Gerry bestowed Mar-Vell's powers on a previously powerless woman through a military accident involving a device called a Psyche-Magnetron.

And thus, the first Ms. Marvel was born.

"I came on board *Mighty Captain Marvel* and *Life of Captain Marvel*, and found myself tasked with giving Carol Danvers her own, more Carol-centered power backstory in advance of the MCU's debut of the *Captain Marvel* film. Forty years down the road, borrowed powers were no longer going to cut it for a blockbuster film headlining hero," Margaret said.

But in 1977, Carol's first costume was a unitard with a bare midriff and exposed back. Whether it was meant to be sexy or stylish, Lorraine Cink, writer of *Marvel: Powers of a Girl*, had a different take. "There is power in a woman like Carol Danvers, especially coming out of the 1970s. There's power in a woman being able to feel comfortable in her own body, to show her belly button, especially in a time where women were not allowed to show 'excessive skin.'"

Carol's code name and eponymous title back that up. In the seventies, the salutation "Ms." was a signifier of the "independent woman" and a marker of the feminist movement. And if you need more proof, look to the pages of the story itself, first written by Gerry Conway and then later by Chris Claremont, where one of Carol's more personal stories saw her fighting for equal pay at her job, struggling to simply be seen, like so many women of the time. That would set the tone for Carol and her story moving forward.

So who *is* Carol Danvers?

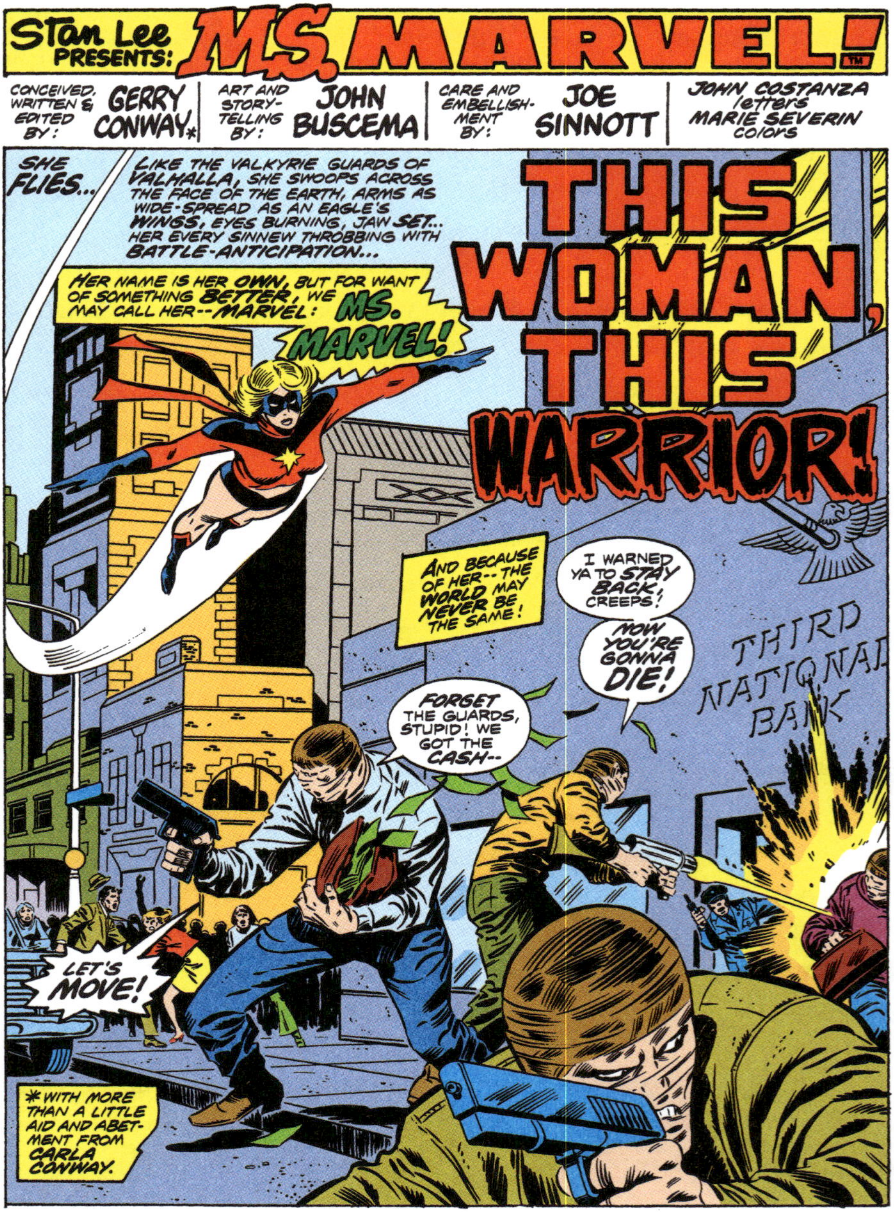

Stan Lee PRESENTS: MS. MARVEL!
CONCEIVED, WRITTEN & EDITED BY: GERRY CONWAY*
ART AND STORY-TELLING BY: JOHN BUSCEMA
CARE AND EMBELLISH-MENT BY: JOE SINNOTT
JOHN COSTANZA letters
MARIE SEVERIN colors
SHE FLIES...
LIKE THE VALKYRIE GUARDS OF VALHALLA, SHE SWOOPS ACROSS THE FACE OF THE EARTH, ARMS AS WIDE-SPREAD AS AN EAGLE'S WINGS, EYES BURNING, JAW SET... HER EVERY SINNEW THROBBING WITH BATTLE-ANTICIPATION...
THIS WOMAN, THIS WARRIOR!
HER NAME IS HER OWN, BUT FOR WANT OF SOMETHING BETTER, WE MAY CALL HER--MARVEL: MS. MARVEL!
AND BECAUSE OF HER--THE WORLD MAY NEVER BE THE SAME!
I WARNED YA TO STAY BACK, CREEPS!
NOW YOU'RE GONNA DIE!
THIRD NATIONAL BANK
FORGET THE GUARDS, STUPID! WE GOT THE CASH--
LET'S MOVE!
*WITH MORE THAN A LITTLE AID AND ABETMENT FROM CARLA CONWAY.

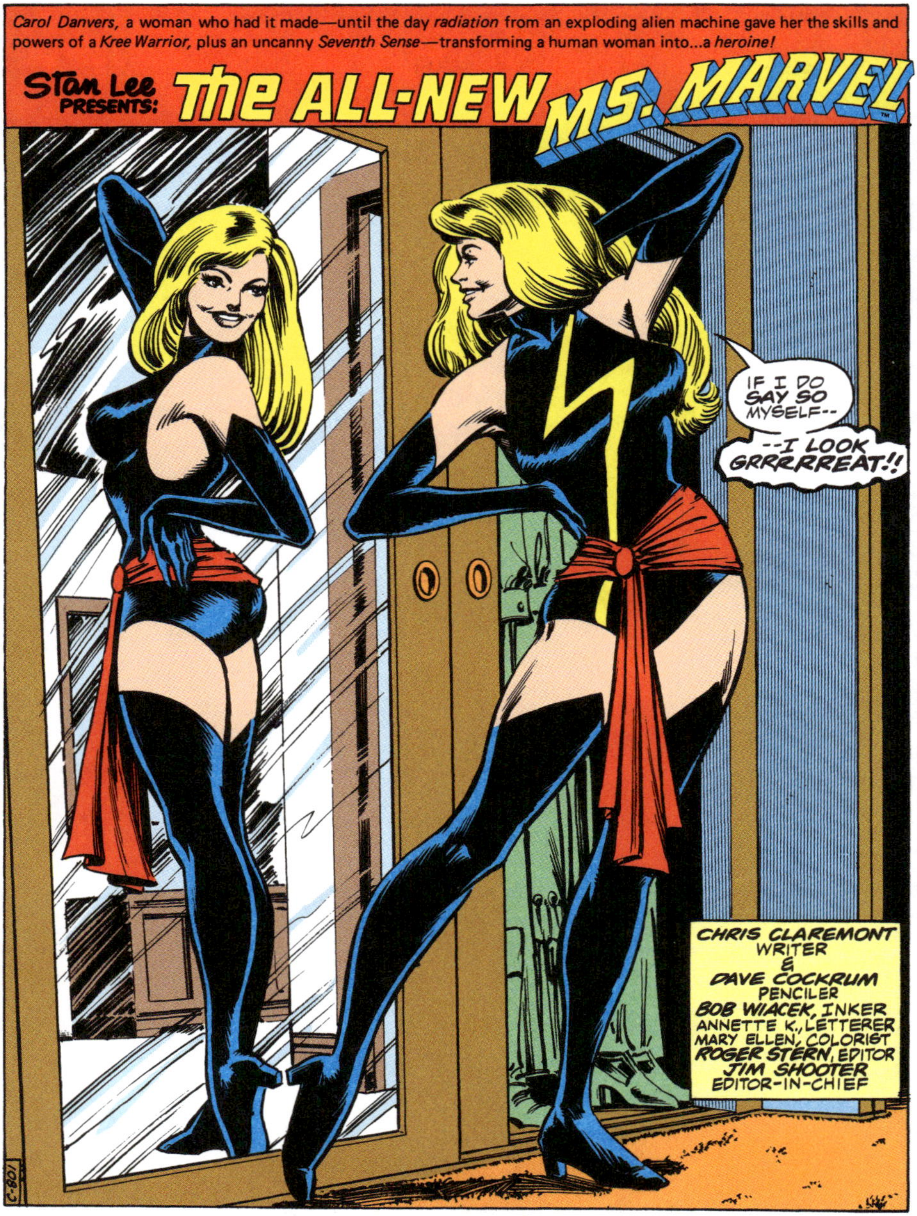
Carol Danvers, a woman who had it made—until the day radiation from an exploding alien machine gave her the skills and powers of a Kree Warrior, plus an uncanny Seventh Sense—transforming a human woman into...a heroine!
STAN LEE PRESENTS: THE ALL-NEW MS. MARVEL
IF I DO SAY SO MYSELF--
--I LOOK GRRRRREAT!!
CHRIS CLAREMONT WRITER & DAVE COCKRUM PENCILER
BOB WIACEK, INKER
ANNETTE K., LETTERER
MARY ELLEN, COLORIST
ROGER STERN, EDITOR
JIM SHOOTER EDITOR-IN-CHIEF

OPPOSITE: Carol's first costume, drawn by John Buscema for *Ms. Marvel* #1 in 1977, was an ode to the vintage heroes before her, including a bare midriff. ABOVE: Dave Cockrum would design her iconic black unitard look for *Ms. Marvel* #20 the following year.

Carol's evolution from Ms. Marvel to Captain Marvel, drawn by Terry Dodson and inked by Rachel Dodson.

A daughter. A sister. A friend. An officer in the air force, then NASA. A fighter pilot. A woman with Kree-given superpowers. Carol is also just a girl from Boston's Back Bay who struggles with anxiety and addiction and a deeply troubled relationship with her father. Not so different from any one of us, excepting the superpowers.

For Ms. Marvel, the highs were high and the lows were low. While considered by many to be Marvel's premier female super hero, a member of the Avengers, alternately an ally and antagonist to the X-Men—playing key roles in the biggest Marvel events, including *The Kang Dynasty*, *Civil War*, and *Secret Invasion*—Carol also suffered from the gender biases of many of her writers, who for thirty years were all men. Some wrote from empathy and saw her as a person first and a woman second, allowing her a fuller range of human emotions and experiences. Others treated her as a device for advancing the larger plot or other heroes' stories, resulting in three decades of mixed messaging, troubling plot beats, and a character who at once inspired hope and cynicism in female Marvel readers.

What does a female creator assuming the reins of a female hero–led book do with all that?

"As one editor friend advised," said Margaret, "as we stood outside in the dark following San Diego Comic-Con one night, after I had poured out some seriously stressed-out feelings on the subject . . . 'You drive on by.'"

CAROL ALSO SUFFERED FROM
THE GENDER BIASES OF MANY OF HER WRITERS,
WHO FOR THIRTY YEARS WERE ALL MEN.

OPPOSITE: Before Carol took on the moniker, Monica Rambeau was the first female Captain Marvel, making her debut in the *Amazing Spider-Man Annual* #16 in 1982, drawn by John Romita Jr.

"YOU'RE NOT writing *Ms. Marvel* . . . you're writing *Captain Marvel!*"

The story of how Stephen Wacker, at the time the executive editor running the Spider-Man group, told Kelly Sue DeConnick that her pitch to write Carol Danvers was approved, is infamous.

"I had been pitching the name [change to Captain Marvel] for a while. I just couldn't buy that the character would call herself 'Ms. Marvel,'" recalled Stephen. "The Captain Marvel name was out there, not being used. I had a feeling that if we didn't do something, someone was going to create another male Captain Marvel, and that's where we would land."

Stephen looked to the history of the character to find inspiration. In 1982, Monica Rambeau, a Black police lieutenant from New Orleans originally debuting in the pages of *The Amazing Spider-Man*, took on the mantle when she, like Carol, accidentally gained powers from an extra-dimensional energy source. Her journey with that code name ended violently, when she was stripped of her superpowers and the name so that Mar-Vell's son could assume the role. Aside from a star turn in the cult favorite *Nextwave* and until her return to the big screen in the MCU's *Captain Marvel*, Carol faded into relative obscurity.

Stephen knew Kelly Sue from her earlier days on the message board forums, and had been following her career. He was thrilled with her acclaimed work on the *Osborn* series, and when the original *Ms. Marvel* series was slated for cancellation in 2010, he knew they had an opportunity.

"I asked her to pitch Carol Danvers," Stephen recalled. "Kelly Sue brought her background of growing up as a military kid and grew it into what she would later call Chuck Yeager."

In an interview with ComicsAlliance in 2012, Kelly Sue expanded on what went into the foundation of the character as she sees her. "If you read her Wiki page and try to extract her character from her biography . . . she

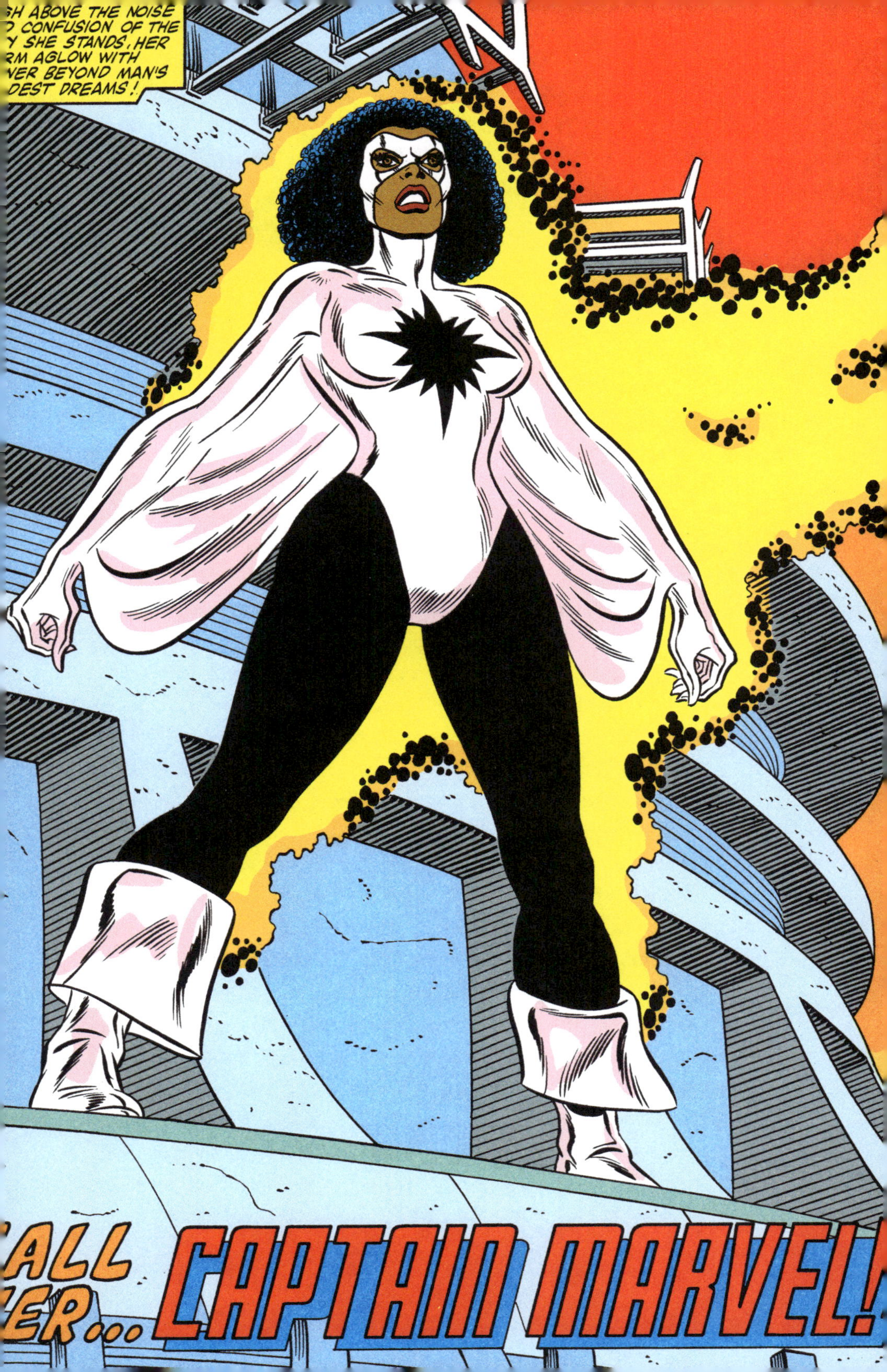
GH ABOVE THE NOISE
D CONFUSION OF THE
Y SHE STANDS, HER
RM AGLOW WITH
VER BEYOND MAN'S
DEST DREAMS!
ALL
ER... CAPTAIN MARVEL!

THE WOMAN I'M WRITING IS A LONG WAY FROM PERFECT, BUT SHE KNOWS HERSELF. SHE TRANSCENDS HER HISTORY.

———

comes across like a walking red flag, like a woman in the constant state of an identity crisis, who literally fights some version of herself over and over and doesn't know who she is. But the magic of Carol is that when you read her, that's not who she is. That's not the woman I'm writing; the woman I'm writing is a long way from perfect, but she knows herself. She transcends her history."

The pitch was a hit in the office and was immediately approved. Stephen, known around the Marvel Bullpen as a jokester, called Kelly Sue and said, "You're not writing *Ms. Marvel* . . . you're writing *Captain Marvel!*"

"I don't think that we understood the gravity of what that character was going to become," reflected current executive of production and development at Marvel Studios Sana Amanat, who, just after the first script was underway, was brought onto the project as associate editor. "I always knew the role, the mantle that she could potentially be fulfilling."

Stephen also saw the value of having a woman on the editorial side who could be a partner for Kelly Sue. "I do believe we are dependent on people, ultimately, being able to speak up and speak their truth, speak their mind," he said. "Coming into Marvel as a fan, I had found Marvel Comics to be a place or fandom open for everyone, not just for the guys. But now, looking back, through the years it was mostly white guys writing those stories. And I see all that now. It was not visible to me when I was just a fan coming up. Then joining the comics industry, I realized that the truth does not always connect with those ideas."

Sana remembered the feeling of being given the space to have a voice in the room. "As soon as I came into the office, he handed it over to me: 'Try your hand at this.' It was awesome because I was finally working on a female-led title. I loved working with Kelly Sue because she believed so much in the project."

In Carol Danvers, she found, like so many female fans did, a sense of righteousness and belonging. "I always thought that was an interesting way to kick off Carol's story—for her, it doesn't matter. 'I'm taking it. This is a part of my legacy and I'm just taking the mantle.'"

Released on July 18, 2012, *Captain Marvel* #1 sold out in less than twenty-four hours.

On July 19, Marvel announced a second printing.

Though the creative team knew they had something special on their hands, the fight to gain ground for women in the industry didn't end with Captain Marvel. It was only the beginning.

The pushback started small and focused at first just on the costume change. "The Cockrum design is beautiful. I don't fault the design at all. But it's also a design that was very much of its time," Stephen said. "I really felt like Marvel needed someone who could stand alongside Wonder Woman. A female character who could stand toe-to-toe just in both silhouette and the iconography with our main heroes." Also, as he would say, an outfit his daughter could look to wear on Halloween. With pants.

The initial designs of Carol's new uniform were done by Dexter Soy, before Jamie McKelvie was brought on to do the final designs. They had an extremely limited budget, and, in true Stan fashion, there was a bit of sleight of hand that the pair had to engage in to bring Jamie on, in a now famous story that Kelly Sue likes to tell, about a phone call where they talked around the issue: "Gosh, it would be a shame if someone were to do a design that everyone in the office loved and we couldn't *not* hire him to do!"

Jamie looked to pay homage to Carol's military roots while utilizing her traditional colors and sash, and the final result was instantly iconic: a stylized flight suit with a simple but effective star design across her chest.

"I get riled up," said Kelly Sue, reflecting on some less-than-favorable opinions about Carol's updated look. "Early in my career, I flipped off a very famous artist at a Marvel party I was lucky to even get invited to. Not exactly a savvy career move, but on-brand, I guess. My *Captain Marvel* had just come out, and we'd taken Carol out of the bathing suit and put her in a flight suit,

"The best and strongest costumes arise from the character's personality and backstory," says Jamie McKelvie of his design for Carol Danvers's new look as Captain Marvel, in 2012.

PEOPLE ALWAYS TALK ABOUT COMICS AS A MALE-DOMINATED INDUSTRY, BUT EVERY INDUSTRY IS A MALE-DOMINATED INDUSTRY.

———

and he didn't like it. He asked me why I hated women. And I lost it. I'd like to think I'd handle it differently today, but I don't know that I would.

"You're always deciding, 'Is this a hill I'm going to die on, or am I just going to make progress?'" Kelly Sue continued. "Yeah, progress is progress, right? So maybe I'm not going to get it to the end zone, but I'm going to get it closer. That's fine. I'll take that. People always talk about comics as a male-dominated industry, but every industry is a male-dominated industry."

BUT IF the Captain Marvel creative team was fighting for progress, they weren't doing it alone. Enter: the Carol Corps.

By 2012, the misconception that anyone who wasn't a cis, straight man didn't read comics had grown roots. But if the internet was a powerful tool for building communities based on hate, it was also an equally powerful tool for building communities based on support. Online, women and nonbinary readers with a passion for comics could find an incognito place to share their love. Whether a reader discovered super heroes from Saturday morning cartoons or newspaper comic strips, from action figures or single-issue comics, the internet—from the original AIM and early message boards to LiveJournal and Tumblr and sites for transformative works (aka fan fiction)—allowed these communities to grow and thrive.

The Carol Corps was one of them.

It started quietly on Tumblr, Facebook, and Twitter. Women, men, and nonbinary fans came together to support Kelly Sue's new version of Carol Danvers as Captain Marvel.

Kelly Sue clocked it right away. "We were trying to welcome in not just previous readers of Carol Danvers but new readers, people who were completely new to the shared universe of comics. And I saw that having a community that would help guide you was incredibly important."

Part of that meant giving this new community a name. "Naming the Carol Corps was huge," says Kelly Sue. "That was, probably next to marrying my husband, the smartest thing I ever did. And you know where that comes from, right? That came from the KISS Army. I enlisted [in that] when I was eight. Someday I'll find my belt buckle."

Kelly Sue could see that giving yourself an identity, and being able to identify yourself the way you want to be seen to the people around you, was key. "I started using #CarolCorps as a tag on Twitter. I was not trying to center [myself] in it, but hold a mirror up and introduce the people tweeting at me to each other. I would look to signal boost anything that was Carol-related, from cosplay to fan art to just conversations. And when I saw other people using it, I knew it had worked."

"I'll admit, I was skeptical of the way she was engaging with the fans," Stephen Wacker recalled. "I totally didn't see the value of that. And she did, and she really used it as a launching point that helped the character, certainly—and helped Kelly Sue. I always love it when creators can find a character that becomes their voice and Marvel becomes their outlet. When they can really pour themselves into a character."

For many new fans, or for those just returning to comics, the Corps became a place to get oriented, especially when the first question was "Eighty years of history. Where do I even start?!" Fans could find their way to reading guides, lists of comic shops to visit, tips for DIY Carol costumes, and even meetups at local conventions, with Kelly Sue leading the charge online via Twitter, and in-person panels.

Judy Stephens, who was a longtime producer at Marvel, is also a proud member of the Carol Corps, known for her cosplay of Carol. If you Zoom with her, you'll see her original Captain Marvel art prominently in the background. "It's an original Terry Dodson and features Carol's three costumes," she will say, following with, "Did you know Terry's wife, Rachel, inks all his work?"

In 2017, Judy and Sana interviewed several Carol Corps members for the *Women of Marvel* podcast. Allison Baker, creator of *The Hangout* podcast, said, "One of my cohosts recommended the new *Captain Marvel* book to me as an entry point to Marvel Comics. I loved it. To me, Captain Marvel—Carol Danvers specifically—represents victory over impostor syndrome: knowing

TOP: Kelly Sue DeConnick poses with her husband, Matt Fraction, and their children, Henry and Tallulah, at the red-carpet premiere of *Captain Marvel*. BOTTOM: More than a decade after her "rebirth," there are countless looks for Carol as Captain Marvel, as a collection of cosplayers demonstrate during a photo shoot at a convention in 2019.

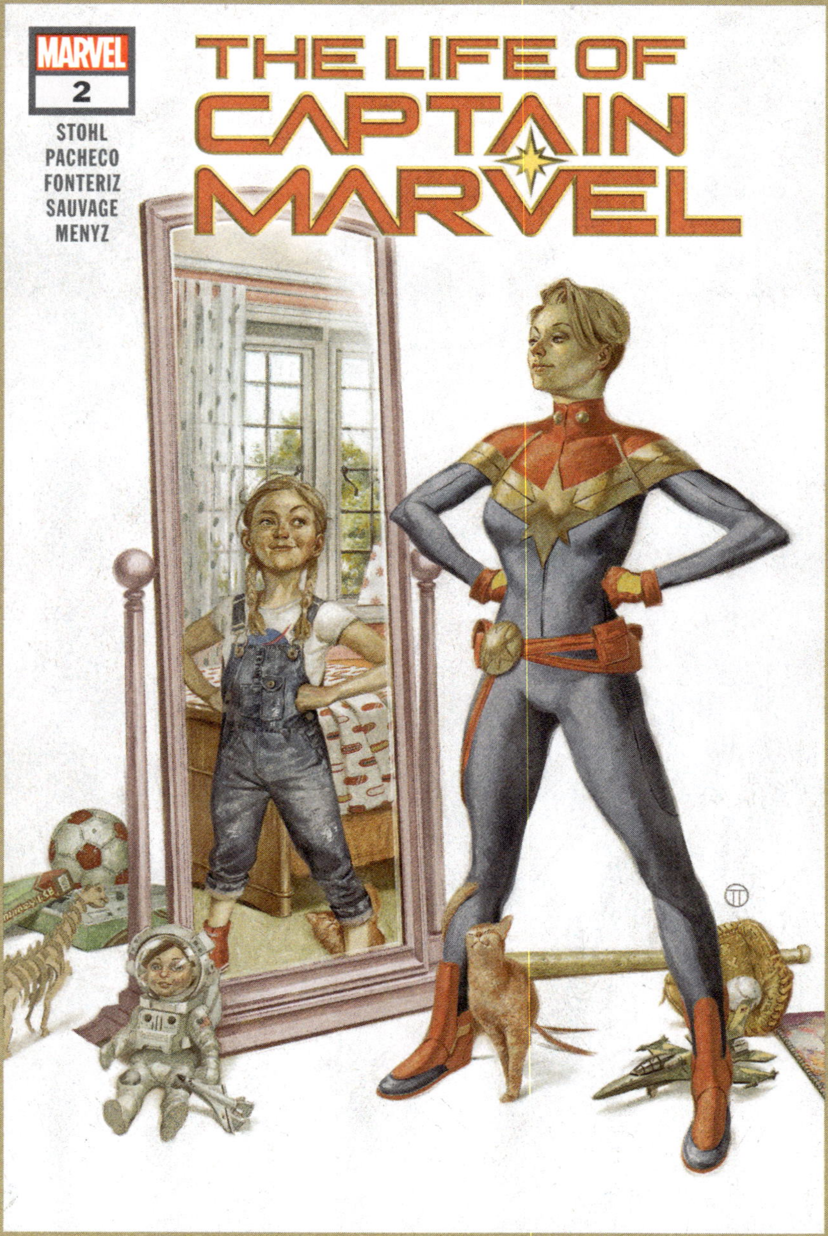
MARVEL
2
STOHL
PACHECO
FONTERIZ
SAUVAGE
MENYZ
THE LIFE OF CAPTAIN MARVEL

OPPOSITE: *The Life of Captain Marvel* #2, 2018, written by Margaret Stohl, cover art by Julian Totino Tedesco.
ABOVE: *Captain Marvel* #1, 2016, written by Michele Fazekas and Tara Butters, cover art by Kris Anka.

you *deserve* to be in the room, not apologizing for knowing your worth, and having the confidence to act without asking permission."

Carol Corps member and aerospace engineer Lisa Kristeena Johnson, a woman of color working in a predominantly white male–dominated field, said, "The Carol Corps was the first time that a nerd group was predominantly women and had so many women of color. That part was so exciting." She discovered Captain Marvel in 2012 with the first issue. "I wrote a very mathematical response correcting her description of Carol's reentry from orbit. . . . For me, the Carol Corps was the nerdiest girl gang I've ever had the pleasure of joining. Carol inspired me to run marathons, take huge career leaps, and live my life the Carol way: stubborn as hell, bold as brass, and never above nerdy puns."

Rafael Rodrigues has run @CaptMarvelNews from Spain since 2010. "It's through Twitter we've been able to expand the Carol Corps around the world. I've made so many friends online and in real life. Now after the first film . . . we keep adding new people to the family. We're at the point that I've always dreamed of, for her character, comic, and within the MCU. Now she's well-known, now she's known around the world.

"It's very important for me, as a man, to show that I'm a fan of female characters, too. That you can identify with these characters no matter your gender, no matter your religion, your color. I'm so inspired by the way Carol overcomes her struggles and the way she turns fears into confidence. I see myself in Carol all the time."

The global advent of the Carol Corps was changing the notions of who was allowed to belong in the comics community, which was clearly growing and evolving. This expansion would become a critical part of building the foundation for the next phase of the Marvel Cinematic Universe.

EVERYONE COMES to Marvel Comics to be a part of something bigger, as the saying goes. The same is true for creators, and taking up the mantle of a particular character also means knowing you will someday put it down.

In 2015, after thirty-five issues of the rebooted *Captain Marvel*— including three issues of *Captain Marvel & the Carol Corps*, a spin-off cowritten with Kelly Thompson, who would one day write *Captain Marvel* herself—Kelly

Sue handed the book off first to Tara Butters and Michele Fazekas, writers of Marvel's television series *Agent Carter*, then, in 2016, to Christos and Ruth Gage. It was that summer at the San Diego Comic-Con when Academy Award–winning actress Brie Larson was announced as Captain Marvel, and that the film would be part of the MCU's Phase 3. The importance of this character continued to grow—in particular, to Margaret Stohl, because in 2017, she began to write Carol Danvers herself.

"I had recently written the prose novels *Black Widow: Forever Red* and *Black Widow: Red Vengeance* for Marvel, and Sana Amanat (who edited both novels and the *Captain Marvel* ongoing comic) reached out to see if I'd like to take on the job. I tried to decline, but when Sana wouldn't take no for an answer, I began my own hero's journey." In 2019, she passed the baton to Kelly Thompson.

"It was time," Margaret said. "When I was given *Captain Marvel*, I felt like I was picking up something from Kelly Sue and carrying it further down the story. Likewise, I felt happy that it went to Kelly Thompson after me. She was able to build on what Kelly Sue and I did—and everyone before us—and then made it her own, which is how it should be.

"As Marvel creators, we are here to tell our part of a sequential story, arguably the longest ever told, at least in the Western culture canon. It is a story that only gets more relevant to and more reflective of the 'world outside our windows' with every telling and with every new voice."

"I don't need to be a figurehead," says Kelly Sue. "I don't want it. It's all right, I'm good. But I think what you're trying to do is give people mirrors. And when you do that, they see themselves, and it feels so good that they think that you did something magic, that you are magic. And you didn't. And you aren't.

"It was them all along."

Oral History

KELLY THOMPSON

Kelly Thompson looks to Kelly Sue DeConnick as a mentor, one of the people who truly helped her break into comics. "In March of 2015, I had the *Jem* debut, and by June I was cowriting *Carol Corps* with Kelly Sue. I still, to this day, don't actually know how that happened. But Kelly Sue is one of a handful of women who were really lovely to me when I reached out, helping me connect to a couple of editors."

That deliberate connection and support would lead to four years of writing for various female-led series, and collaborating with a growing number of women in both editorial and other creative roles. By the time Kelly wrapped her *Captain Marvel* run in June of 2023, she had written fifty issues, a longer run than any other "Captain Carol" writer.

Interior pages from *Captain Marvel* #1, 2019, pencilled by Carmen Carnero.

140 / SUPER VISIBLE

JUDY STEPHENS: Before you go, we also want to talk to you about the room. Kelly, you were the third female writer to join a Marvel Creative Summit, right? G. Willow Wilson was the first. Margaret "Margie" Stohl was the second.

KELLY THOMPSON: I was the third woman in the room?

MARGIE STOHL: You were.

KELLY: It's startling if you hear you're the third [female creator] to have ever been in the room, and you sort of want to shake someone and be mad about it. But at the same time, I don't think there's anyone at Marvel going, "Keep those women out of the room!" It's just a thing that sort of happens. It's like, "Oh, well, we only put exclusive people in the room, and we don't have any women who are building at the architect level yet and we're looking for them." I don't think it's like a nefarious plan for the most part. It's just a reality that we all need to work our best to push forward and change, you know.

Did I Replace Her?

KELLY: Tini Howard was in the room with me previously, and I was really glad to see it, not just because Tini is great, but because, Margie, you and I were in the room together one time. Yeah. And then you weren't there at the next one. And I was like, "Did I replace her?" I had a real gut check feeling of like "Wait a minute, is there only room for one? Did me being there last time force Margie out?" Like, I don't feel good about that. So I was glad when Tini came for *X-Men*, and so now there's a couple of women in the room and I'm still there and she's there.

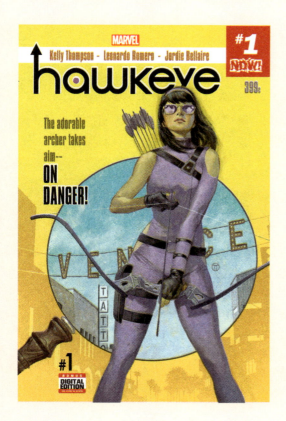

Hawkeye #1, 2016, cover art by Julian Totino Tedesco.

MARGIE: I never held you accountable for that. It's not the one-girl chair. And you didn't take it from me. So please don't feel like that at all.

KELLY: I hoped that you didn't feel that way. You've always been incredibly kind and generous to me and supportive.

MARGIE: It's a community that we are sharing with each other. MacKenzie Cadenhead just talked to us about how important it was for her to be able to look across the table and see another woman.

KELLY: At that first summit I went to, I was so glad you were there. It meant everything to be able to look across the room and be like, "Oh thank God. Thank God there's another one." And there are always a lot of female editors, and that's actually gotten a lot better, where I feel like Sarah [Brunstad] and Alanna [Smith] and others are graduating to the main table. And that helps, too. But there's still a difference in that room between the creative and the editorial, you know. So it meant a lot, meant a lot having you there.

MARGIE: So you were three, Tini [Howard] is four, and Leah [Williams], then, is five. Is there anyone else in that? I think it's important to get that list down.

KELLY: I think that's right. Vita [Ayala] is a really important voice [for Marvel]. I hope they get the chance to really tell some stories there.

A Long Way to Go

KELLY: I think there's a thing that happens, unfortunately, where creators who are from more diverse backgrounds, that are so needed, when they can't get through [i.e., approval for] those stories that they want to tell, that are more personal to them, they end up sort of getting driven out.

Not that anyone's firing them or anything, but just that they can't get the content they're interested in producing out there. And that ends up creating an environment that continues to be mostly straight, white, and male.

It's easier for me to stick around because I'm a white woman. It's a little easier for me than a woman of color, in part because all the heroes I get handed are white women. And I try to be the best ally I can. But until that room and until those stories are more diverse, we just still have a really long way to go.

And the only way that really changes, no matter how much everyone intends, the only way that really changes is to change the makeup of the people creating.

Angela Bassett and Letitia Wright in *Black Panther: Wakanda Forever*.

CHAPTER FIVE

THE BILLION-DOLLAR CLUB

Keeping Comics Relevant in a Sharply Contracting Market

Released in March 2019, almost exactly a year after Marvel Studios' *Black Panther*, the *Captain Marvel* feature film was a bona fide juggernaut. It became the seventh out of the twenty-one films so far in the first three phases of the Marvel Cinematic Universe to join the Billion-Dollar-Worldwide Club, the new marker of big-budget success, right after *Black Panther* and *Avengers: Infinity War* became the fifth and sixth, respectively.

Black Panther and *Captain Marvel* were two of the three films in the early phases of the MCU to be headlined by heroes who weren't white men. *Black Panther* debuted first, shattering multiple records in one fell swoop: with a $242 million North American box office in its opening weekend (and $426.6 million globally), it nabbed the record for second-biggest four-day North American opening of all time, fifth-biggest three-day domestic opening of all time, biggest ever February opening, and the biggest bow for an African American director.

As of the writing of this book, it also holds the record for sixth-highest-grossing movie in domestic box office history. This was all for a movie that was the first studio tentpole to feature an almost all-Black cast.

The diversity of its audience was unheard of, with Black moviegoers showing up at 37 percent, and a whopping 45 percent of ticket buyers were women, spurred on by the word-of-mouth that much of the action was driven by a cast that was largely Black women.

"People are so hungry for different kinds of representation," said Roxane Gay, a bestselling writer and professor who focuses on intersectional women's issues, and the cowriter of the comic book *Black Panther: World of Wakanda*. "But—people have said this before—bigotry is expensive and they are leaving a lot of money on the table."

SOME PEOPLE STILL DEFAULT TO WHAT THEY KNOW AND HAVE NEVER HAD THE MOMENT IN WHICH TO INTERROGATE THAT OR UNLEARN CERTAIN BEHAVIORS.

———

In an interview with *The Guardian* in 2011, Idris Elba (who plays Heimdall, the Norse guardian of the Bifrost, in all four *Thor* films) said, "Imagine a film such as *Inception* with an entire cast of Black people—do you think it would be successful? Would people watch it? But no one questions the fact that everyone's white. That's what we have to change."

Cate Shortland, director of *Black Widow*, vehemently agreed. "When you're in a boardroom having a meeting, you might have twenty men at the table and two or three women. But then all the women sitting against the wall behind—all the assistants—are women. Not that much has changed. And we have to change it. We have to demand, I suppose, that we work with women."

Marguerite Bennett, a multiple GLAAD award–nominated writer who exploded onto the Marvel scene with *Angela: Asgard's Assassin* and who went on to write *X-Men: Years of Future Past* and *A-Force*, thinks often about identity and expectations, and what both shapes and perpetuates biases in the industry. "Some people still default to what they know and have never had the moment in which to interrogate that or unlearn certain behaviors," she said. "And look, we all do it. It's the kind of thing where, 'Oh, I never realized that that might be a problem.' Where you default to because of your upbringing or your worldview or the place in time that you exist. And so with comic book art, it was just a given that everything is going to be, like, mega-horndog material."

Gail Simone launched the website *Women in Refrigerators* in 1999 in order to take on the work of that interrogation, and encourage others to do the same. "The *Women in Refrigerators* site was never meant to create shame," she said. "It was a question. I loved comics. I was always hearing guys say, 'Why don't more women read comics?' So I asked about it. I think there was

Marguerite Bennett teamed up with G. Willow Wilson to write the *A-Force* series in 2015, featuring an all-women team of Avengers.

a feeling that female readers were like unicorns—they were so rare, so there was no real point to trying to appeal to them. Which is odd, because for decades, everyone had read comics. The idea that they were only for young boys and teens and male collectors is a very recent proposition."

This proposition continues to threaten the health of a comics industry that, with the rise of streaming services, the game industry, and smartphone-friendly, all-access digital media, needs a constant influx of new readers to remain competitive. As Gail wrote in 1999, "My simple point has always been: if you demolish most of the characters girls like, then girls won't read comics."

Similarly, Kelly Sue DeConnick recounted for us how often fellow creators—"who were not idiots"—perpetuated the same biases, telling her, "Women don't want to write super heroes," to "We have all the female readers we're going to get," and even, "Women don't like comics—they're not very visual."

In our conversations for this project, the women and nonbinary members of the Marvel community—probably not unlike most people who work in comics, read comics, or even just like fantasy or sci-fi—were looking for the same things the men of comics do. To be seen on the page. To feel connected to the fandom. To be, returning to the familiar refrain, a part of something bigger.

OPPOSITE: A hero from film to screen to comics, actress Ming-Na Wen poses with the *Agents of S.H.I.E.L.D.* comics during a visit to the Marvel offices in 2015.

"My mom brought me and my brother to the United States when we were little kids," recalled actor Ming-Na Wen, who portrayed Agent Melinda May in Marvel Television's *Agents of S.H.I.E.L.D.* from 2013 to 2020. "We didn't even know where we were flying to. I had to learn English at seven. I grew up in a very white suburbia, part of Pittsburgh, always feeling like I never fully belonged. I had a weird Chinese name, and I was one of the few, if not the only Asian girl growing up in Mount Lebanon. So I tried to change my name a couple of times, anglicize it. That didn't work.

"I read Larry Niven, I read Jerry Pournelle. I read all of them. That carried me through. They made me believe in possibilities, that there's a future that I need to live for. Fantasy is great for that. And I think that's why we still have so many fans. We all strive, I think, for that fantasy life."

It's a deliberate change, one that ultimately requires intersectional parity, or at least an attempt at it, in the rooms where decisions are made. Films like *Black Panther* and *Captain Marvel* are a direct result of that, a true reflection of Stan Lee's "world outside your window."

Kimberlé Crenshaw, the American law professor who first coined the term "intersectionality" in 1989, said, "All inequality is not created equal." Only in recent decades has intersectional feminism, and the deliberate centering of the voices of women of color, become an integral part of growing our collective creative industry.

But growing that industry is a commercial imperative, particularly for Marvel, because super heroes are a truly global business, and because underrepresented super hero characters, particularly women of color, have historically been written by creators who did not themselves share these identities.

Marvel Studios' *Black Panther*, based on a Marvel Comics character created by two white men, but released as a film in 2018 under the stewardship of two Black men, is a case study in exactly that. A massive commercial and critical success, the film was nominated for Best Picture at the 2019 Academy Awards, and it became the first Disney film to have a cross-nation release in Africa.

AND IT HAS NOTHING TO DO WITH FRAGILITY. . . . ON ALL LEVELS IS COMMUNITY. IT'S LEANING ON MY SISTERS, WITH MY FELLOW WOMEN.

Black Panther also became a driving force in changing how the public viewed the Marvel Cinematic Universe. The Academy Award–winning production design, costume design, and score brought to life a wholly unique corner of the Marvel Cinematic Universe, a fully realized, living Wakanda that not only redefined itself, but also changed and expanded the creative terrain of the larger Marvel Universe.

"You're not going to change everything," said Ruth E. Carter, costume designer for *Black Panther* and *Black Panther: Wakanda Forever*, and the first Black woman to win an Academy Award for Costume Design. "But when it comes to my lap and they say create it? Then I get to choose.

"The fact that a young person growing up in the neighborhood with nothing can put on one of these costumes of their own making and feel amazing in it is where it all starts," she continued. "That's what they relate to and that's what they see in themselves. That makes the biggest impact. That's who they want to be and who empowers them."

As Stan Lee was famous for saying, anyone can be a hero. It takes another kind of hero, however, to support them.

"Community and congregation," said Zoe Saldaña, who stars as Gamora, Thanos's adopted daughter and one of the most dangerous women in the universe, in the *Guardians of the Galaxy* and *Avengers* films. "Community and congregation. Let me tell you something. And it has nothing to do with fragility. . . . On all levels is community. It's leaning on my sisters, with my fellow women. It's that congregation of these spirits that are holding my hand, and I am learning to hold theirs more and more."

TOP: Angela Bassett, nominated for an Academy Award for her role as Queen Ramonda in *Black Panther: Wakanda Forever*, brilliantly costumed by Ruth Carter. BOTTOM: Ruth Carter, a two-time winner of the Academy Award for Costume Design (for both *Black Panther* and *Black Panther: Wakanda Forever*). Ruth was also the first African American to ever win an Oscar for Costume Design.

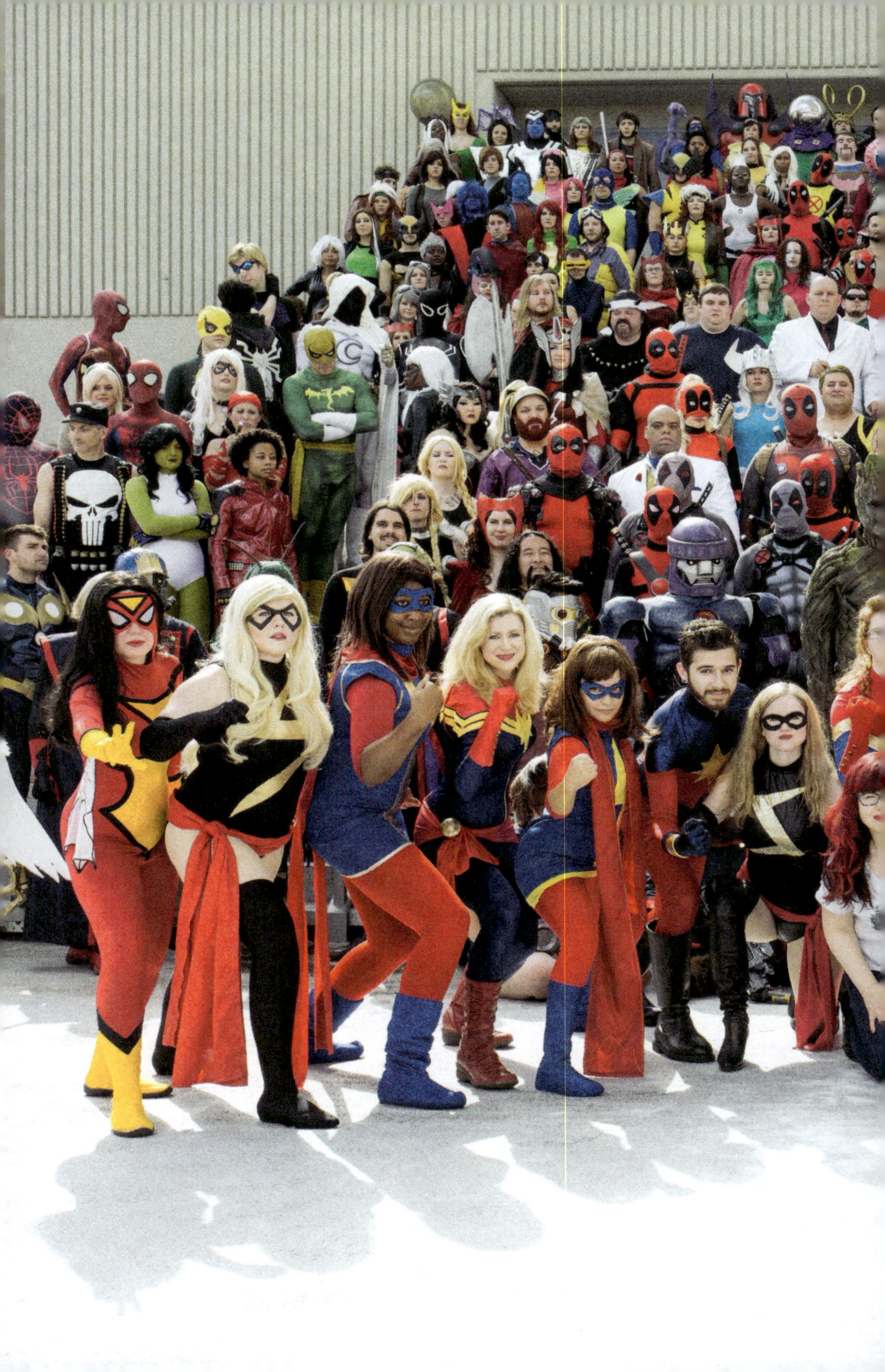

Kelly Sue DeConnick poses with the Carol Corps at the Dragon Con Marvel Gathering in 2014.

PART THREE

THE CALL IS COMING FROM INSIDE THE HOUSE

PAY ATTENTION TO THE WOMEN BEHIND THE CURTAIN

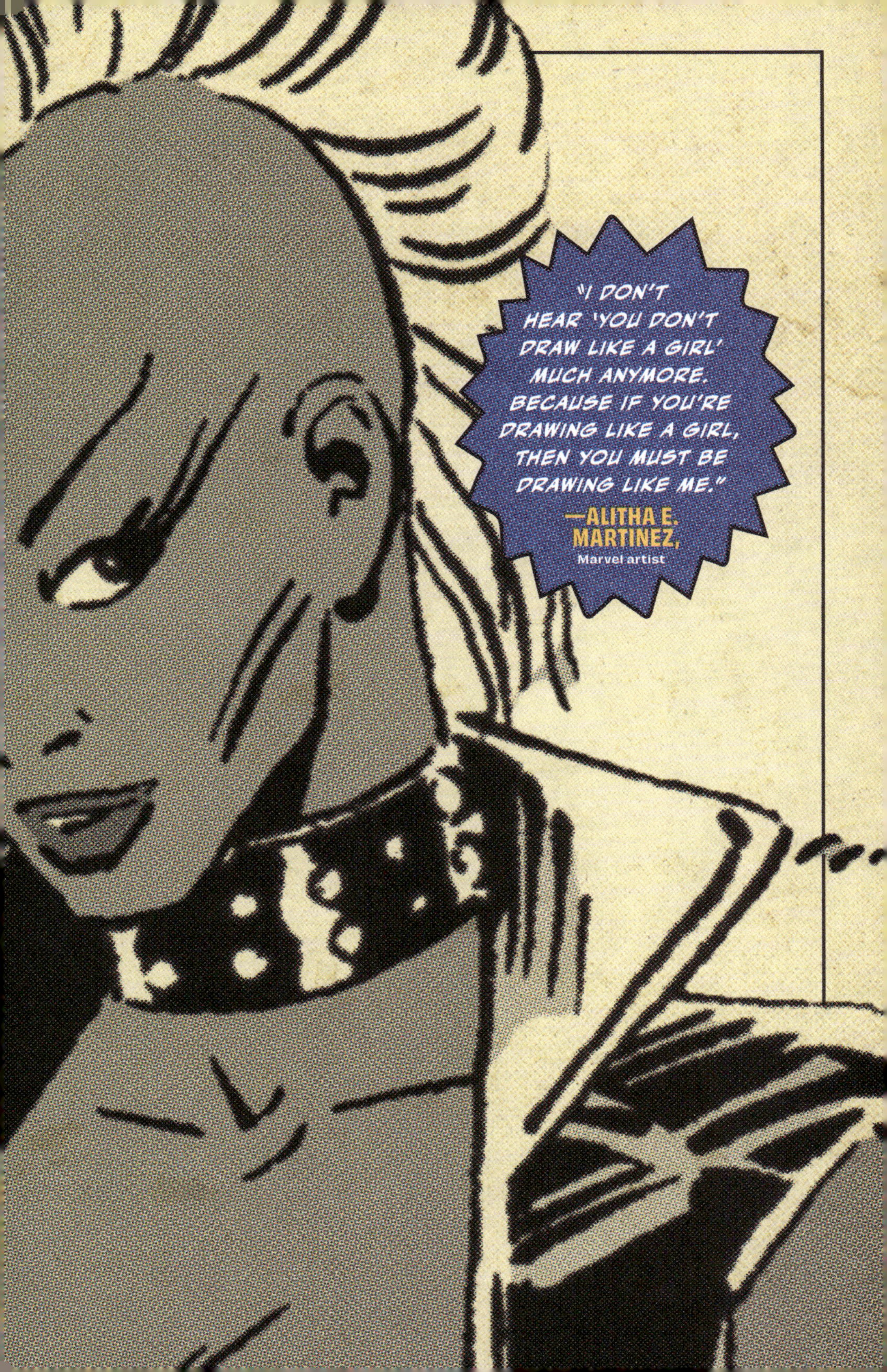
"I DON'T HEAR 'YOU DON'T DRAW LIKE A GIRL' MUCH ANYMORE. BECAUSE IF YOU'RE DRAWING LIKE A GIRL, THEN YOU MUST BE DRAWING LIKE ME."
—ALITHA E. MARTINEZ,
Marvel artist

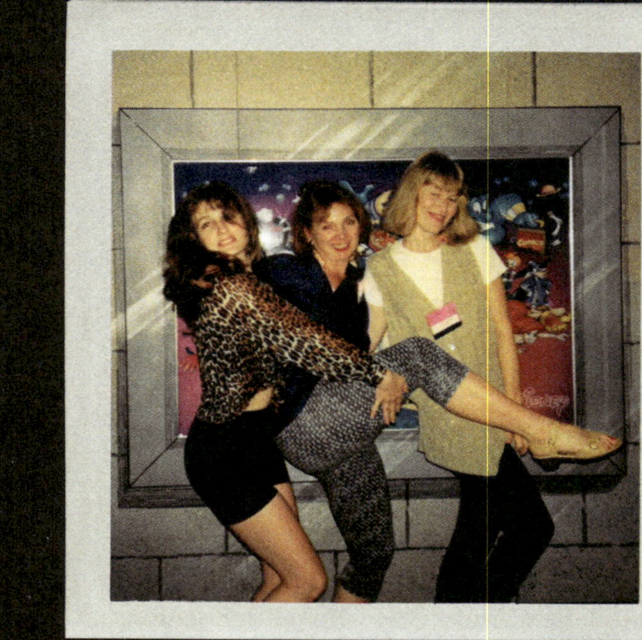

CHAPTER SIX

MEET ME IN THE BATHROOM

How Women Find Each Other
in an Industry That
Prioritizes Male Spaces

Anna Boden, director of *Captain Marvel*, has spoken specifically about how most spaces on a movie set aren't built for vulnerability.

The same holds true for many other spaces in comics, whether it's in the office or on the convention floor. These communities of creators had to find their own spaces, and what better space than the one that—historically at least—has been the least-used?

The women's bathroom.

"**For** most of my career in video games, I have been the only woman in the room, sometimes on an entire floor," said writer Margaret Stohl. " So bathrooms also became my safe places, almost like my private office. There were so few female employees that each one had her own monogrammed hand towel. I still recall when a rare female leader instituted the then-radical policy of keeping free tampons in the bathroom."

"It was my favorite place to cry!" former Marvel editor Jeanine Schaefer said. "Sometimes Sana [Amanat] would come into my office to talk about something else, take one look at my face, and say, 'Okay, bathroom,' before marching me down the hallway."

"Thank God it was all the way in the back, behind the freight elevators," Judy Stephens said of the Marvel offices on Fifth Avenue.

Writer Irene Vartanoff recalled a treasured moment between her and Marie Severin in the bathroom. "On my birthday, I kept saying it was my birthday, so Marie taped business cards inside each toilet stall saying 'Happy Birthday, Irene!' A little secret only for the women in the office to see."

Jess Reed, a project director at Insomniac Games who worked on *Marvel's Spider-Man*, talked at length about how the feeling of being not only the

FOR MOST OF MY CAREER IN VIDEO GAMES, I HAVE BEEN THE ONLY WOMAN IN THE ROOM, SOMETIMES ON AN ENTIRE FLOOR.

——

only woman in the room but also the only minority in the room can make it hard to ask important questions. She spoke of the power of seeing someone who looks like you in "The Chair," and the importance of feeling like you are not alone.

"I remember I was at a previous studio and I said to somebody, 'This is the first time there's a line for the women's restroom!'" she said. "This has never happened in the history of me working in games. And I remember the day it happened. It feels like we have so many women working here now that there is actually a line for the restroom, the way there's always one for the men's restroom. . . . It just felt memorable."

"I do remember running into [Cate Shortland, director of *Black Widow*] in the bathroom, which from the beginning of my time at the Marvel offices was an important space," Anna Boden recalled. "As people started joining our team, and more and more women in particular, those offices became fuller. By the time Cate started, there [were] lines for the women's bathroom."

Cate says her relationship with Anna was crucial not only to her creative process, but her well-being as a person, and their friendship was cemented in those quiet moments in the restroom.

"At really hard times, I would call her," Cate said. "And at times, I'd run into her in the bathroom. And then I'd just . . . Because there's a thing about being a woman, being a female director, where you have to be strong and you have to not show emotion and not be a hysteric and all this kind of stuff. With

Anna, I could let all those walls go down. And she could see me, and the state I was in, and what was going wrong, and help me put it into perspective and leave the bathroom a whole person."

It's important to note that this book is not written in a vacuum. Women's restrooms in this community can be a safe space for *all* women, cis and trans, as well as any nonbinary or gender-fluid folks who feel more comfortable using those facilities, and the hope is that more such spaces will follow suit, to account for the needs of the ever-expanding demographics of both fans and creators.

In 2015, Emerald City Comic Con became the first major convention to offer all-gender restrooms in addition to women's and men's rooms, and after they saw lines as long as any other, in the years since have greatly expanded the number of them, with other conventions following suit.

"Bathrooms were crucial for cosplayers," said Judy Stephens, who, in addition to being a Marvel producer, has made a name for herself as a cosplay photographer and, more recently, as the most recognizable Captain Marvel cosplayer. "Whenever you needed a hand, help with a zipper, a safety pin, or just a safe shoulder to lean on if you had a bad experience on the floor."

"At a con, the bathroom was our golf course," Jeanine Schaefer said. "We'd talk so much business between panels, or just have an opportunity to connect with each other."

Vita Ayala, current *X-Men* writer, talked about the bathroom as a place to actually get to meet editors at a convention, as meetings on the show floor became increasingly impossible. "I was going to a bunch of conventions and meeting editors," they said. "Mostly in the bathroom, women network in [there]. I have access to women's spaces because I have boobs [and] I need to go to the bathroom. And we just hit it off because we were all in these really stressful situations; how do we survive?

"Especially in these high-pressure situations where you're not allowed to have emotion—you just have to be chipper and on all the time. That is exhausting. And the bathroom becomes that safe space."

Even as lines for the women's room become longer, as more women work in previously "male" creative industries, the bathrooms have remained a space for commiseration, as created by and for the community who needed it.

IT SHOULDN'T seem revolutionary to hear that hiring women leads to hiring more women; like a snowball rolling down a hill, momentum doesn't make things smaller.

"When I started at Marvel [in 2001], I was the only female editor, and also the only woman of color on the editorial staff," editor Jenny Lee said. "I knew what it felt like to be an outsider. And at the time, [we were starting] to hire more women, which is how we got people like MacKenzie Cadenhead and Nicole Boose. When they started, I wanted them to know, 'I'm here, I'm another woman. I know what it feels like to be the only woman in the room. And I'm here for you.' Because I didn't have anybody doing that for me when I started at Marvel. I knew that if we created a community, it would allow this next generation of female editors to focus on their job, and not create an atmosphere of competition. And MacKenzie and I just got along famously from the start. We knew that the office was a stressful place to work, and knew that together we could be each other's support system.

"Just like with the safe spaces created in the bathrooms, women were trying to create a culture that would support them. That meant being deliberate about hiring women and other marginalized creators, carving out a space for them to succeed, and standing firm in the knowledge that more women, and more diverse points of view, was a necessity, in an industry that often chided women for taking up too much space."

"Molly Lazer, an associate editor on the Avengers books, was the first woman at Marvel I ever met, at a Women in Comics panel at MOCCA [the Museum of Comic and Cartoon Art], when I was an assistant editor at DC Comics, around 2005 or so," said Jeanine Schaefer. "I got to know her and [editor] Nicole Boose and just got to chat about the environment of the office at Marvel. They loved it there, and a lot of it was the relationships and the camaraderie that they had with each other. And with MacKenzie being there, she had such a strong sense of mentorship, rallying the team together and making everyone feel like they all belonged there, especially women.

"So when I got the call from [then executive editor] Stephen Wacker, saying a job was available, it was a no-brainer."

Women hiring women is in the DNA of Marvel, from the minute Flo pulled Linda Fite's letter to Stan Lee and personally put it on his desk.

Irene Vartanoff remembers her being hired directly because of Michele

Editor Jenny Lee would build a community and safe space for the women who would follow after her, including fellow editor and now-lifetime friend MacKenzie Cadenhead.

Wolfman (née Kreps). "My sister went to high school with Michele, and we took her with us to conventions. I went home and to graduate school, and then Michele married Marv Wolfman [co-creator of *Blade*]. And one day, Michele called me up and said, 'Hey, there's a job here. Do you want it?'

"I said okay. That's it."

It's a similar story to that of Nanci Dakesian, lead editor of the groundbreaking Marvel Knights imprint, and her assistant editor, Kelly Lamy.

"Yes, Kelly was one of my hires," Nanci said. "We had worked together for about seven years at Archie Comics, before she had left. Once I started at Marvel, I gave her a call. 'How'd you like to work for me again?' We balance each other out, between our skill sets, to run the entire office, from insurance to bookkeeping."

The two women were, as Joe Quesada put it, "a two-person wrecking ball."

Hildy Mesnik was the lead editor on the Barbie licensed books in the early nineties, a line that was given to her specifically by Renée Witterstaetter when Renée left Marvel. "I had powerhouse women writers and artists on the Barbie books," she said, "I just had this dream team of strong women."

One of them was Amanda Conner, now a superstar artist and best known for her action-packed, engaging, and often-times hilarious cover work as well as her reinvigoration of Power Girl at DC Comics. Amanda credits Hildy, her editor on *Barbie*, as the woman who gave her the shot that catapulted her to the next level of her career.

"When I first got into comics . . . I'm like, 'One of these days I'm going to do *X-Men*.' But at the time they were looking for a particular style, and I didn't have that," she says. "Hildy eventually asked me to do the *Gargoyles* comic, where I really got to flex my drawing muscles. If there weren't books like *Barbie*, Disney titles, and *Gargoyles*, I may not have had the chance to work as much as I did. Eventually the work that she assigned to me led to being given an *X-Factor* story with Kitty Pryde, and *Suburban Jersey Ninja She-Devils*. Hildy looked out for me and made sure I would get these really juicy Marvel stories to work on."

Kate Herron, director and executive producer of the Disney+ series *Loki*, recalls her pitch meeting with Kevin Feige.

"When I pitched on the show, Kevin Feige asked me, 'What are your terms?' Which was so funny to me, because I was like, 'I'll do it for free.' But one of them, I said, was I wanted a fifty-fifty split across our crew."

I JUST HAD THIS DREAM TEAM OF
STRONG WOMEN.

TOP: Interior page from *Excalibur* #80, released in 1988, pencilled by Amanda Conner. BOTTOM: Sophie DiMartino and Tom Hiddleston playing different versions of Loki, in the critically acclaimed series *Loki*, created by Kate Herron.

Marvel delivered on that promise, and the *Loki* set had almost perfect parity, with many of their department heads also women.

"Autumn Durald, my DP [director of photography], and I were the first female director and DP team across Marvel," she said. "There was also Christine Wada as costume designer, Monique Ganderton as stunt coordinator, Amy Wood as head of hair, Emma McCleave as editor, Natalie Holt as composer, Michele Blood as production manager, and Sandra Balej as VFX supervisor. And obviously our writing team included Elissa Karasik and Bisha K. Ali."

Kate said the different atmosphere that parity created was palpable. "It was really nice to see a mixture of women, and of backgrounds. It was very comforting to me, because I've so often been—on my previous jobs—one of the only women on set. So it was amazing to just have a slightly different experience in that sense, on this and hopefully beyond it."

Sophia Di Martino, who plays Sylvie, a Loki variant who distances herself from the Loki name, told us about being able to feel that energy. "Honestly, Kate Herron made it so easy. I've worked with her previously and know what a huge champion of women she is. As part of that, she aims to hire as many women as possible, including the amazing director of photography and the costume designer. So, to start with, the set was really mixed, not mostly white men (how it often is), which brought a nice energy and experience. Plus, she just championed me from the beginning. I always felt really supported."

Samira Ahmed, writer of *Ms. Marvel: Beyond the Limit*, knows that the only way to make progress is to do what you can when you have the power, and then pass that power onto the next person, especially when it comes to women of color.

"There's people who probably wanted someone else besides me to take the *Ms. Marvel* job. But I knew, 'I'm going to do a good job with it, so I'm going to take it.' We are making progress, even though it's not linear. You start with G. Willow Wilson and Sana Amanat, and now me. Each of us is doing our best to push it out there. We make the path by walking, and the more people we can have join us on the path, the easier it is going to be to walk, especially for the people who come after us.

"That's an important part of just being in publishing, even broadly, as

THAT'S AN IMPORTANT PART OF JUST BEING IN PUBLISHING, EVEN BROADLY, AS A WOMAN, OR A WOMAN OF COLOR. YES, WE HAVE TO HOLD THE DOOR OPEN AND PUT A HAND OUT.

———

a woman, or a woman of color. Yes, we have to hold the door open and put a hand out."

The women of Marvel whom we have spoken to have made a habit of throwing open every door they can find and, when they run out of doors, stocking up on dynamite to bring the walls down.

"You know, I went to work on staff at DC because I realized no woman had gone from one comic book company to another," said Irene Vartanoff, about her move from Marvel to DC in the mid-seventies. "So I said to myself, even though I really don't want to work in comics anymore, I'll go there anyway, so other women can follow me."

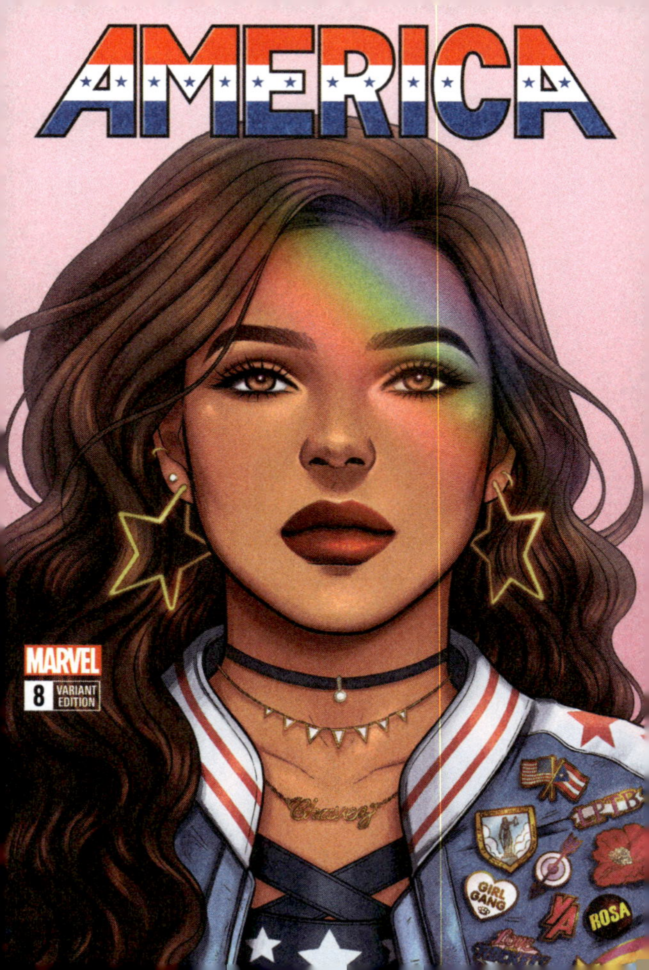
AMERICA
MARVEL
8 VARIANT EDITION
GIRL GANG
YA
ROSA

CHAPTER SEVEN

DRAW LIKE A GIRL

Gatekeeping, and the
Repositioning of Stories
for a Broader Audience

"Comics to me as a kid were very appealing because I loved fantasy. I loved sci-fi," said Mackenzi Lee, the bestselling author of *Loki: Where Mischief Lies*. "But I just didn't feel like I could access them. Part of it was because they felt like such male spaces. It felt really gate-kept. And I didn't know where the gate was."

It is a struggle to know how to talk about harassment of women in the comics industry while still encouraging women to join it. However, the increase in online bullying that we saw as more and more women began to openly work for and with Marvel—and throughout the industry, generally—was so definitive it cannot be dismissed.

"Something about the books we've made is threatening for some reason I don't understand," said Kelly Sue DeConnick, who, as the writer of *Captain Marvel*, has taken the brunt of this most recent wave of pushback, even after she left Marvel to create her own comics and her own production studio.

"The worst was actually a SyFy interview I did that I deeply regret," she said. "But it is what it is. I did it, like, two or three years after I had left *Captain Marvel*. They asked me about the online harassment in the interview, and I said, 'I don't understand—if you don't like my books, don't buy them.'

"Why is that controversial? But there's all this disingenuous outrage, suggesting I was throwing other creators who worked on my books under the bus because I was saying not to buy their books. Or that I was personally responsible for comic shops closing. I don't know. It doesn't make that much sense. Somehow I killed the industry because I said, 'If you don't like my books, maybe don't buy them.'"

OPPOSITE: Alitha E. Martinez has been drawing for Marvel for over two decades, including being brought in to assist on Joe Quesada's books.

She went on: "You know, there are a lot of comics that exist that I don't like. I don't buy them. I don't feel the need to harass their creators."

Social and cultural justice have been a foundational aspect of Marvel's ethos ever since the days of Stan Lee and Jack Kirby—"Stan's Soapbox" is a demonstrable by-product of that. But legend also says that upon hearing that a Nazi sympathizer—furious at Marvel's portrayal of Hitler—was downstairs in the lobby of their offices looking to start a fight, Jack rolled up his sleeves and went to the elevators to give it to him.

Historically, comics have never been created for any one particular audience, but somewhere along the way—after the Senate hearings of the fifties, after the gutting of the mainstream comics industry, after the Red Scare and the Space Race and Vietnam, as America began to sense its collective mortality—comics were seen by ever-growing segments of their readership as vehicles for fantasies of power.

"There's not even anything inherently masculine about power fantasies!" Kelly Sue said. "I'm a five-foot-tall woman! I can school any man in any room about power fantasies!

"I had the opportunity to meet a comics writer I admired, and he said that he knew my *Captain Marvel* run. And I'm gobsmacked! He's actually read it! And I'm like, '*Holy*, this is so cool!' And right then, when I'm walking on clouds, he adds, 'Yeah, you know, most women can't write super heroes. I don't know what it is, but you can.' And I just . . . deflated.

"It was like, 'Oh, buddy, I need to rewind this conversation thirty seconds and forget this bit ever happened. Because what you're saying is that I

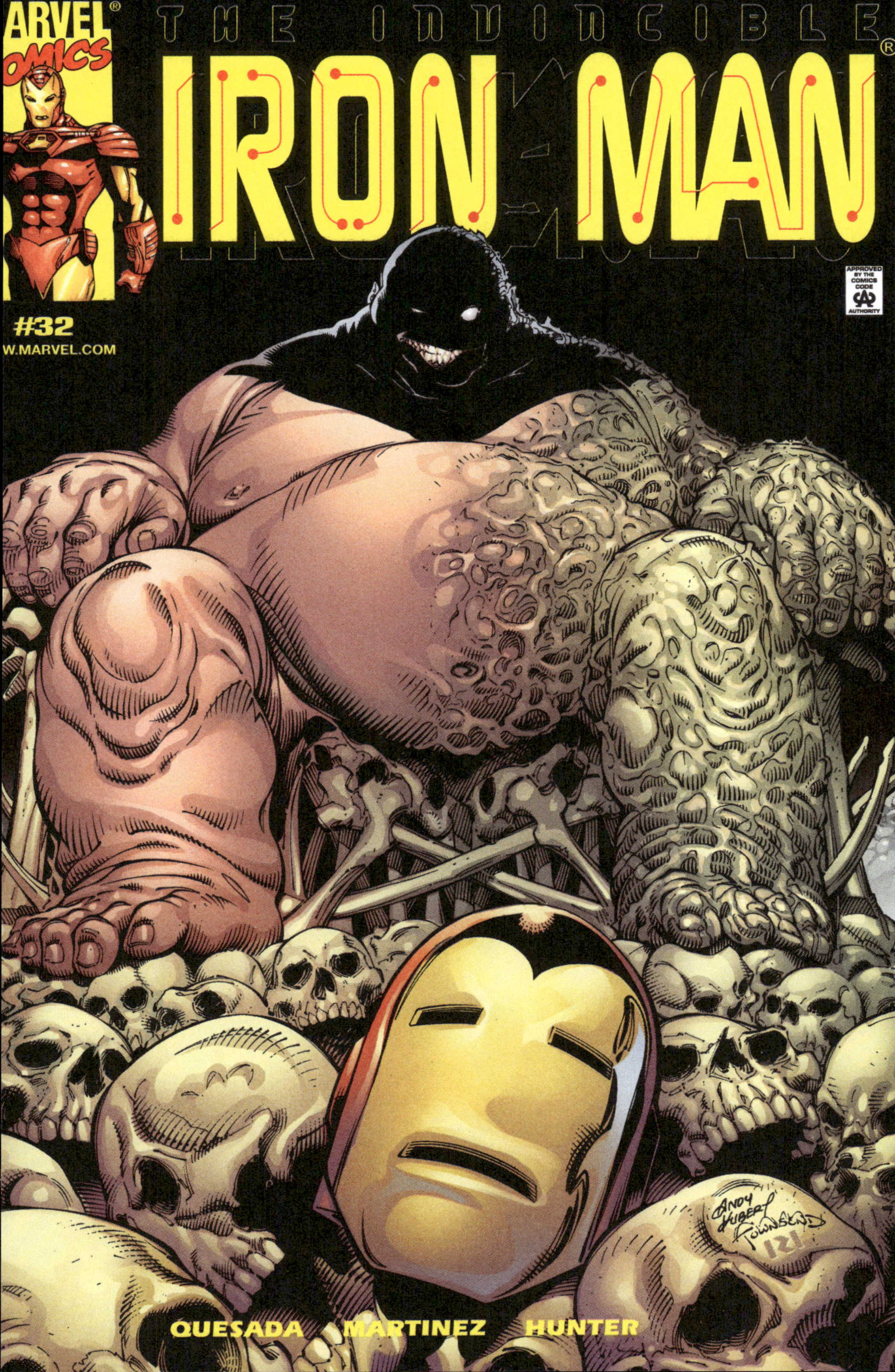
MARVEL COMICS
THE INVINCIBLE
IRON MAN
#32
W.MARVEL.COM
APPROVED BY THE COMICS CODE AUTHORITY
QUESADA MARTINEZ HUNTER

Jen Grünwald owes her love of
comics to her dad, seen here
with her as a child.

have somehow miraculously transcended my gender's inherent otherness to the human experiences that we examine in super hero comics, and that, my friend, is not a compliment.'

"There is nothing inherently masculine about heroism."

For marginalized groups who were just discovering comics at a time when the medium's audience was narrowing, it could be extremely lonely. And the more intersectional your identity, the lonelier it was.

"I moved here by myself," said Alitha E. Martinez, an artist who started in the Marvel Bullpen in the nineties before moving on to *Iron Man*, *X-Men*, Cable, and, most recently at Marvel, *Black Panther: World of Wakanda* with Roxane Gay. "I heard there was the School of Visual Arts. And I told myself I will go to this school. . . . I was the only girl in the cartooning program.

"It's so funny, because I actually teach at the School of Visual Arts now, and my class is 90 percent girls. I might have two boys in my entire class . . . which is amazing because that's, like, a huge explosion flip. But back then, I had male students who didn't want me to critique their work on the wall because I'm not serious—I'm here just to shop. Apparently, that's what I'm here for.

"So you're hypersexualized. You're called crazy. You're called [*****]. You're followed home. And I just had to block it out to say, 'I'm going to go and I'm going to stay in class and I'm going to come home. I'll be fine.'"

Shannon Hale, the *New York Times* bestselling coauthor of the *Squirrel Girl* middle grade series (written with her husband, Dean Hale), said the expectation was that she wouldn't make it writing. "I grew up in a culture where it was not expected that I would ever actually succeed at something. I was expected to be a wife and mother. So it's not that big of a risk if I try to become a writer, because who cares? I'm a woman. I'm not supposed to support a family anyway. So in some ways that cultural misogyny gave me freedom to try something impossible."

The flip side to the expectations of what women should or should not do, or should or should not like, is that of what a comics fan should or should not look like.

"I was ten or twelve, and my dad put on the *X-Men* cartoon, and I instantly fell in love with Rogue," said Jen Grünwald, director of production and special projects at Marvel. "It started with that. And then my dad would get me the comics every week. One distinct memory I have from being into

THE CREATIVE TERRAIN OF SUPER HERO GENRE WORK HAS BEEN SEEN FOR SO LONG AS A STRAIGHT, WHITE, MALE SPACE.

---

comics as a kid was when, in between junior high and high school, I had this summer school, to get ahead, because I was a nerd. And this one kid was talking about comics, and I was like, 'I love comics, I love *X-Men*.' And he goes, 'No you don't.' He literally said it."

Preeti Chhibber, author of young adult titles like *Avengers Assembly* and the *Spider-Man's Social Dilemma* trilogy, as well as the cohost of the *Desi Geek Girls* podcast, along with the *Women of Marvel* podcast, remembers not knowing how to approach other kids in her high school who read comics. "You're just like, 'Oh my God, I don't want to be embarrassed. I don't want to be made fun of because I'm asking a question about something that's supposed to be so obvious.' Right?"

This early form of gatekeeping—often called the "credibility check"—is something most women and girls experience as they dip their toe into comics, and for many it stays with them, even after they experience professional success in the industry.

"When I started working for Marvel, I really felt like I had to have my résumé ready at all times, or my reading list," Mackenzi said. "And I had to have names and references and all of these things ready. I was quizzing myself on the history of Loki, of the character. Ready for that moment when somebody is going to try and discredit me and try and prove that I shouldn't be here for some reason. And I don't think male writers have to do that."

The creative terrain of super hero genre work has been seen for so long as a straight, white, male space, that the soft mandate becomes "bring diverse faces in, leave diverse content out." Navigating the genre rules that make up the unchallenged creative status quo of the most successful franchises in the Western world often requires self-inflicted identity erasure from underrepresented creators. Historically, no matter who you were, creators and readers were asked to project themselves into a default story,

New York Times bestselling author Roxane Gay took her turn at writing Marvel comics with her work on *Black Panther: World of Wakanda*, drawn by Alitha E. Martinez.

rather than consider the possibility of changing that story to make space for a new perspective. A creative turf war, except only one side has all the turf.

But that is slowly changing.

"I've questioned how we bring visibility to a broader range of lived experiences," said writer Roxane Gay of her work on *Black Panther: World of Wakanda*. "So to have the opportunity to be able to write queer Black women into a canon that has historically been the purview of heterosexual white people was really exciting.

"I think when you give them visibility, you also give them a sense of normalcy, which is incredibly important. It doesn't feel like, 'Oh, this is the Other anymore.' This is just another story about two characters who are pretty badass and awesome.

"And I want to say it is just another story, but it's also very specific and I think that's important. Oftentimes, when we talk about representation and how we're all human, people overlook the fact that this is a specific experience that no one else will have other than Black women. As universal as I hope that the appeal is, I'm very much still telling a very specific story."

"*Ms. Marvel* really got me through high school," says actress Iman Vellani of her Disney+/Marvel character counterpart. "She always felt so different than all the other Muslim teenagers I've seen in mainstream media. And Kamala Khan represents everything about nerd culture. That's what makes her such a universal character. She's a fan just like us. And that's why we root for her.

"Her excitement and her fascination about the Avengers and super heroes is so, so real. And everyone can see themselves in her. You don't have to be Brown, right? That's the main thing for our show. It's not about a Pakistani American Muslim teenager. It's about this Avengers-loving fanfic-writing nerd who happens to be a Pakistani American Muslim teenager. Balancing all the things that make her can be difficult and confusing, but that's life."

Defining what is canon becomes a more interesting and natural proposition when formerly underrepresented creators can assume responsibility for the authenticity of a character. Though hard-core comics fans historically considered adaptations of classic comics into films, games, or television as "lesser" forms, the reverse is true when it comes to the work of minority creators. Because most women super heroes were not created by women

Sam Maggs was a fan first, here in a Ms. Marvel cosplay, before becoming a writer of comics, prose, and video games.

creators, the adaptation of these comics into other formats becomes a critical chance to involve transformative female creative talent. So the writing of specific canonical characters by creators who resemble them becomes an act of re-creation, or as writer Margaret Stohl calls it, identity reauthentication. "When a woman is writing a female character from her point of view, some things become incredibly different," she said.

Sam Maggs, writer of comics, prose, and video games like *The Unstoppable Wasp* and *Marvel's Spider-Man: The City That Never Sleeps*, says, "It actually wasn't until I got to college that I discovered *Runaways*. And that was my first step into really getting into comics. Because it involved teenagers and queer characters and characters of color and people who kind of looked and talked and acted like me." And I thought, "Oh, this is for me."

"Seeing yourself in comics attracts readership and talent," Dan Buckley agreed. "Miles Morales, in many ways, really signified the beginning of it. . . . Having those characters that attract a more diverse readership, that has begun to feed down through the talent side. The editorial team has been

Jen Bartel brings her vibrant and industry-defining style to this cover of *Marvel Comics* #1000, 2019, featuring the many looks of Storm

THE ISOLATION OF BEING "FIRST" OR EVEN "FIFTH" CAN WEIGH HEAVILY, EVEN AS THEY TAKE IT ON TO CARVE A MORE DELIBERATE PATH FOR OTHERS.

———

much more proactive on that recruitment over the last five to seven years, so it's created a [chance for a] lot more women in the room." Though he does acknowledge, "We're not quite as there in Black and Latino representation and other underrepresented communities."

For those creators, the isolation of being "first" or even "fifth" can weigh heavily, even as they take it on to carve a more deliberate path for others.

"I had no idea that I was the first Black nonbinary person to work both at Marvel and DC. I'm the first person. In 2021," marveled Vita Ayala. "And Alitha Martinez as the first Black artist. It is wild. It is ludicrous that she has had a lot of firsts and she's not that much older than me."

Eve L. Ewing had a similar reaction when she discovered she's only the fifth Black woman to write for Marvel comics. "I'm living history right now, and I'm just out here trying to do these doofy things," she said of her work on *Ironheart*. "I'm lucky number five. *E* is also the fifth letter of the alphabet. So it's a good number for me."

Jen Bartel is an award-winning comics artist, creating covers for *She-Hulk* and *Star Wars*, as well as the designer of Captain Marvel and Thor shoes for Adidas × Marvel. After winning her first Eisner Award for Best Cover Artist in 2019, she reflected on the necessity of intersectionality when it comes to hiring. "I don't have a specific list of goals or benchmarks that I've laid out for myself, but my level of conscientiousness has definitely gone up because of everything that happened over the last four years. We went through a time where people needed different types of heroes. But now I've seen the conversation shift from 'We need to hire women, we need to hire women.' Once we had gotten more women into the industry, then it became time for 'Okay, let's go to the next step and let's talk about where are disabled women working in the industry, where are all the women of color, where are queer women, what are their perspectives?' It's the quest that I've been on."

Former *Ms. Marvel* writer Samira Ahmed has seen the direct value of that quest, of working to make a character who might have once been considered "the Other" now the status quo. "One of my friends texted me a picture of their kid and grandma, who were both dressed in a homemade Ms. Marvel costume, holding my first issue. This is exactly what Ms. Marvel means. That this girl who was in sixth grade could share it with her grandma."

"I know how important representation is because I have felt that isolation and loneliness that comes with not feeling represented or seen," said Iman Vellani. "I believe film and TV literally shape how we see people. And an accurate representation is, frankly, long overdue. So why not have it starring in the greatest franchise ever?"

Marvel Studios executive producer Trinh Tran agrees. When the *Hawkeye* TV series was green-lit at Disney+, she knew she had an opportunity to get more women involved on a show that needed as many different women's perspectives as possible.

"I was inspired by one of the most memorable moments of working on *Infinity War* and *Endgame*, what we called the 'Women of Marvel Day,' when we shot all of the women coming together in that epic shot of them running.

"It was one of the most powerful days I can remember. Being on set where everybody gathered together. So many women crew members came together on that day, because they just wanted to be part of that experience.

"I can't even describe just standing there on set and going, 'I'm so grateful to be able to experience this—but also to actually have everybody experience it, all the crew members, including the cast.' That level of energy that you felt, so different than any other day.

"Some female crew members came up and said things like 'Thank you for making this happen. It doesn't go unnoticed.'"

REPRESENTATION MEANS POSSIBILITY—
IF SHE CAN DO IT, I CAN DO IT.

———

"I DIDN'T realize till I was nineteen years old that there are women making comics," said writer Vita Ayala. "Louise Simonson's a whole person. No idea. Because when you're a kid, you don't look at the credits."

It's a moment that many marginalized creators can point to, seeing the name of someone who looks like them in the credits and feeling like they've been struck by lightning.

Iman Vellani felt the same way about seeing Sana Amanat's name in the credits of *Ms. Marvel*, and noting a face that looked like hers rise through the ranks. "She has inspired me so much in high school, and I thought she had the coolest job in the world. The fact that we both come from very similar backgrounds gave me hope that maybe one day I could work at Marvel, too. And now we're very close. She's like my older sister, and I couldn't be happier to have her in my life. She literally will call me over and make French toast for me."

What's the power of seeing a woman's name in the credits of a comic, or a video game, or a movie? Did it matter?

"Oh, it was a huge deal for me as a kid," said Gail Simone. "I followed every female creator I found back then. If Marie Severin, Annie Nocenti, Colleen Doran, Jan Duursema, Louise Simonson, or any of the other greats of that era were involved, I would find the money to buy it. Again, I lived in the boonies, so I didn't find out about indie and underground female creators until later, and I again became an incessant follower of all that I could afford."

Hannah McLeod, narrative designer at Crystal Dynamics, who worked on the 2012 *Marvel's The Avengers* film, said it directly contributes to getting more women into comics. "Knowing someone like you worked on something you love is extremely powerful. Representation means possibility—if she can do it, I can do it."

"When I was young," recalled *X-Men* writer Tini Howard, "I would read old Vertigo books and see Jill Thompson's and Shelly Bond's names in there and [think], 'Those are girls. Those are girl names. There are girls in this book and not just on the cover, but making them.' And that was super exciting to me. I've had the opportunity to tell both Jill and Shelly that. And maybe I'm that for someone, maybe some little teenage girl who is reading *X of Swords* and is like, 'I can write *X-Men*.'"

Letterer Janice Chiang had that very experience, learning from Bernard Chang that seeing her name in the credits had encouraged him to pursue his own career. "He said, 'You know, I saw Larry [Hama]'s name in the credits. I saw your name. I saw Jim Lee's name. And then I knew there was opportunity for me. There are people like me there. I can strive.'"

That lightning-bolt moment is what, in 2010, sparked the idea of an all-women-created anthology, when Marvel launched the Women of Marvel Initiative, and was developed into *Girl Comics*. Marvel handed the reins over to the women in Marvel editorial, telling them they could set the tone, the format, the collaborators, and, most controversially, the name. "Oh my God, the name!" Jeanine Schaefer said. "Men said we were 'doing reverse sexism,' whatever that is. And women said we were infantilizing women in comics, the assumption being that the men at Marvel forced the name on us."

But the idea was theirs; they wanted to have fun with it, take a name from an old Marvel comic, as was tradition, and subvert it a little. Instead of romance comics written and drawn by and large by men, it would tackle all genres, social issues, and tones, and would, of course, be made top to bottom entirely by women.

"Not just the creative team," Jeanine stressed. "Editorial, the book designers, the production and prepress artists, the proofreader—Flo, of course—the logo designer, Irene Lee. Everyone who touched the book was a woman. We wanted to show it was not just possible but necessary that women were given a platform."

Janice Chiang explains to the reader how a letterer works, from a back story in *Ka-Zar* #25.

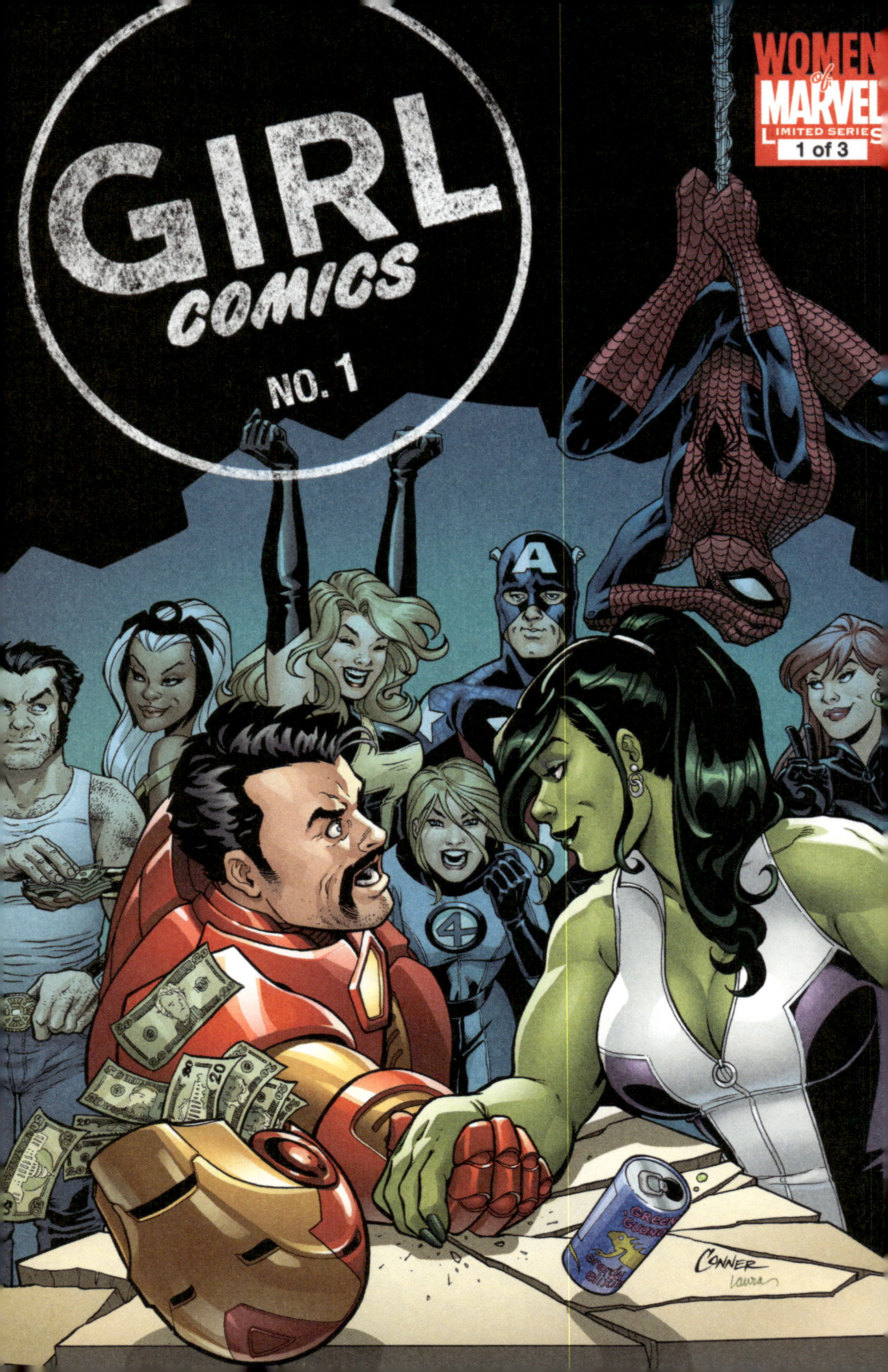
GIRL COMICS
NO. 1
WOMEN of MARVEL
LIMITED SERIES
1 of 3
CONNER
Laura

OPPOSITE: The cover of *Girl Comics* #1, 2010, an entirely women-driven and -created anthology, art by Amanda Conner and Laura Martin.

It's something the women at the company talked about a lot as they planned the revamped panels, the press, the podcast, and *Heralds*, an event book written by Kathryn Immonen and starring a ragtag assembly of female heroes who have to learn to work as a team. The story addressed themes of identity, how you're perceived versus how you see yourself, and the burden of legacy—all the things we've come to associate with super hero comics, but topics that women don't often get to explore in that space as *women*.

"As Nick Lowe [*Spider-Man* executive editor] likes to say, 'How do we be the change that we want to see in the world?'" said Jeanine. "For the industry, Marvel is the kingmaker. I understand that obviously it's a business, but on some level, if you take a male creator and you put him on *Avengers*, everyone goes, 'Oh, that guy must be important. He's on *Avengers*.' I'm not saying just chuck anyone on it, but it can't just be that there's only ten people who can do *Captain America*, *Batman*, *Superman*, *Spider-Man*. It can't just be those same ten guys."

There is power in a name, seeing it in print.

As writer Marguerite Bennett told us, "When I broke in, one of the pieces of advice that I was given was to go by just my first initials, because Marguerite is such an obviously feminine name. . . . They told me, 'You will do better if you just go by M. K. Bennett.' And I refused that. And when I showed up at conventions, I showed up in cocktail dresses and heels, and I put flowers and a bowl of candy on my table. You're going to come on *my* terms."

"I would almost say for a long time they can't even get past my first name," said artist Alitha E. Martinez, who might be the most prolific woman of Marvel, but who has remained in the greatest obscurity. "That it's too flowery and ethnic for print. I'm like, what? But no, I wasn't going to change it. I didn't get into comics to hide behind a male name. If you hide, then the next girl that comes along is also going to have the same fight.

"I don't hear 'You don't draw like a girl' much anymore," she said. "Because if you're drawing like a girl, then you must be drawing like me."

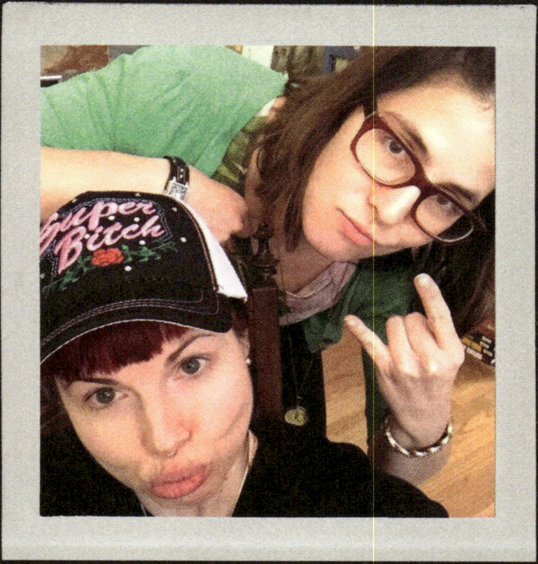
Super Bitch

ouilt at Marvel last a lifetime.
timates editor Lauren Sankovitch
e DeConnick at their production

CHAPTER EIGHT

THE NETWORK

Mentorships,
Friendships, and the Women
of Marvel Identity

Comics, like any industry where women and other marginalized groups find themselves in the minority, has something of an informal spiritual phone tree, where information is passed along, often by mouth only, to help a community navigate what can be a hostile work environment. It is a fancy way of saying we all talk. Which we do.

In the past five to ten years, however, the network has become a place used more for active support and mentorship. A place to pass along gig openings, to promote work and each other. It takes the form of breakfast meetups at comic conventions, showing up for each other's readings and signings, even covering a fellow creator's table at a show so they can run out to use the restroom. It means making a note of the names in the headlines or at the panels or in the credits—and the names left out of them—and especially in the case of the latter, seeking each other out to say, *Hey, I see you. I see the work you do.*

"You find each other in the room," said writer Vita Ayala, "you meet each other once, and then whenever you enter a new room, if you see each other, you're just like, 'I got you. Here are the exits. Here we are. We have hand signals now, we can coordinate.'"

"There's an amazing, really supportive group of women in London called the Cinesisters," said writer and director Kate Herron. "And they're all female directors, and we're all coming up together. We were all at the first steps in our careers from making shorts, to directing television, to even making their first feature. I think honestly that was kind of what inspired me. I was seeing women just a few steps ahead of me, and in a way, it made the distance for me seem more achievable. That was when I started to feel I had a seat at the table, making shorts and just finding my community, and helping out in friends' films and them helping out in mine."

The idea of mentorship at Marvel Comics is the cornerstone of not just crafting and sustaining an almost one-hundred-year-old universe, but making sure it can evolve and grow with its audience. This kind of growth requires getting institutional knowledge in the hands of diverse caretakers, through a hiring process that is deliberately inclusive, and a careful fostering of the future. "The greatest tool an editor has," Marvel executive editor Tom Brevoort used to say, "is their opinion. We can teach you everything else."

"Not all mentorships evolve into deep-seated friendships, but that mentorship is key for everyone's development, and is especially important in teaching the craft of comics storytelling," said president of Marvel Comics and Franchise, Dan Buckley. "There are not a lot of places to go to truly acquire those skills. The idea of mentorship versus training has become much more important to us over the past decade and is an underlying mantra of Women of Marvel."

If in the 1960s, women had to incept the idea of hiring other women into the office, the 1970s saw perhaps Marvel's first attempt at organized mentorship, under the watchful eye of Marie Severin and her army of women colorists. The tradition has continued, even though colorists are now freelance and not on staff.

Christina Strain, now a screenwriter on critically acclaimed projects like *The Magicians* and *Finding 'Ohana*, was one of the most in-demand colorists in comics; in her eight years at Marvel, from 2003 to 2011, she worked on everything from the Avengers to the X-Men. As a young artist, Christina remembers meeting award-winning colorist Laura Martin at the CrossGen Comics offices and feeling that she was being passed institutional knowledge that would shape her future career. "The first time I visited the office, I sat down and watched Laura color for, like, four hours straight. She just walked me through it, showed me how she did stuff, and talked to me about her color choices. It was the first time I had ever seen a coloring tutorial. This was like

> **I WAS SEEING WOMEN JUST A FEW STEPS AHEAD OF ME, AND IN A WAY, IT MADE THE DISTANCE FOR ME SEEM MORE ACHIEVABLE.**

---

a sacred moment for me to sit behind Laura Martin and watch her color a double-page spread."

Three years earlier, as a college sophomore, Christina had met artist Amanda Conner, whom she credits for her own decision to take the plunge and do what she loved for a living. "I had with me a small sketchbook that I did a lot of drawing and coloring in, and my friends pushed me to go talk to Amanda. She asked me, 'What are you getting a degree in?' And I said, 'Well, I'm going to be a programmer.' And she was like, 'Why are you wasting your time? You clearly want to work in comics.'"

In a career spanning from the mid-1970s to the mid-1990s, production manager Virginia Romita was another highly influential mentor for the Marvel Bullpen, setting a high bar for the two additional female production managers—Dawn Guzzo and Sue Crespi—who followed her. While Sue's father, Danny Crespi, had also managed the Marvel Bullpen in his day ("Keeping it in the family," Sue said), Sue remembers Virginia vividly. Alternately terrifying editors or reading romance comics, always looking out for her people, Virginia gave Sue much more than the holiday ornament that landed on her desk every year. Sue has a quieter manner than her predecessors, but still credits her ability to manage over seventy books a month, and the loyalty with which she protects her Bullpen, as inherited from Virginia.

"I think I might have rather been yelled at by Virginia Romita than disappointed Sue if and when my books were late," recalled *X-Men* editor Jeanine Schaefer. "She would move mountains to get these books out, and did it without burning out her crew."

"I started at Fifth Avenue, worked temp upstairs on the eleventh floor, and I remember coming down to the tenth floor," Sue said, referring to the Marvel offices. "I mean, like, this is the cool floor. Corporate was always afraid to come down. They were scared of us."

Lynn E. Cohen Koehler was an administrative manager and associate editor who started in 1982 when, as she puts it, "I must have been in the three-by-five card box that Dorothy Marcus, the head of personnel, accumulated from the New York State Department of Labor of people who were unemployed. She pulled me out of the box and said, 'Oh, this person might be good to work here as a secretary.'"

She remembers the divide between "corporate" and "creative" very well. "I was sort of the liaison between upstairs, downstairs. I had a lot of friends that were in the business department, including Francine Grillo."

She also revamped Marvel's now-vaunted internship program, which at the time only pulled from local high schools, to include college students. "The internship program is the thing I'm most proud of, because it lasted and helped careers for many students," she said.

Another woman who loomed large in the office as a spiritual mentor: Nanci Dakesian. The stories about Nanci are legendary—like how she drove four hours to an artist's house and showed up on his doorstep and said, "I'll wait," when their pages were late ("I also learned that he actually had a fax machine," she said cannily, "which means he couldn't lie to me anymore about not being able to send [pages]"), or the time she locked artist Mark Texeira on the roof of the Marvel offices when he snuck out there instead of doing the work he promised he was completing.

THE INTERNSHIP PROGRAM IS THE THING
I'M MOST PROUD OF, BECAUSE IT LASTED AND
HELPED CAREERS FOR MANY STUDENTS.

Recently celebrating twenty years with Marvel, Jen Grünwald joined the team after college, and over her time became a beacon of light for fellow women in the office.

"Every time we had a creator late on a deadline," said Jeanine Schaefer, laughing, "the girls, we would always ask each other, 'What would Nanci do right now?'"

"I used to laugh because our office was right next to Jen Grünwald's," said Nanci with a big, fond grin. "I would hear Jen yelling at people, and Kelly, my assistant editor, would go, 'Oh, that's a young you. That's you when you were twenty.'"

Jen Grünwald, director of production and special projects, decidedly does not have a quieter manner than her predecessors.

Because she hails from Queens and Staten Island, Jen's love language is yelling (when she and Jeff Youngquist have creative differences, the interns in the trades division ask in hushed whispers if they are fighting or not, because they can't tell); and she might know every single person in the industry. "If you ever see her at a convention, it's like there's a light shining on her, drawing everyone in," said Jeanine Schaefer.

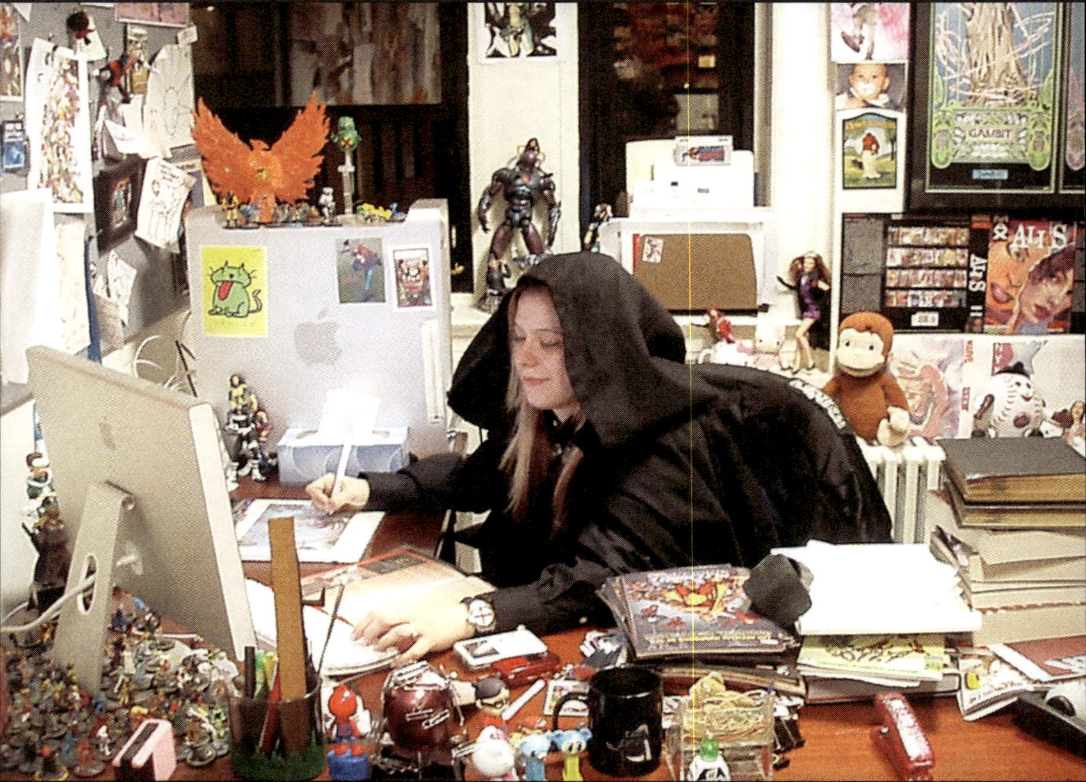
GAMBIT

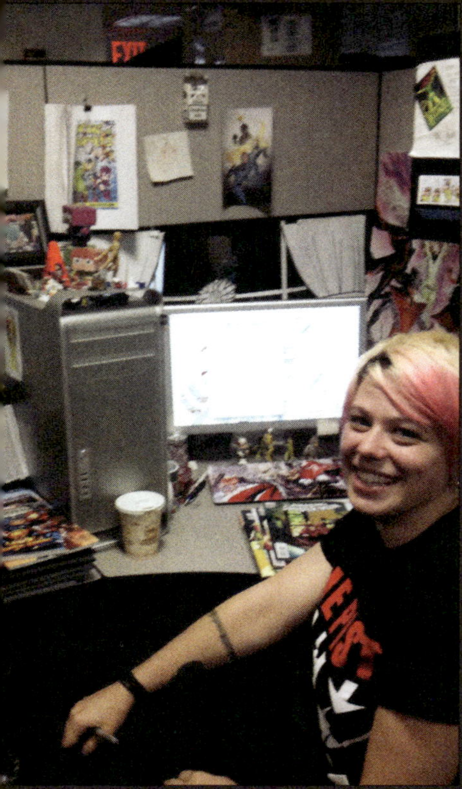

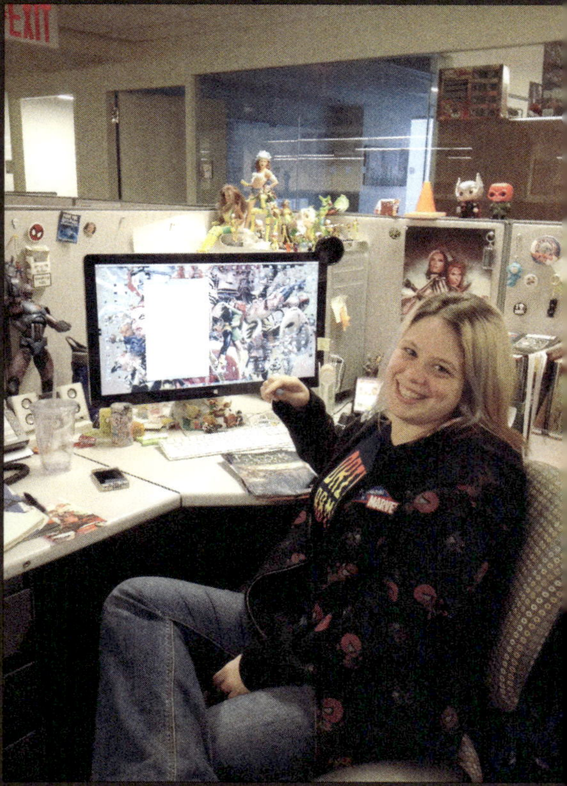
EXIT

Yet, on a recent Women of Marvel panel, Jen tells this story: "I remember [former editor in chief] Joe Quesada years ago giving a tour to someone. And he came to my cubicle and said, 'This is Jen. She's what I call the heart of Marvel.' After the panel, some [attendee] came over [and said], 'I can't believe that someone would call a woman the heart of Marvel.'"

A self-described tomboy, Jen says most of her significant female friendships happened through Marvel, and they've lasted the entire twenty years and counting that she's been there, through office moves, job changes, and the Covid-19 pandemic lockdown. "I feel like it's as much of a girls' club as the boys' club comics can be. And I think that's probably because the girls find each other."

The strength of the friendships and mentorships between women at Marvel through the years cannot be understated, as, year after year, the women in the company pulled together to hold each other up and push each other forward.

"As soon as I started at Marvel, it was Jenny Lee who told me, 'I got you, you're with me,'" said MacKenzie Cadenhead. "At the time, there was one woman in each editorial office, and Jenny and I would organize lunch outings for the women editors, for us all to connect. We were the early Women of Marvel. Plus Flo."

Many women who worked there at the time said they could feel the culture shift with the united front that MacKenzie and Jenny presented, and there's a direct line through all the women in editorial, starting with Flo Steinberg and running all the way through to the staff there today, as they deliberately passed along the mentorship they got from the woman before them.

MacKenzie had worked with Sana Amanat at Virgin Comics, and when Sana told her she was thinking of leaving the industry, MacKenzie remembered Jenny's words and her deliberate mentorship. "My experience at Marvel, then and now, has been filled with a lot of creative support. And I did not think that Sana had gotten that experience where we had been [. . .] and "I said, 'Great, I'm not going to let you leave comics. . . . Your voice needs to be heard.'

"Plus, I loved her so much as a person, and loved working with her. She was so good at it, and I knew the industry needed someone like her. I knew she was going to make interesting stories, plus she was going to make stories

TOP: Sana Amanat, Sarah Amos, MacKenzie Cadenhead, and Jen Grünwald. BOTTOM: Associate editors Annalise Bissa and Lauren Amaro at the Marvel booth at New York Comic Con 2019.

Introduced thanks to MacKenzie Cadenhead, Sana Amanat and Jeanine Schaefer became fast friends.

that I liked. When you find people who do things that you enjoy, you just want them to do more things so you can enjoy more of their work."

"It was such a formative experience being at Marvel, and there were so few women there," said Jenny. "Being in the minority really bonded MacKenzie and me. We share a lot of the same beliefs and we're both feminists. She was part of an influx of this generation of younger women who were coming in. Before then, I had been so isolated there. . . . When MacKenzie started, I basically was so excited to see another woman, that I decided we were going to become friends."

MacKenzie passed that on, working to bring more women into the company and into each other's orbits even after she left.

"I remember we went out for a coffee: me, MacKenzie, and Sana," said Jeanine Schaefer. "MacKenzie had requested it because she was like, 'Okay, if I'm not going to be at Marvel, you're going to be best friends, it starts here, let's go.' She was right!"

202 / SUPER VISIBLE

"When you're working on something that's so meaningful to you," said MacKenzie, "you develop this deep relationship. Especially when you meet someone who puts themselves all in the same way that you do. It never felt like a mentorship. Now when we talk, [Sana] mentions how I mentor her, but it doesn't feel like that. For me, it was just such a reciprocal relationship from so early on because I got so much out of working with her. And still do."

"Sana is amazing," said Jeanine. "She just wants to know you. And it is such a cool thing when you meet someone like that, because you feel like you're meeting a genuine person. She has such a strong sense of what she wants to do, the kinds of stories she wants to tell, the kinds of people she wants to work with, the kinds of stuff she just wants out there in the world to try to make the world a better place. Truly make the world a better place, and everything that she went through to get to where she is, I just don't think people understand how difficult it was."

"I think that's what I find the most incredible about her," said Judy Stephens. "This was an opt-in battle for her. Every day there was some new bull, and every day she decided, 'I am doing this.' And she tried to keep an open communication about it all."

Just before Jeanine's and Sana's hiring, starting with Nicole Boose, Molly Lazer, and Lauren Sankovitch, it felt like the floodgates had opened.

Lauren Sankovitch was an editor on the *Ultimates* line and formed fast bonds with the other women in editorial when she joined, like Nicole and Molly. She calls the experience of working at that time, "Powerful, that I could look at someone and be like, 'Oh, I can see myself in this person, I know that we have on some level shared experiences,' and I had lots of shared experiences. And we even lived in the same house for a while."

"Lauren was certainly the welcoming party in editorial," said Judy. "She loved to go to the different offices and departments and meet everyone. When I was hired, I was so young and didn't know how to connect, so she helped organize a running club, and I even attended Baltimore Comic-Con with her. I'm so grateful to her."

"Lauren is a great friend and mentor," said Ellie Pyle, who went on to be the executive director of audio and story at Marvel Entertainment, but who back then was a new assistant editor starting out in the Spider-Man office. "She had a huge influence on me, particularly building relationships with

> ## I'M DEFINITELY INVESTED IN HOW WE MAKE
> ## PEOPLE FEEL LIKE THEY BELONG HERE AND GIVE THEM THE
> ## TOOLS THAT THEY NEED TO KEEP RISING.

talent. When we'd go to conventions, she'd always include me in things and introduce me to people.

"[And] you could always walk down the hall and have a conversation with Jeanine about anything," she went on. "That was a very different kind of perspective, just kind of being a woman in this industry. She had a different perspective than some of the male mentors I was working with."

Sarah Brunstad was hired as an intern, and then got a part-time gig cleaning up old digital files. ("The true Marvel way," said Judy Stephens. "When your bosses like you and your work ethic, they do their best to provide work to keep you around till an actual job comes up. The same thing happened to me.")

"Sarah is really wonderful because she works very hard to make sure that there's a community between the various female editors and also editorial employees that work together, that we have a way to network and address issues and just vent to each other if something is frustrating us," said Alanna Smith, *Captain America* editor. "She's really a wonderful person to have in the company—I'm very grateful to have her."

"I always try to be really open and welcoming because what drew me into Marvel was the atmosphere," Sarah said. "So I'm very invested in bringing up a generation that way by giving people tools to move forward, because I think that comics has a retention problem. Which might be why we don't have a lot of female editors. It's not that we don't hire them—it's that they don't stick around. So I'm definitely invested in how we make people feel like they belong here and give them the tools that they need to keep rising."

About their editors, and who they would point to as champions of their work, Vita Ayala said, "Listen, I work with some really great dude editors. Really solid guys. But, if not for Annalise [Bissa] and Lauren [Sankovitch] and Shannon [Andrews Ballesteros], nah. No way. I quit a job working at a museum as a security guard with a union so I could do comics, and I would not have done that if not for all these women. I just would not have done it. There's no way."

Many women have left Marvel to pursue other passions. It feels like often we see men leave the company but remain in the industry in one way or another, while many women turn the page when that chapter is over, or find other ways to integrate comics into their lives. Molly Lazer went on to teach high school English and publish short stories; Jennifer Smith, a one-time assistant editor in the X-Office and an invaluable voice for women at Marvel, has just now returned to comics as an editor, after getting her PhD in media and cultural studies; Emily Shaw, an associate editor who helped develop a new iteration of *Moon Girl and Devil Dinosaur*, left to pursue her master's degree in business administration, and now works as a product manager at Netflix.

Lauren Sankovitch was also one of those women. After she left Marvel, she became the longtime managing editor for Milkfed Criminal Masterminds, Kelly Sue DeConnick and Matt Fraction's production company. Currently she's getting her master's degree in geology and works for the United States Geological Survey. She says that her time at Marvel has shaped her life, and that the "Network" is never far from her. Once you're a Woman of Marvel, you're a Woman of Marvel for life.

"My time with the women there allowed me the latitude to explore that identity, [and] it allowed me to understand why it was important for me to understand these things. Why it was important for that representation to be happening, and representation in general, and how to celebrate that. And so I'm grateful to the women I got to interact with, both the creators in editorial and staff, because it made me the very quiet, radical revolutionary that I am today."

Oral History

ANGÉLIQUE ROCHÉ

Angélique Roché is a true journeywoman: an attorney, an educator, a political consultant, a journalist, and a producer. From 2018 to 2023, she joined Sana and Judy as a cohost of the *Women of Marvel* podcast, alongside launching and hosting the *Marvel's Voices* podcast. We spoke to her in May of 2021 as she was deep into her own research on her book, *My Super Hero Is Black*, a history of Black characters and creators at Marvel Comics.

ANGÉLIQUE: It's very interesting, throughout the sixties and seventies, because it's not that folks weren't there, it's just like how they were created, how they were utilized, the depth of the characters, where they sidekick, where they are not a sidekick.

And then comic books are just full of tropes. Right?

But when you're dealing with the character being the only one . . . it just makes such a difference and it just makes much more of an impact.

And there is just so much to this concept of a difference in understanding of the implications of race and ethnicity and gender and gender identity within comics at that time.

JUDY: Totally! And we've known each other for so many years, but I don't actually know your story of coming to Marvel.

ANGÉLIQUE: As you know, I came from politics . . . from law. I had finished up a campaign in Ohio in 2014, and had planned to join Hillary [Clinton]'s campaign, but instead I ended up taking a different job and moving to NYC. While there, I ended up meeting Tom Brennan, who used to work for Marvel.

And just so you know, there is a much longer version of this . . . but through Tom and his improv friends, I met Lorraine Cink. A couple of years go by, and eventually I am burnt out. Just burnt out of the nine-to-five life, and thinking of what is next.

Then in 2017, I get a random email from Lorraine asking me to send her my reel. And it had been a crazy time, as I was preparing to leave for the Middle East for a monthlong trip.

And I remember getting this email from Dan Fink while we were on our way to the airport in Bahrain.

They were looking for a cohost for *Wolverine: The Long Night— The After Show*, and it was during the process of emails and meetings, that Chloe [Wilson] goes, "Hey, there's this other show. It's called *Voices of Marvel.* Would you be interested in that?"

It was in that moment that I just knew.

ORAL HISTORY

Angélique would become a regular face within the Marvel community, seen here with fellow host Josh Saleh after moderating the Marvel Games panel at New York Comic Con in 2019.

So a couple of weeks later, I signed my first six-month contract that turned into the *Luke Cage* premiere that turned into Comic-Con, that turned into a yearlong contract. And I've been at Marvel ever since.

JUDY: Amazing. And obviously you were a fan. . . .

ANGÉLIQUE: My first introduction to Marvel was *Howard the Duck*. I was a child of the eighties. But I actually got introduced to comic books by my brother-in-law, who had them in his dorm room, and my dad gave me my first trade for Christmas, which was *The Death of Superman*. . . . I remember him telling me, "I couldn't afford these when I was a kid, but it looks important and I thought you should have it."

ANGÉLIQUE ROCHÉ / 209

With multiple red carpets under her belt, Angélique poses with her fellow women of Marvel Lauren Bork, Lorraine Cink, Tamara Krinsky, Christine Dinh, and Sarah Amos.

And by the time I signed my contract, I was a huge fan. I was a huge fan of the movies. Going back to the *X-Men* and *Spider-Man* movies. And it was during the Obama campaign I remember going to see *Marvel's The Avengers* with one of my colleagues.

JUDY: You know that was also a great moment for our team, as we had started to get this influx of new people. And they brought with them a new perspective. When you started, what did you think you could bring to the table?

ANGÉLIQUE: I wanted to bring my passion for stories from a very particular perspective, and I knew there was a possibility for that when Chloe said we're going to do a show to spotlight artists, creators, and fans of color.

And to my knowledge, I was the first Black woman host at Marvel. And the first Black woman that was on the red carpet for a Marvel movie [on behalf of] Marvel.

And even now, there aren't a lot of us in this space.

I think, for all intents and purposes, I wanted to bring my desire to learn and get better and do and bring stories and bring fans in.

But also bring in my years of being an attorney, my BA in journalism, my curiosity to want to profile people and know who they are and what makes them tick and to spotlight their stories. I even learned a lot of those skills on the Obama campaign . . . how do you help people find their personal story and how do you bring that personal story to other folks?

For many, it's their first access to something you love so much, and it's the first opportunity for them to find themselves in this vast, crazy, bonkers, what-if-loaded multi-universe. And for them to realize there is something for everybody.

And when I walked in, there were these pods that were just women. And I knew that as a normal.

JUDY: Yeah, and that makes me think of the story we're telling of Tini, Leah, and Vita. How they became friends through Marvel and writing comics, and how supported they've felt working in the X-Office.

ANGÉLIQUE: You know, the X-Men office is how we got *Marvel's Voices*. The actual comic book came out of that office and Chris Robinson. And thinking about the X-Men, I don't know what X-Men team that doesn't have a woman on it, or even two or three women on it.

And it can't be coincidental, because we know things in print, social, politically, reflect in our brains. Those things have an imprint. And so when you think about it, all those teams had women on them.

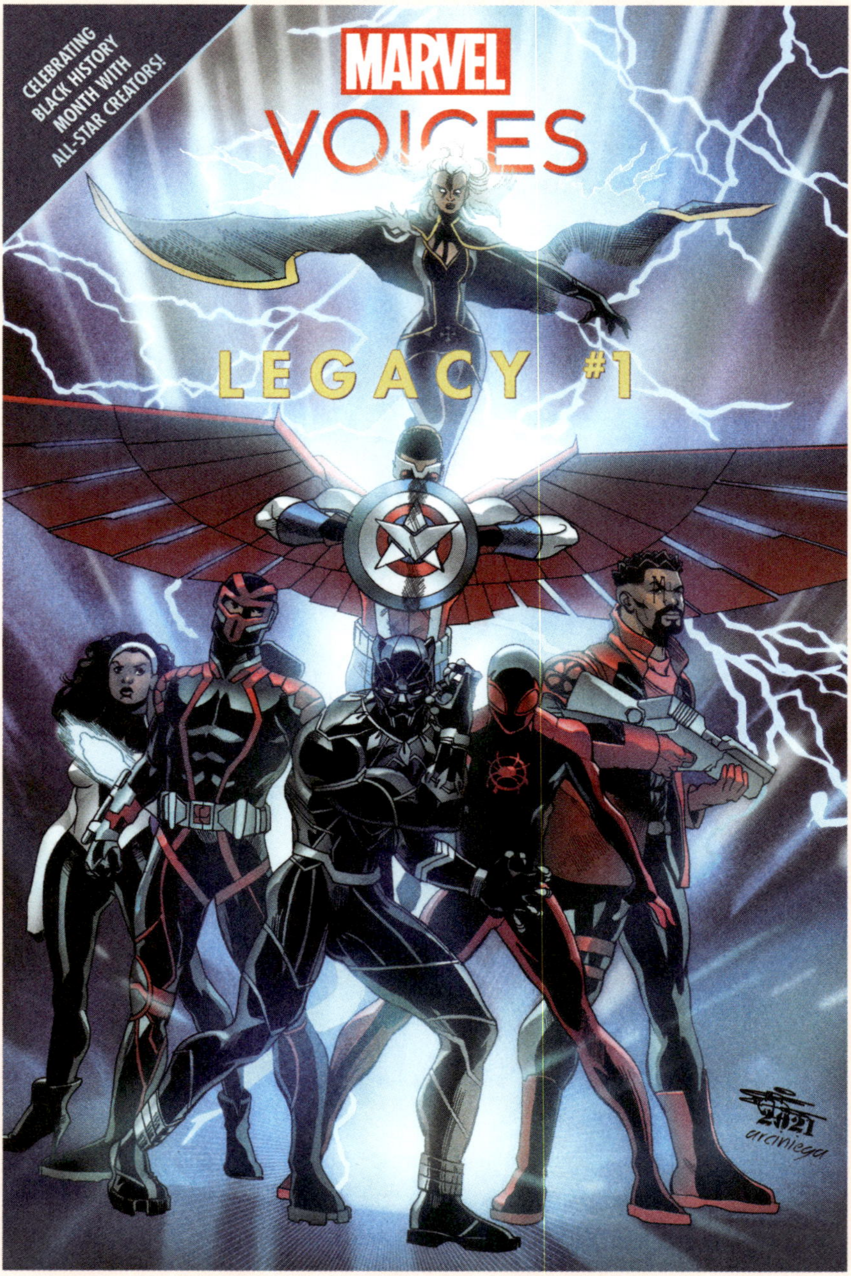
CELEBRATING BLACK HISTORY MONTH WITH ALL-STAR CREATORS!
MARVEL
VOICES
LEGACY #1
2021
arciniega

OPPOSITE: *Marvel Voices: Legacy* #1, 2021, cover art by ChrisCross.
ABOVE: *Marvel Voices: Pride* #1, 2023, cover art by Nick Robles.

JUDY: And even if we just look at race culture in America, we have so much farther to go. And yes, comics are much quicker. It's easier to make a comic. It's not as costly as making a movie, but we're still struggling to just have even a woman in the highest seat at Marvel.

ANGÉLIQUE: Please note that I [used to] have conversations at least once a week about how technically [I was] the only Black woman editor at Marvel and I am a consulting editor.

JUDY: Wait. . . . Are you the first Black woman editor ever?

ANGÉLIQUE: I think I am. If true, that's bonkers.

JUDY: When you first started, did you feel very supported?

ANGÉLIQUE: So I walked in with friends, I walked in knowing some people. My dev person, Chloe, was a woman. The entire graphics team were women. And Brandon [Grugle, podcast producer] was dope.

But, like, to be very honest . . . having [former Marvel executive producer] Sarah Amos there, when I walked in the door, who's a contemporary of mine—we are of similar age, similar background, both went to all-girls schools. So yeah, I felt my voice was heard.

And slowly but surely that expands out to the Marvel.com team. Because Jamie [Frevele] started at the same time. Of course, you were there. There was also Larissa. And we just had so many amazing women, in addition to the men who were there that I didn't feel like, "Oh, I'm the weird one person who identifies as a woman who's here."

And then there was the editorial floor, where Dan's office was always open, but also Sana's office with Ashley and her bright face. And Ryan Penagos is the greatest cheerleader ever. I think he's a great ally.

And so on top of being supported by a bunch of women, I knew that there would be folks in the room who supported me. Like Sana.

So I had known of Sana, going back to my days in DC. It had to be 2015, the last year of Obama in office. And I remember being at the Women's Day at the White House with my boss. [She said], "I hired you to be the pop culture person and understand comics." So she brought me over to meet Sana, who had just presented the Obama comic book cover at the White House.

And I have this picture of Sana and [me] from the White House that day. True story.

I was definitely just geeking over comic books and the fact that Sana was one of the coolest, hardest-working people I had met, and that we were contemporaries and she was doing it! And then Sana ended up being the first interview I did for *Marvel's Voices*.

And she's, man, she's so amazing. She's such a genuine, amazing, supportive human being that I'm really glad she was the first interview.

JUDY: And with *Marvel's Voices*, looking back, what did you see the story of *Marvel's Voices* was in the beginning?

ANGÉLIQUE: No one was talking about it in depth in a way that was nuanced. They just weren't.

So when I walked in, I think *Marvel's Voices* initially was supposed to be every two weeks . . . the show that was bookending *Women of Marvel*. It was only supposed to be about thirty minutes [and] two hosts that alternated. But then after I did my voice test, they decided, "Nope, Angélique is the host."

And I've thought about it a lot, and it was always on my mind as we were developing the show, from what the logo looks like to the tagline to who we would bring on the show.

I did all the background research on questions because it was a very different kind of space. And we were kind of just testing

Angélique celebrates the fifth anniversary of Kamala Khan as Ms. Marvel with game director Shaun Escayg, voice actor Sandra Saad, writer G. Willow Wilson, and Marvel executive Sana Amanat.

it out. But what I always knew about the show and the potential of the show was that . . . everyone's story has power.

Creatives and creators, whether or not they want to admit it or not, are impacted by their own personal stories. How they grew up, their traditions, the way they see the world, the perspectives that develop, and whether they want to tell it from that perspective or if they want to reinvent what the world should look like or could look like. The possibilities are endless, but inherently unique.

Hearing these personal stories—like Martellus Bennett saying he thought about Luke Cage when he was in the locker room before he won the Super Bowl, or how Dungeons & Dragons impacted Greg Pak to think about diversity differently as a mixed-race kid from the South—aren't just interesting [so much as] impactful. Stories about how Mariko Tamaki viewed art and theater growing up in a Japanese family in Toronto or even how Vita Ayala found their first comic book in a bodega and thought Wonder Woman was Puerto Rican show how their art and lives intersect with the content we know and love.

These are the stories that connect us, right? These are the stories that someone hears. And I go, "Oh, man, that person is just like me. Well, I kind of want to do that thing. I can do that thing."

Their perception of who can tell stories suddenly changes because there is another level of storytelling, which is how it either impacted someone or how it came to be or why it came to be right.

That's what it was always for me. What *Women of Marvel* is about, and what we wanted *Marvel's Voices* to be about, too. It gives our guests who are newer to the industry a platform to speak from, a place for them to tell their stories.

And at the end of the day, you never know what's going to inspire another person.

Then there are these folks who are established, brilliant folks. Having Eve Ewing talk about comic books is one of my favorite things in the whole wide world, because [of] her sociopolitical deconstruction of comics and the impact [Marvel has] on popular culture.

I think the profound impact at the end of the day is that you get to know the people who are writing the story. You get to connect to those people, and I think to a certain extent connect even deeper with the characters and the stories that they tell.

And one day you'll be able to look back and you'll be able to see what the full articulated landscape of the Marvel creative universe was. . . . You'll be able to see Roxane Gay and Vita [Ayala] and Brittney Williams and Nic Stone and Stephanie Williams and Tochi Onyebuchi and Saladin Ahmed and Alyssa Wong. All of these amazing, brilliant people, award-winning people . . .

You shouldn't have to go dig in the back of a file cabinet to get their story.

PART FOUR: THE AMBASSADORS

OUTREACH, AND GIVING OURSELVES NAMES, FACES, AND VOICES

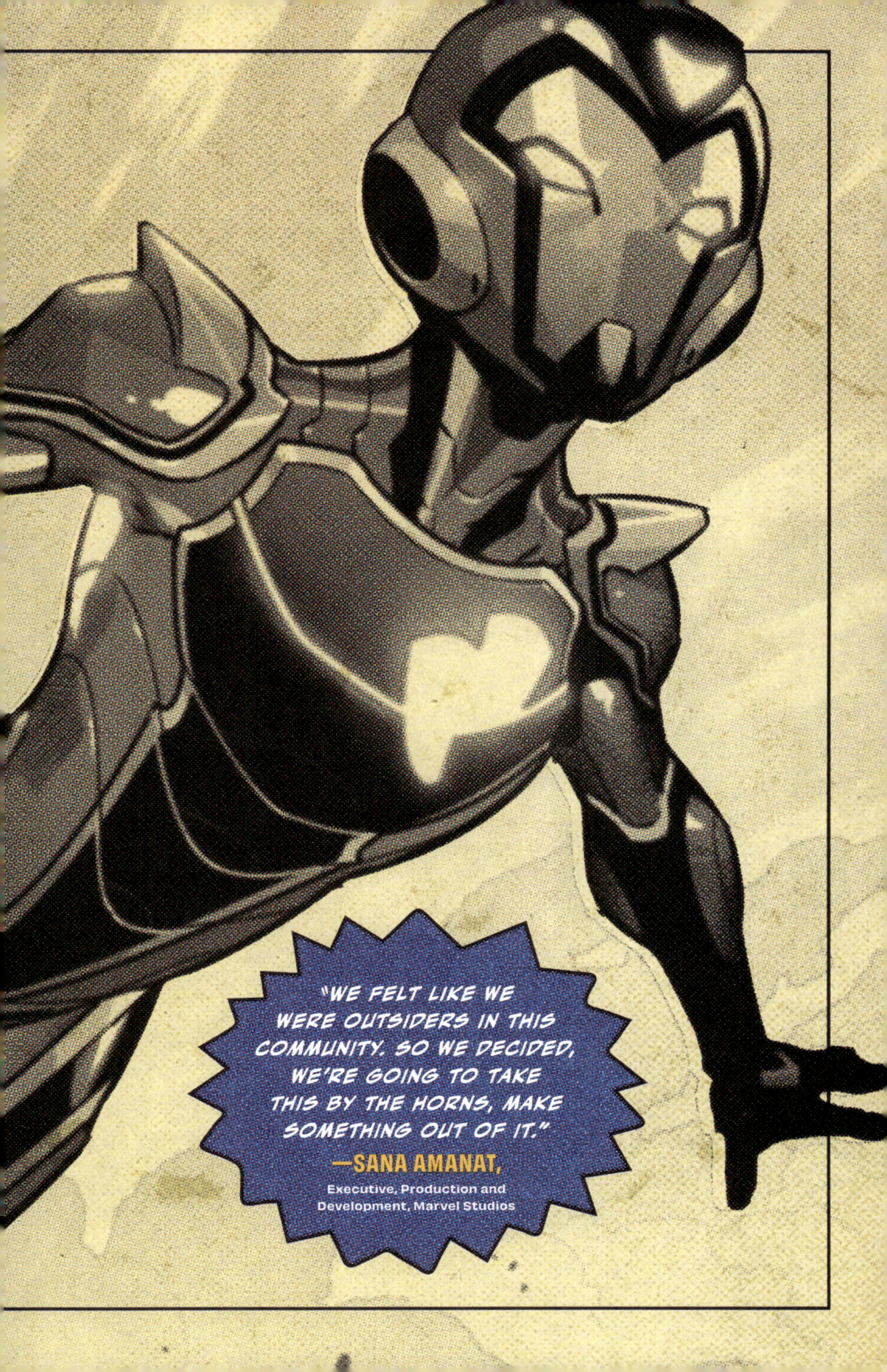
"WE FELT LIKE WE
WERE OUTSIDERS IN THIS
COMMUNITY. SO WE DECIDED,
WE'RE GOING TO TAKE
THIS BY THE HORNS, MAKE
SOMETHING OUT OF IT."
—SANA AMANAT,
Executive, Production and
Development, Marvel Studios

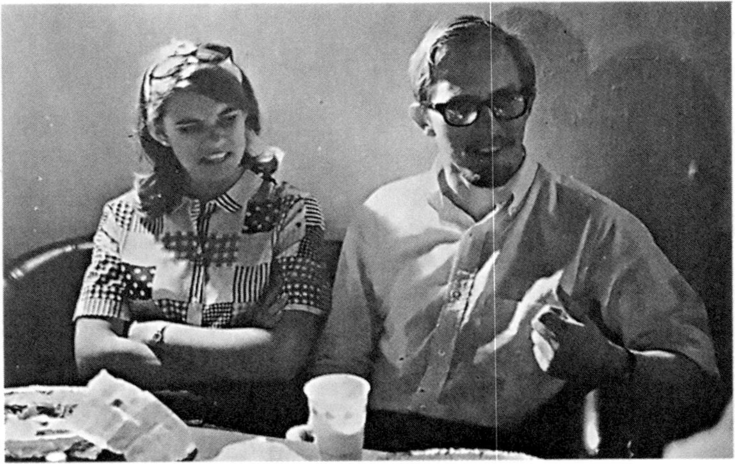

CHAPTER NINE

POP CULTURE IS CULTURE

Identities, Found Families,
and Finally Getting to Own a
First-Person Point of View

"*Every comic is somebody's first.*" "*With great power there must also come great responsibility.*" "*Hulk smash!*" If Stan Lee was widely known for his quippy sound bites, less well known is the advice he gave insiders in the House of Ideas, oft-repeated in informal Marvel creative guidelines. What makes a super hero both inspirational and relatable? "*Feet made of clay!*" What should a Marvel world feel like? "*The world outside your window.*" How is Marvel different from the guys down the block? "*[The Distinguished Competition] is a soap opera where a fight breaks out, Marvel is a fight where a soap opera breaks out.*"

A soap opera, or a family drama. Either way, Stan Lee knew that the secret to powerful characters was less about the super than the human.

"I had never liked super hero comics and found them boring," says comics historian Trina Robbins. "But the Marvel Renaissance, and the new characters . . . they had problems. They were human."

"With a lot of projects at Marvel, there's a depth to the characters that exists regardless of gender," agrees artist Jen Bartel. "I feel like the reason why so many of the female characters at Marvel resonate with women—and people in general—is because they're more complex than you would expect a super hero to be. It's nice to see people get to branch out into writing characters in ways that reflect how complex they actually are."

Oftentimes, women don't get to be flawed—they get to be, as previously mentioned, "strong." Sometimes they get to be "bad," but often without the layers of empathy that we offer men who are considered the same. Most of the time, heroic or not, women characters need to be the one thing that governing cultural norms have decided is acceptable for them to be.

MOST OF THE TIME, HEROIC OR NOT, WOMEN CHARACTERS NEED TO BE THE ONE THING THAT GOVERNING CULTURAL NORMS HAVE DECIDED IS ACCEPTABLE FOR THEM TO BE.

———

And as Mackenzi Lee, who wrote Marvel's *Loki* prose novel, pointed out, that applies to all underrepresented characters, as well. "Rather than addressing the fact of the difference between women and men in super hero comics, we just don't acknowledge it at all.

"That's always a big question, I think, too, within LGBTQ literature. . . . How much do we want books to be about queerness and identity and coming out and homophobia and things like that? And how much do you want it to just be, 'Here's a super hero who also just happens to be queer'?

"The answer is, you want to find something in between, because as a queer person, there's nothing about you that isn't influenced by that piece of your identity. But at the same time, it's not the only or defining feature of everything you do.

"It's figuring out how to put the background music of it in. And that's a hard thing to do, because, I think, when you tell those stories, then [you hear] 'It's not queer enough or it's not Black enough or it's not feminist enough.'"

"We're in this golden age of comic storytelling and revitalization and bringing in all these new readers, all these new audiences," said Marguerite Bennett, cowriter of *Angela: Asgard's Assassin* and *A-Force* (and GLAAD Media Award nominee). "And so we're getting a lot more voices and a lot more talent to the table to tell stories that are just not that same repeat of 'On the team there's the main character, here's this cool best friend, there's the fat funny one, and there's the girl.' We're not just stuck with one girl anymore."

Angela: Asgard's Assassin #1, 2014, written by Kieron Gillen and Marguerite Bennett, cover art by Stephanie Hans.

Actress Sophia Di Martino felt the truth of that while playing Sylvie on *Loki*. "Marvel characters are so well written that they can show how important vulnerability is as well as strength. Just me being a part of *Loki*, and getting to play a character that kicked ass, was actually really exciting and healing for the ten-year-old girl in me who never really got to reenact that as a kid. . . . For me, it was really important that we look at [Sylvie] as more than a 'female' character, just as a person, dealing with her own experiences, like any other character."

Paige Pettoruto, former lead game designer for *Marvel Puzzle Quest*, said, "I think, in my mind, I had this preconceived notion that [comics] was filled with Mary Sue super heroes who are omnipotent. And that wasn't too interesting to me. I didn't see the fun in that. But as I got into college, I was surrounded by more people who were interested in Marvel and DC, specifically. And through them, I started to see this [other] lens of the stories that were being told in that space, and understood that they were actually more complex and interesting and about flawed people and complex people and not just bland demigods. And that's what sunk Marvel's claws in me."

OPPOSITE FROM LEFT TO RIGHT: Marguerite Bennett poses with
Kieron Gillen, who helped open the door for her at Marvel.
Game designer Paige Pettoruto, who built *Marvel Puzzle Quest*,
spent almost nine years at Demiurge Studios.

"I was focusing on the authenticity of these characters, and I knew that that's what the fans wanted to see," said Stephanie Maslansky, costume designer for the Netflix-aired *Daredevil*, *Jessica Jones*, *Luke Cage*, *Iron Fist*, and *The Defenders*. "And I really threw myself into the project as a person enjoying the idea of these very flawed, realistic, complicated, complex human beings who happen to have these superpowers that they never ask for. And I loved all that complexity. To me they felt like people in New York, who are just complex individuals—there's a reason that so many people are drawn to New York and it's not because it's easy."

It's what letterer Janice Chiang remembered most when she looked back on her time in the Bullpen. "I still have Marvel friends who say, 'Our office back then was such a melting pot, because we reflected New York,'" she said. "It did not matter if you were a man or woman, only if you had the talent and the discipline to do what was needed, you belonged. At that time, it was 'We gotta get this thing out. All hands on deck. Let's run.' It was always nice to walk in and see new faces. I did feel like I was in the right place, that I belonged."

Paige Pettoruto agreed. "It's about humanism at the end of the day," they said. "And that's what appeals to me in [Marvel's] books."

"I think everyone grows up feeling like they're a part of the family when they're reading Marvel," said president of Marvel Comics and Franchise, Dan Buckley. "When my dad died, when I was ten, Marvel storytelling had a great influence on what I thought, and what I thought my moral code should be. It was very much part of who I was."

Unsurprisingly, the word "family" appeared more than two hundred times in the transcripts of our conversations for this project.

When former Marvel writer Jean Thomas (who was at one time married to Roy Thomas, Stan Lee's first successor as editor in chief of Marvel Comics) spoke to us, she pointed out how bittersweet that feeling of a Marvel found

> OFTEN, WOMEN AT MARVEL SPOKE OF NEEDING
> TO COMPARTMENTALIZE THE DIFFERENT ASPECTS OF
> THEMSELVES WHEN THEY WERE IN THE OFFICE.

family could be. "The flip side of a place with a family feeling is when you're no longer part of the family, you're really out of the family."

Truly, most of the people we interviewed rarely spoke about their time at Marvel as just a job. An honor, a choice, a calling . . . but rarely a job.

The idea of the Marvel found family is even captured in the pages of Marvel's first super hero team comic, *The Fantastic Four*, created by Jack Kirby and Stan Lee. As "Marvel's First Family," Reed Richards ("Mr. Fantastic"), Sue Storm Richards ("The Invisible Woman"), Johnny Storm ("The Human Torch"), and Ben Grimm ("The Thing") remain bound together in all the definitions of family, found or otherwise—blood, marriage, friendship, and a shared history—continually choosing each other, to stay together, over and over again.

Not unlike the character of Sue Storm, women at Marvel often mentioned finding it harder to be seen as complex individuals (or sometimes, like Sue, "seen" at all!) than their male counterparts. Often, women at Marvel spoke of needing to compartmentalize the different aspects of themselves when they were in the office, particularly during the earlier decades.

"Hearing Louise [Simonson] talk about being a mom during that time, and her struggles," said producer Juliette Eisner, when asked what she found the most affecting in the interviews they did for the "Women of Marvel" episode of *Marvel's 616*. "I have a lot of respect for her in what she's done and how she handled herself back then. And she's just really impressive. Her whole life was comics, with her husband, Walt, also being a part of the Marvel world.

A regular on the *Women of Marvel* podcast, costume designer Stephanie Maslansky with her design partner and fellow Designing Women Award 2017 recipient Sharon Globerson, and *Luke Cage* costume and wardrobe supervisor Pashelle L. Latino.

"It was just really interesting to hear her talk about being a mom in that context, which I don't think people always really realize. Many think of [Marvel] as a fun playhouse, and it still is, but also [the people who worked there] were real humans with a family back home."

That compartmentalization, and the fact that many women found it so necessary, seems to work only until it doesn't.

"I was so afraid it would make people see me differently," said then *Wolverine* editor Jeanine Schaefer, about being pregnant while working at Marvel. "I didn't tell anyone for the longest time—well, except for Sana [Amanat], who took one look at me the morning I found out and knew something was up."

Looking at the comics, Jeanine was struck that there weren't many Marvel characters who were mothers, and none who had the experience she was having with a newborn. "So when I got the chance to relaunch *X-Men* with an all-female team, I thought maybe this was a place I could share that point of view."

Like the *Girl Comics* discourse, men and women alike complained about the mere presence of a baby, because it was too stereotypically "girl stuff."

In the intervening decade since *X-Men*'s relaunch in 2013, and with more women integrating the different facets of themselves into their creative work in what was once a male-dominated space, the accommodation of "girl stuff" like motherhood has become a vital part of ensuring gender parity.

"Christine Wada, the costume designer [on *Loki*], was a real hero. She's a brilliant woman and did everything she could to make me as comfortable as possible," said actress Sophia Di Martino. "She also had the genius idea of putting easy access zips into the torso piece so that I could breastfeed my baby milk during the working day. The best! It felt empowering because I can run, kick, feed a baby, and do anything else that I need to in the costume, and at the end of the day, whip it off quickly. It made working mum life a lot easier!"

Marvel costume designer Stephanie Maslansky agreed. "One thing that I remember thinking when I first started, as I'd never done a super hero production before—I realized how there are so many people in real life that are super heroes, that they become super heroes in their own ways.

"I liked thinking about people like that, and how it was reflected back on these characters who were real-life people [and], through no fault of their

I WANT COMICS TO REFLECT THE REAL WORLD.

———

own, were super heroes. And that's how the audience needed to see them and did see them. And to think about how so many people in their lives, whatever they do, whether it's philanthropic or just helping or doing things against all odds, you can really look at a lot of people as super heroes. And they don't necessarily have to put on a costume."

We know Marvel was meant to be "the world outside your window," as Stan Lee liked to say, a real-world universe of heroes, both relatable and aspirational for all readers, even the most underrepresented individuals. By extension, *the world inside your window*, the world of Marvel as a company and Marvel creators as a community, needs to share those same inclusive values. As Eisner-winning writer Marjorie Liu said on the New York Comic Con Women of Marvel panel in 2012, "I think when you look at the diversity of the readership, all the different people who love comics, I want comics to reflect the real world. I think Marvel does a good job of trying to do that, but I don't think there's ever an end point when it comes to creating diversity and creating stories that people can relate to."

Marvel novelist, comics, and game narrative writer Sam Maggs (Marvel's *The Unstoppable Wasp, Marvel Action: Captain Marvel, Spider-Man: The City That Never Sleeps*) emphasized this when we spoke. "The truth of the matter is that Marvel is modern mythmaking. They are eternal stories. I think they are what people will remember about our generation of literature forever, and it is important that we see the real world and people's real perspectives represented in the modern myths. And so I think it is important.

"It has a lot of influence over culture. Because pop culture *is* culture."

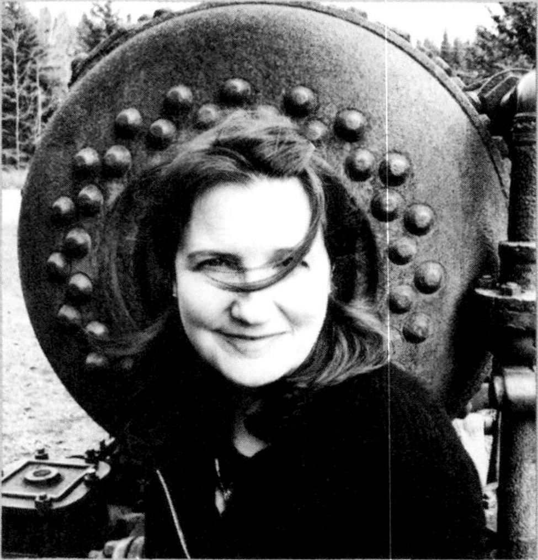

CHAPTER TEN

UNLIMITED

Comic Shops, and the Advent
of Marvel Digital

COMICS ARE FOR EVERYONE. That was the slogan that colorist, writer, and community-builder Jordie Bellaire and designer Steven Finch collaborated on for T-shirts in 2014, in the wake of the latest wave of hate directed at women in comics. It quickly became a phenomenon, with creators and staff from every company repping it, and a hashtag going viral.

It's a simple statement, and one that seems like it wouldn't garner much pushback. But in the year that the world outside of comics fans grew hip to the fact that women and other underrepresented groups were, in fact, reading and creating comics, it felt revolutionary. It had exposed the slow but steady narrowing of the comics audience over the years, as well as the work that needed to be done to gain that ground back.

"The suitability for a boy versus a girl simply did not enter my mind," said Irene Vartanoff of the comics from the sixties that she remembers reading growing up. "If you read the house ads at the time, they would say *boys and girls*. They expected that girls would read comics."

Newsstands were once the major distributors of comics in the 1930s and '40s. Over the next few decades, you could also find a spinner rack in most grocery stores and pharmacies, and there were robust subscription services, so your favorites could be mailed directly to your door.

When Irene first started reading—by filching the comics her brother had bought and already read—she held out as long as she could before she had to do something about it. "I don't know how long it was, but eventually, within a year or two, I figured out that I was missing just about every other issue of every monthly comic. So I got subscriptions. And I read comics on the newsstands. I mean, that's how I discovered Marvel, ACGs [American Comics Group], all the others, because you had read every comic you had and there was nothing else to read."

In the 1960s, the underground comix scene spawned the first comic shop in the United States: the San Francisco Comic Book Company (where Flo Steinberg worked for the year she lived out West). The shop sourced mainstream books from newsstand distributors, and then would stock local zines from the collectives that were springing up throughout the area.

In the 1970s, with comics sales falling at newsstands, Phil Seuling and his partner, Jonni Levas, had an idea—what if they bought directly from comics publishers at a discount, and those books were then sold through specialized comics shops? By the end of the decade, only 6 percent of Marvel's sales were through comics shops, but a funny thing pinged on the radar of those who were watching closely: Marvel books, the legend goes, were outperforming other companies at the shops, and titles like *The Uncanny X-Men* in particular were among the only books at Marvel showing real growth because of its sales at these shops.

Inside the House of Ideas, there was a woman overseeing this "direct market experiment" and carefully watching the trends. She saw what was happening and rightly identified that the health of the direct market was essential to that of the industry. Her name was Carol Kalish.

In an oral history at GamesRadar+ in 2020 titled "The Most Important Comic Book Figure You've Never Heard Of," Paul Levitz, former president and publisher of DC Comics, called Carol the "first ambassador" between publishers and retailers. Kurt Busiek, award-winning writer of *Marvels*, and Carol's assistant in the sales department at the time, said she brought "sensible business practices to an industry that, when she started, largely worked out of cigar boxes. She modernized the comics industry in a lot of ways." Her partner and comic artist Richard Howell said she "was probably the second-best marketer in the history of the business, behind only Stan Lee."

She was extremely hands-on. She sourced cash registers in bulk and got Marvel to subsidize them, in order to help shops who couldn't afford one themselves. She traveled around the country, showing retailers how to use display racks and other marketing tools, and innovated store purchase bags

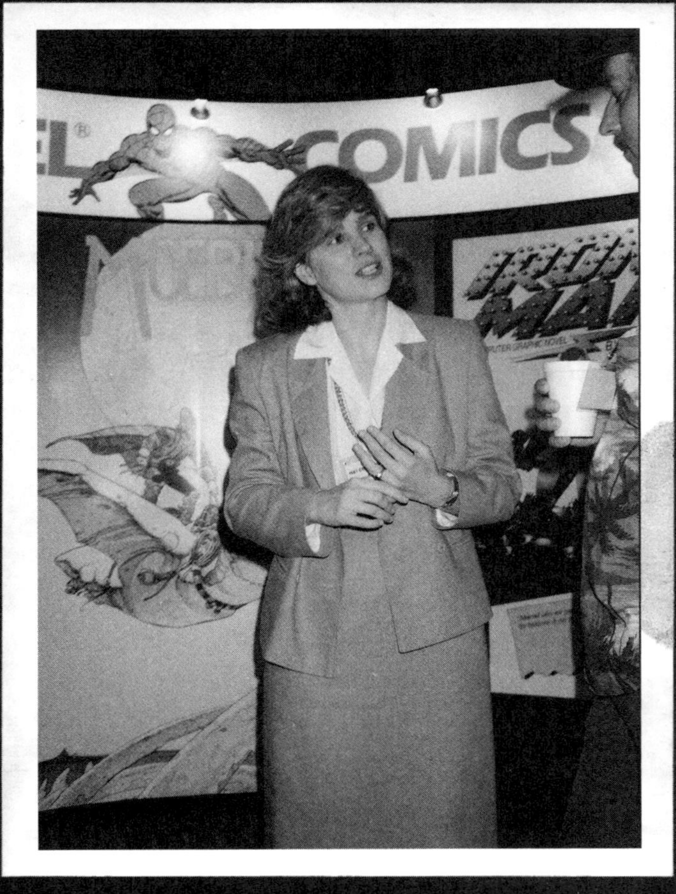
COMICS

NOBODY AT THE LIBRARY . . . THEY DIDN'T HAVE ANYONE WHO COULD TALK TO ME ABOUT COMICS AND TELL ME WHERE TO START.

———

with Marvel art printed on one side and the shop's address on the other. She also instituted a cooperative advertising program, where Marvel would subsidize ads for groups of retailers in the same region, so they could do a larger-scale promotional push better than they'd be able to do on their own.

She also created Marvel Masterworks, a publishing program that reprinted, with restored art, out-of-print Marvel classics in a collectible format. "That's a program that's still going thirty years later," says Sven Larsen, vice president of licensed publishing at Marvel, who worked under Carol in sales. "At that time, that material had never really been collected in any sort of permanent format. She was very forward-thinking that way in terms of what type of product the direct market would support."

Under Carol's guidance, Marvel's presence in the direct market boomed.

Then came September 5, 1991, the day that writer Peter David, once Carol's assistant direct sales manager, called "The Day Comics Stopped." At the age of thirty-six, Carol died suddenly of a pulmonary embolism, collapsing outside Penn Station on her way to work. In an interview with Dan Gearino for his incredible and incredibly moving history of the industry, *Comic Shop*, Jim Hanley, founder of the famous comics shop Jim Hanley's Universe, remembers the news ripping through the industry, shop owners calling each other in tears. "She was the patron of the art of comic retailing," he said.

1991 started a decade of turbulence for the industry, the height of its peaks matching the depth of its valleys . . . and it was also when the shine of the ease of access at shops, which people like Carol could see the potential in, started to tarnish. Comics shops as a concept got the bad rep they would go on to carry for many years: that they were spaces at best incidentally unfriendly to anyone not considered a "serious" comic reader, and at worst, openly hostile. And much of the time, these "unserious" readers would be identified as women.

"Throughout the eighties and nineties, there were all these adult male–driven stories because the comic book retailers were attracting readership similar to them, so the books they ordered reflected that readership," noted Dan Buckley.

"I've got my local shop, Hot Comics, who is super kid-friendly and welcoming," said Jen Bartel, an award-winning artist and designer, who currently illustrates *She-Hulk* covers, and is well known for her sold-out run of Avengers-themed sneakers for Adidas. "But when I was younger, in college, it was pretty rare to walk into a comics or a specialty, nerd type of shop as a woman and feel comfortable."

Preeti Chhibber remembers wanting to learn more, but feeling she didn't have anywhere she could turn. "That's what was so frustrating, because I was into all the other nerd culture stuff. All the other nerd culture stuff was so accessible, whether it was *Star Wars* or fantasy books or whatever . . . I was into all of it. But comics were just, 'I don't even know where to start.'"

Mackenzi Lee agrees. "I could never figure out how to read [comics] and how to start. And I remember seeing the comic book section at our local library and going to try and pick some of them up and just being like, 'I don't know who any of these people are. I don't know these stories.'

"Nobody at the library . . . they didn't have anyone who could talk to me about comics and tell me where to start. And I was also too shy to ask. I felt like comics were a very uncool thing. I remember feeling like all of my nerd obsessions I had to keep very secret."

Pat Redding, a Marvel editor and inker in the 1980s, remembers going into a shop that sold comics as a young girl and seeing Black Canary for the first time, drawn in fishnet stockings. "It always bothered me because all the men in comics were fat and old and bald," she said. "And their wives were really shapely and always had dresses and high heels on and perfect hair when they were vacuuming or whatever. And I said, 'Mom, why do they look that way?' And she just said, 'Oh, that's an example of male chauvinism.'"

Mackenzi had a similar experience. "My grandma lived by a comic book store when I was growing up. And I think I went in it, like, two or three times.

And it was just totally staffed by dudes. I'm a thirteen- or fourteen-year-old girl there who already feels out of place. And then you're surrounded by these supermasculine comics and characters. And the only place that I saw women were these super sexualized versions of them."

"When I was growing up, a comic book store was not the place that you would take your young daughter. I still remember seeing this giant cardboard cutout of Red Sonja and thinking, 'This is not where I'm supposed to be. I should go to KB Toys. I don't belong here,'" said writer Marguerite Bennett.

Amanda Conner was an early adopter of the comics shop as a place where women could find each other; seeing the reputation that a small number of stores were giving the rest of the market, she opened up her own comic book shop in the early nineties with her now ex-husband, that's still open, even if she no longer runs it: FunnyBooks in Lake Hiawatha, New Jersey.

"At that time, comic books had a horrible reputation amongst girls and women, which was disappointing, as I love them so much," said Amanda. "And there were many great options to read, from *Elfquest* to *X-Men*. I tried to make our store really female-friendly. Bright, colorful, nonthreatening. And I realized, 'If I work here, nobody will feel threatened.' We had fun with the shop, and slowly but successfully, girls came into our store."

Kelly Thompson said having a good comics shop experience when she was younger set her up as a fan for life. "I was really lucky. The shop that I ended up going to was owned by a woman, and so it was very naturally inclusive. It was Night Flight Comics, which, when I was a teenager, was in the Cottonwood Mall. That was our shop that we made our home.

"Because my first experience at Night Flight was really good, and because I felt really embraced, it gave me confidence. It didn't even occur to me that I wasn't really welcome in comics. I had a very different experience from what a lot of women have. And I think it was probably surprisingly integral to me staying in the fandom and not feeling excluded."

At the New York Comic Con Women of Marvel panel in 2012, Jordie Bellaire called comics shops a home, too. "I think it's important to establish ownership and a home. Build a community in your store."

But for years, starting in the mid-nineties with the arrival of the computer as a mainstay in homes across the globe, women in fandom had been building their community elsewhere: online.

Jeanine Schaefer kicks off the Women of Marvel panel at New York Comic Con in 2012.

Said Rainbow Rowell, "Without the internet, I didn't know many other girls who liked the same things. I did have one friend, Jennifer, who we bonded over a love of *Star Wars*. And I think that is one reason why we became so close, because we were able to read all the *Star Wars* novels together. And it was so rare and special to meet another girl who was really into science fiction."

So how could we merge this diverse, thriving online community with the mainstream comics community?

"For me, my job has always been about making things accessible," said Lorraine Cink, director of creative content at Marvel and the host of the *This Week in Marvel* podcast. "Having eighty years of comics for a lot of people is intimidating. . . . I try to ultimately serve our audience by letting them in on the stuff that I wish I knew when I came up to it or when I first encountered it. Because I think everybody just wants to be part of the community, and it's sort of like, 'Hey, here's the key to the door. You don't have to break the door down.'"

Christine Dinh worked in digital marketing and strategy as an editor for Marvel.com. She said she would listen to the *Women of Marvel* podcast as she drove to work, at another comics publisher in Los Angeles. "At the start

TOP: Rachel Paige, Alana Hermnson, Faith D'Isa, Christine Dinh, and Haley Conatser at the Marvel booth at New York Comic Con in 2019. BOTTOM LEFT: Author Mackenzi Lee poses with her first book with Marvel, *Loki: Where Mischief Lies*. BOTTOM RIGHT: Hosts of the *Desi Geek Girls* podcast, Swapna Krishna and Preeti Chhibber, with Vishavjit Singh, the Sikh Captain America.

HEY, HERE'S THE KEY TO THE DOOR. YOU DON'T HAVE TO BREAK THE DOOR DOWN.

of my comics career, it was isolating. There were times when there were so few women that I would latch on to, like, any woman in comics." She loved the message, and the method, and when she heard about an opening at the company, she put herself forward. After five years with Marvel and building up her outreach team, she and her team are seen as a direct line to the fans.

"We are for every single faction of a Marvel fan, whether they love just games or they love the character or if they do pick up the comics or if they're a kid whose parents introduce them, we've run the whole gamut of this audience," she said.

"I've realized I have power in my experiences, especially as they've tried to silence me before. It's important to understand, I think that the struggle a lot of women have is, the understanding that we all have power and that our voice and our experience and our knowledge [are what] we bring to the table."

In 2007, Ryan Penagos, now vice president and creative executive for Marvel New Media, but at the time a member of the newly formed Marvel Digital Media Group, was one of the first adopters of Twitter as a tool to create a brand. Over the next six years, his account would grow to over a million followers, and Marvel's Digital Media Group would become a vital part of fan outreach.

Adri Cowan started her career with Marvel right in the middle of the New York Comic Con. "I feel like I might have been in a shock," she said, laughing. "For, like, the first year, at least!"

By that point she was only the third person who managed the official social media channels for Marvel. Her predecessors, Margarita Montimore (née Vaisman) and Janna Zagari (née O'Shea), wrangled the company's feeds when the platforms were still basically the Wild West, and the foundation they laid provided Adri with the opportunity to come in and build a structure.

Though it was her dream job, there was the necessary realignment of the fantasy of the job versus the day-to-day realities. Marvel is notorious for operating as lean as possible, which is how they're able to innovate and execute ideas so quickly. But the social media team at that point was leaner than most. "It felt like the original vibe that Marvel was built on," Adri said. "We were definitely allowed to get away with more things than we are now."

Adri brought creative and brand strategy to the digital team on her way to her main objective: to position Marvel's online presence as a piece of the overall lifestyle brand. "What Stan and Flo were brilliant at was knowing how to talk to fans where they were, and in the ways that would truly reach them. I hope we're continuing to do that through the platforms that exist today . . . continuing the legacy of building a community—a community that at its heart is a family. I hope we're doing Stan and Flo justice."

THE RISE of the comics/pop culture conventions, and the slow but sure pulling back of the curtain about women's attendance and their history with them, is credited by many of the women interviewed for this book as the bridge from feeling a need to keep their fandom a secret to being active and public participants in the shaping of the entire industry.

"The first convention I remember going to was run by Dave Kaler," says Carole Seuling. "There was a costume parade, believe it or not! The convention was held in a hotel in downtown Manhattan, I believe . . . in 1965."

The Academy Con was—depending on who you're taking to—either the third or fourth "official" comics convention ever organized, held the weekend of July 31–August 1, 1965, at the Broadway Central Hotel in New York City, in what is now NoHo. The show ran for three consecutive years and also featured the first instance of industry awards, called the Alley Awards, modeled after the Oscars.

TOP: Social media director Adri Cowan poses with her team at the Marvel Studios' *Black Panther: Wakanda Forever* red carpet.
BOTTOM: Controlled chaos: Nicole Ciaramella, Tamara Krinsky, and Lorraine Cink backstage at the Marvel booth.

The Alley Awards would go on to give way to the Shazams, which ran from 1970 to 1974, when Marie Severin and Glynis Wein (née Oliver) became the third and fourth women to win a comics award for their work—Marie for pencilling and Glynis for coloring (the first two were Tatjana Wood [née Weintraub] for Best Colorist for her work at DC Comics in 1972, and Gerda Gattel, DC Comics' production coordinator, who won a Special Achievement Award after her retirement in 1973).

Carole Seuling recalled, "In 1967, we went to the World Science Fiction Convention in Cleveland. My husband was so impressed by the way they ran the convention that he decided to do exactly the same thing for comic books. He picked a hotel in NYC and borrowed the format. That was 1968."

Carole would handle the business aspects and behind-the-scenes work, running the "super hero masquerade," selling tickets, handling the guests' flights and hotel rooms, or even putting them up in their own home, while Phil Seuling was the face of the show. "[I] met a lot of very interesting people," she said fondly. "Hal Foster, Isaac Asimov. We truly had some great guests. It was an experience."

They named it the Comic Art Convention, and it was held annually in the summer in Manhattan from 1968 until Phil's sudden death in 1984.

The impact of these shows can't be understated. Will Eisner, creator of the groundbreaking comic *The Spirit* and the godfather of the graphic novel, credits the Comic Art Convention with his return to the medium. Phil tracked him down to the job he had left comics for: chairman of the board of Croft Educational Services, a curriculum and education legislation publisher, and invited him to attend as a guest in 1971.

Eisner, in his keynote address at the 2002 University of Florida Conference on Comics and Graphic Novels, remembered it fondly. "I went down to the convention, which was being held in one of the hotels in New York, and there was a group of guys with long hair and scraggly beards, who had been turning out what spun as literature, really popular 'gutter' literature if you will, but pure literature. And they were taking on illegal [*sic*] subject matter that no comics had ever dealt with before. I came away from that recognizing that a revolution had occurred then, a turning point in the history of this medium."

For women in particular, the 1974 show is also the first instance of a

I CAME AWAY FROM THAT RECOGNIZING THAT A REVOLUTION HAD OCCURRED THEN, A TURNING POINT IN THE HISTORY OF THIS MEDIUM.

———

Women in Comics panel (which could also be seen as the first instance of a Women of Marvel panel). Panelists were Flo Steinberg, Marie Severin, Jean Thomas, Linda Fite, and Irene Vartanoff, who was there as a fan representative, before she started working full-time at Marvel.

"I found out about fandom through letter columns," said Irene. "I started writing to Billy Joe White, who had the *Batmania* fanzine. Somehow or other, I discovered Dave Kaler was running a convention up in New York City.

"The first convention that I went to required a hotel—Mother came, too. It was clear that we were being properly chaperoned, that we were young ladies, and the boys that we met were young gentlemen." We had a good laugh at the idea of boys at a convention as young gentlemen, considering the chaos of what cons have become.

"It was a totally different thing!" Irene exclaimed. "It wasn't a very large event. I met a number of very nice boys, who have been my friends actually all my life, including Marv Wolfman, Len Wein, Mark Hanerfeld, Stan Landman, Eliot Wagner, Rich Rubenfeld. Rich is a retired professor of art history and he was all [about] the comics. He just loved them. And Andy Yanchus, who was a modeler [for Aurora] and then worked at Marvel in the coloring department. [. . .] Everyone dressed up. Boys had jackets on. Pretty much everybody was wearing suits.

UNLIMITED / 247

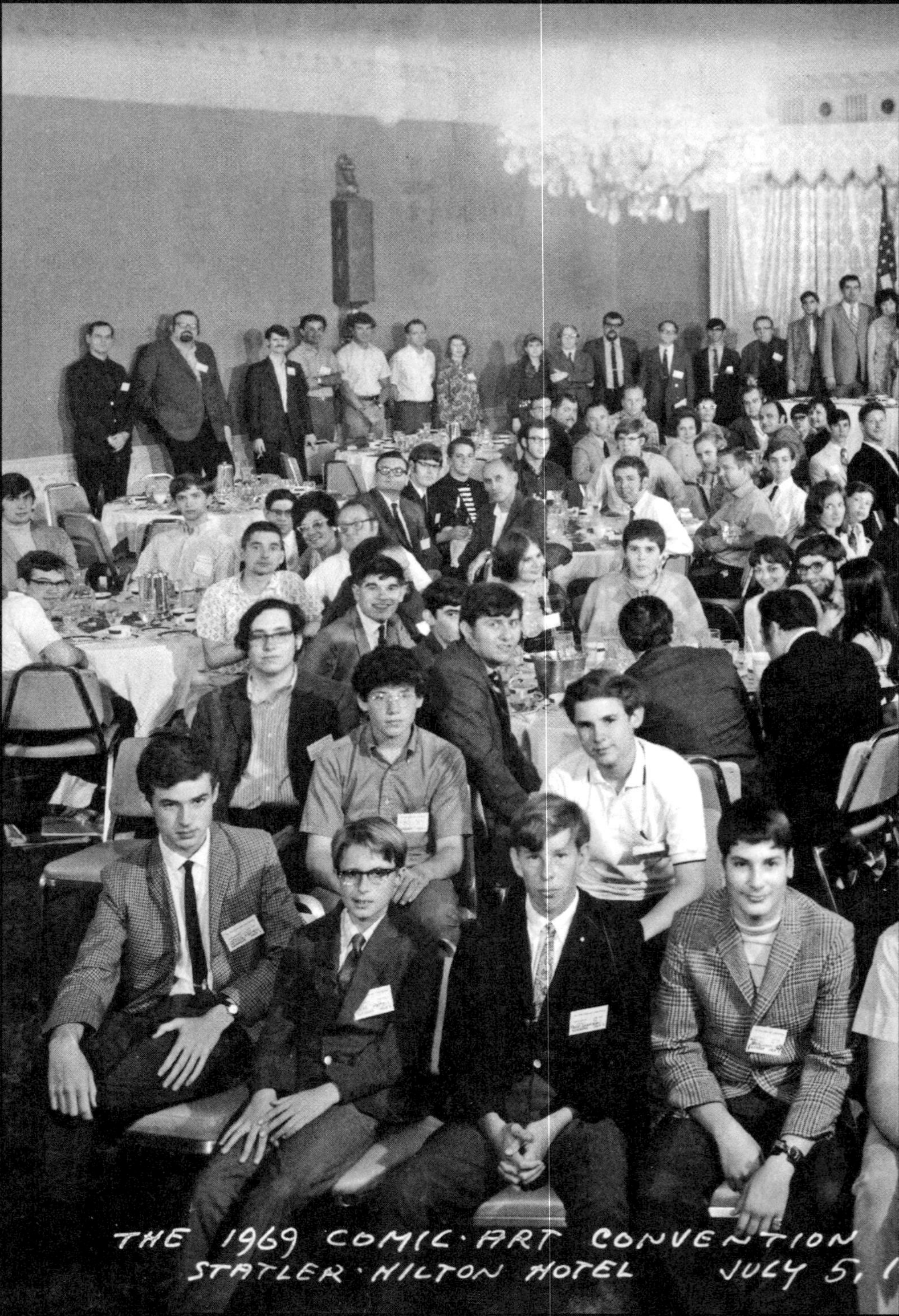
THE 1969 COMIC·ART CONVENTION
STATLER·HILTON HOTEL JULY 5,

All the attendees at the 1969 Comic Art Convention Luncheon.

OPPOSITE TOP: 1982's Women in Comics panel at San Diego Comic-Con, from left to right: Jan Duursema, Trina Robbins, and Carol Kalish. BOTTOM: As Mary Wilshire hand-titled this photo from her scrapbook, 1980's "ill-fated panel on Why Women Read Comics." From left to right: Ann Nocenti, Mary Wilshire, Lee Binswanger, and Trina Robbins.

"There were a few women and girls—there was my sister, and then there was Andy's sister, Pat Yanchus. Margaret Gemignani (also a science fiction fan), and that's it for the young female fans. But I looked around and I said, 'Okay, we're all weird.'"

"If there were a litmus test for being involved in the organization, it would be passion," said David Glanzer, chief communications and strategy officer for Comic-Con International, the organization behind San Diego Comic-Con. "And we know that passion for comics and related popular art transcends all descriptors. Specifically, in terms of gender, our staff and board are 53 percent identifying as female, and 47 percent identify as male."

In 2018, another milestone was reached: Kristina Rogers, vice president of ReedPop, the organization behind multiple nationwide conventions like New York Comic Con, C2E2, and Emerald City Comic Con, shared with us that at Emerald City Comic Con that year, female attendance outnumbered male. A long way from Irene Vartanoff looking around in 1966 and being able to count the number of women on her hands. But conventions now are also a long way from total numbers in general; where those first shows saw attendance in the low hundreds, events in San Diego and New York regularly see numbers ranging from 130,000 to 200,000, with New York Comic Con topping off at a whopping 260,000 in 2019.

"There used to be a convention in New York, which we called Church-Con," said Amanda Conner, talking about the Big Apple Comic Con of the mid-nineties, which was held in the basement of Manhattan's St. Paul the Apostle Church. "We'd walk around and see who was attending, and then go out for long lunches to see friends. You could get [an exhibitor] table next

Jen Bartel during a signing at the booth during San Diego Comic-Con in 2019.

to one of your friends and chat till a fan came up asking for a commission. It was so much more relaxing back in the day. Not that it's not fun now—it's just different. Attending conventions was more of a recreational thing, but now it's a marathon, working three to four days."

"In 2016, I started tabling at comic conventions," said Jen Bartel. "And there are certainly men who would come to my table every now and then, and more so now that I've branched out of the initial work that I was doing. But in 2016 and 2017, most of 2018, I was selling my work pretty much exclusively to women. And it was not a small number of women, either. Every show I did, I was consistently shocked by how many women were physically walking around the convention and making it a point to stop at my table and support what I was doing."

And it's not just fans who were supporting her. The year before, Jim Demonakos, the co-creator of Emerald City Comic Con, reached out and offered her a half table, in an effort to get more newcomers into Artists' Alley, the section of comic conventions where creators sell their art, merch, take commissions, and generally make themselves available to meet fans in a more casual setting than on the show floor.

"For me, personally, [Artists' Alley] has always been the crown jewel of that show because it's community-driven. Jim gave me a chance and I just took it.

"[He] had put me next to Tamra Bonvillain—who is the most amazing colorist. We tabled side by side, and Tamra was so kind to give me a little bit of extra space because I had stuff overflowing on my table. I'd gone into that experience fully expecting to not break even, but by day one, I had broken even.

"So that was my first introduction to comic conventions, and the following year, Jim's wife, Andrea, approached me about running [my] online store. Jim basically opened the door for me, and then Andrea and I partnered. This is why when people in comics [say], 'Women don't read comics,' I [say], 'I think they do. And they're at comic conventions buying my stuff.'"

In 2019, Jen won her first Eisner Award, the premier comics achievement founded in 1988 and awarded annually ever since at the San Diego Comic-Con, for Best Cover Artist.

"I definitely did not expect to win an Eisner," she said. "Even as they were reading [it] out, I thought that I had misheard at first. And had to be told, 'Jen, you have to go up there.' It felt as if something had shifted in the universe after that. All of a sudden, people who had been dismissive of me just the day before were, 'Okay, I guess we should take her a little more seriously now.' After I won that Eisner, I felt all of a sudden there were a bunch of men that kind of talked to me a little differently."

Jen became only the third woman recognized for her cover work in the award's thirty-one-year history, after Fiona Staples in 2017 and Sana Takeda in 2018. But a funny thing happened then: the next three awards would also be given to women, with Emma Ríos, Peach Momoko, and Jen Bartel again, in 2020, 2021, and 2022, respectively.

"I think the best way to put it is, in 2016, it felt to me like the most important thing was having strong female characters," she said, reflecting on why that night felt like such a sea change, in just the three years since her first convention. "Having these women on the pages of comics that girls and young women could aspire to look up to and admire, who were infallible. And by that time, it stopped being exclusively about just having strong women on those pages, and it became more about having complicated women on those pages. It also coincided with the #MeToo movement. There were just so many conversations happening that made a lot of us think about what feminism meant to each of us."

"I think 'access' is the right word," said *X-23* and *Ms. Marvel* artist Sana Takeda, when we asked her why she thinks conventions, and women's place in them, are such a driver of the health of the industry. "Before this, the space didn't exist. And even if it did, no one felt that they had access to it. That's the wonderful thing about conventions—it's this accessible place [where] you can go and find people like you. They're right there. They're in Artists' Alley or walking through these crowded panel floors or sitting on a panel. And they're also equally excited to be there. It's very thrilling."

THE HISTORY of women and cosplay, a Japanese portmanteau for "costume play," goes all the way back to the first recorded appearance at a convention, in 1939. Myrtle R. Douglas—more popularly known to the fan community as Morojo, a science fiction fanzine publisher—designed "futuristicostumes" based on the 1936 sci-fi film *Things to Come*, for herself and the legendary Forrest J. Ackerman, a sci-fi literary agent and the man credited as the founder of sci-fi fandom, which they wore to the first World Science Fiction Convention.

Morojo was a force in sci-fi fandom (she also wrote for what appears to be the first all-female sci-fi fanzine, edited by her niece), and by the next year, the convention had an official masquerade added to the programming.

"Cosplay is one of the few professions on the planet that is dominated by women," said Yaya Han, a costume designer, author, and arguably the most well-known cosplayer in modern fandom history. "I think that's very profound."

Having been in cosplay professionally for over twenty years, she feels the genesis of that comes down to two factors, the first of which is the credibility check, which women have historically had a harder time passing, especially in the days when modern cosplay was coalescing.

"Cosplay was so small in the early 2000s," said Yaya. "And when a community is so small and so underground and also very misunderstood, which we were back then . . . we were considered the really obsessive fans back then, we weren't the 'cool fans.' We just were the little kids that just ran around with our hot-glued-together outfits and horrible wigs." She laughed. "Or sometimes no wigs at all!"

TOP: Yaya Han's Scarlet Witch cosplay as part of the Marvel Cosplay Covers program. BOTTOM: Caught in flight, *Marvel 616*'s Marc Schwerin in his Wiccan cosplay.

The creator of the Superhero Costuming Forum, Allen Wolf, poses with his wife, Mary Cahela, in their Doctor Strange and Clea cosplays.

The second factor, she noted, is the reliance on skills that were a barrier of entry for many men. "Crafting and sewing is traditionally considered a female activity, and less men were willing to open themselves up to crafting. And the thing is, every costume is sewing-based. It doesn't matter if it's a full suit of armor—you still have to wear something underneath it. It has to have a base. So knowing how to sew is a huge advantage. Also doing makeup and styling wigs."

Marc Schwerin, a costume and prop designer whose work has been featured on *Marvel Becoming* as well as the cosplay episode, "Suit Up," for *Marvel's 616* series, said a lot of it has to do with how the perception of identity in cosplay naturally makes it more accessible for traditionally marginalized groups. "For a lot of people, cosplay offers this opportunity to put on, or to try out, or to interact with identities that are not your own. And I think that that can apply to gender, to sexuality, to a type of person.

"I think for a lot of people, maybe they feel shy, or they feel a way about themselves, or a way about the world, and being able to put on the identity of a hero, in particular—I think this is really common in the Marvel community—is really empowering for people. That they're able to embody a character that they see things about, that they maybe are inspired by, or maybe help them feel more comfortable."

As for Marvel, with its long history of heroes who grappled more with their civilian identities and their place in the world than they did as their costumed counterparts, cosplayers found a new world opened up to them with the arrival on the scene of the Marvel Cinematic Universe.

"Oh, it's more than just an entry point for cosplayers," said Yaya. "I think the Marvel movies specifically have made comic fandom grow. [. . .] I felt that as a cosplayer almost immediately. Once we had *Iron Man* and especially when we had *Avengers*, it was this collective door opening for fans around the world. Looking back at the first half of the 2010s, there was such an explosion of super hero costumes. From Black Cat to Captain America to Scarlet Witch to Tony Stark. And I certainly got caught in that explosion."

She grinned. "It was just cool to be a Marvel character."

"Fandom was the first step in people being, 'Oh, we can make content and interact with each other and complete this loop. We are consuming something that we love and then we are finding a way to also put something back out,'" said Marc. "And I think cosplay was a part of an outlet for people to consume media and then put something back into the community."

And cosplay has reflected fandom's joy tenfold.

Danai Gurira, the actor who played Okoye—the leader of Wakanda's all-female army, the Dora Milaje—in *Black Panther*, said fandom's embracing of her character in that movie, and of what the Dora Milaje represent, has been a blessing. "The whole perspective that Marvel had and that [director] Ryan [Coogler] had was to really give these women a very powerful presence. And I think that was really achieved. And to see that really resonates with young girls and women.

"I have seen so many women cosplay Okoye. For that to represent strength and femininity, fearlessness, a protection and guardianship of a very sacred nation, and for people to really have taken to that the way they did . . . the defiance of a mainstream ideal of feminine beauty in the form

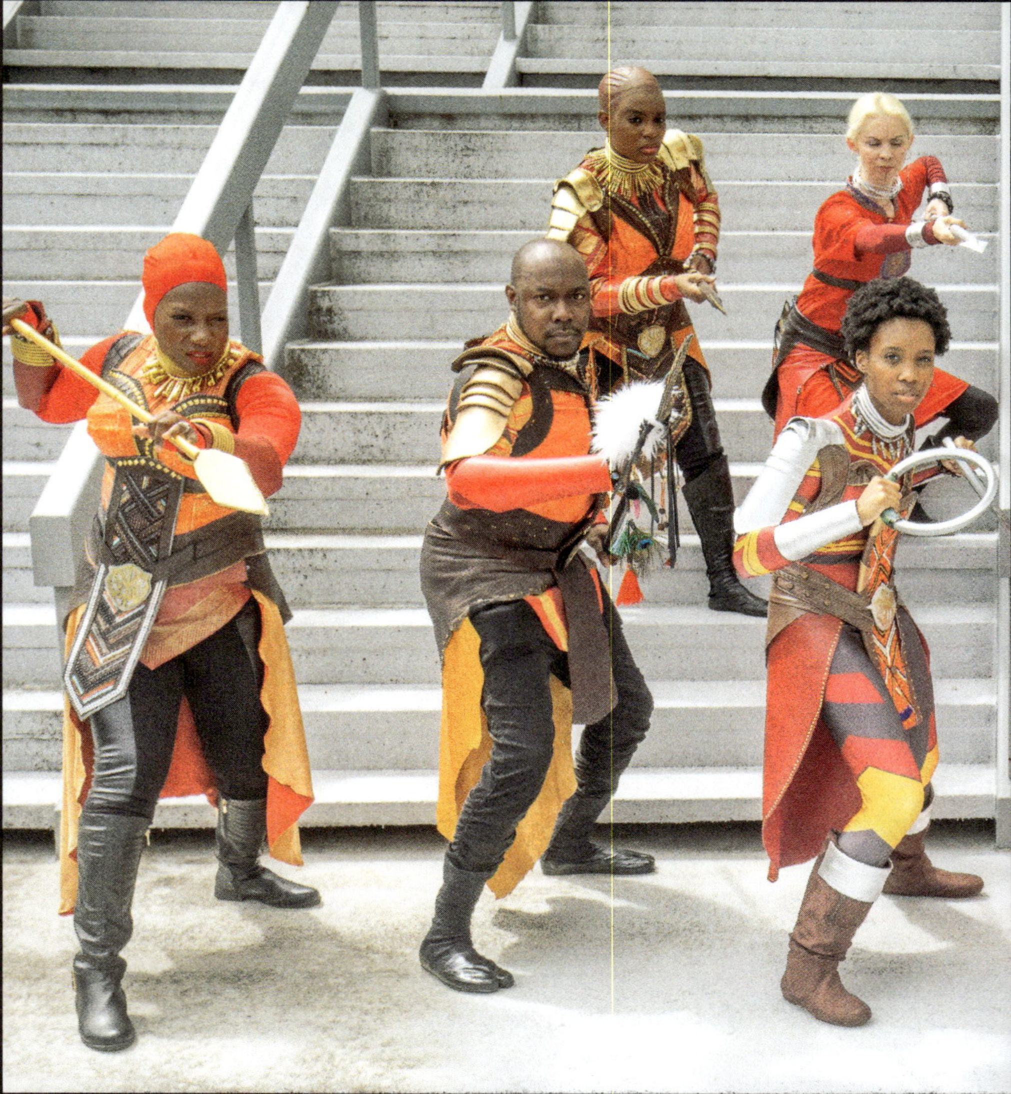

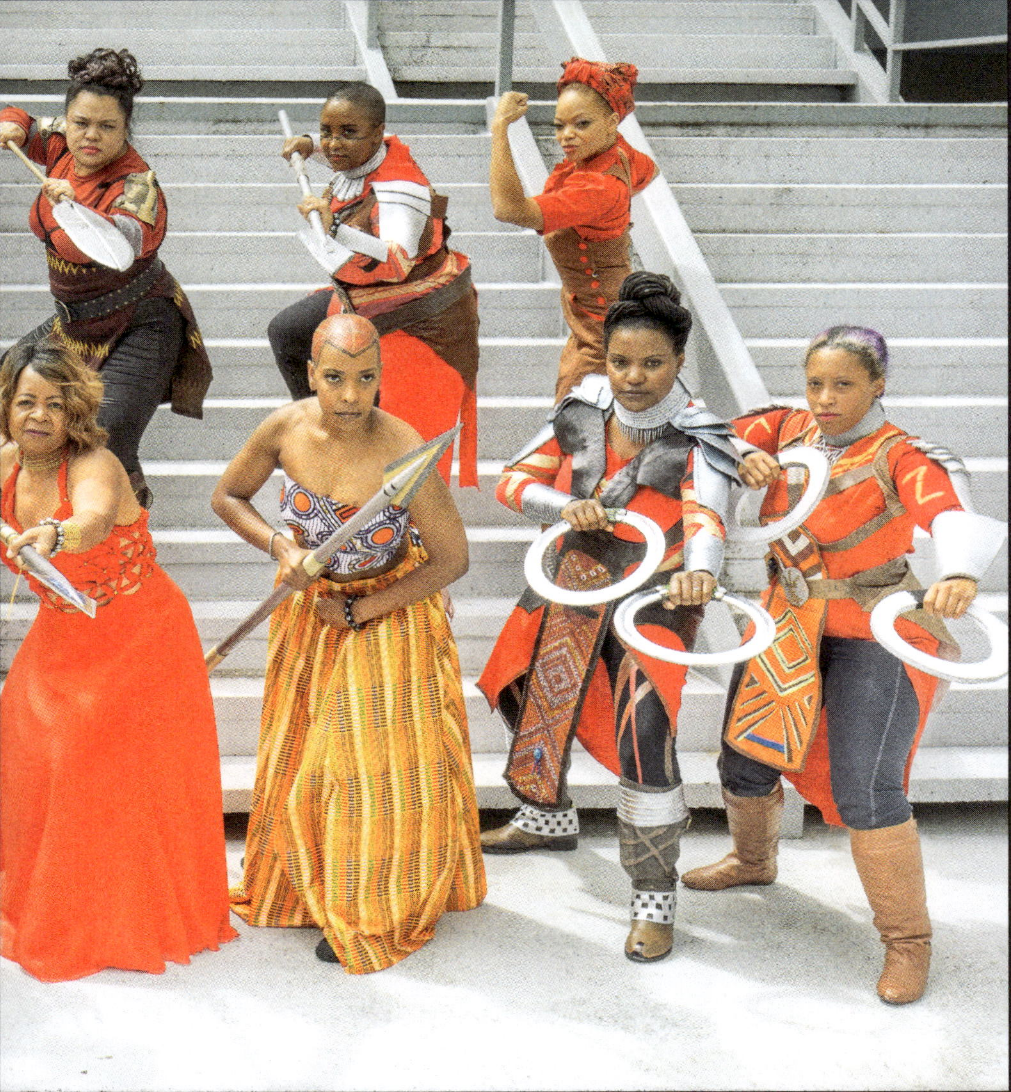

of the bald head and the tattoos on the head, while still having big lashes and red lips . . .

"It is a gift to women and girls. We hope that they receive it that way."

Anna Boden felt the same sense of awe when they started the *Captain Marvel* press tour in Singapore. "I just remember so many young women and girls wearing their homemade Captain Marvel stuff. It was so exciting, just seeing thousands of people—I mean, I've never been in a position to contribute to something that was that powerful, in terms of how it reached people. It was more than about the movie, but it was about the fact that the movie was made. And to be part of that felt very special."

Ann Foley is the costume designer for *She-Hulk*, and was the designer on seasons one through four of *Agents of S.H.I.E.L.D.* After seeing young fans in costume at Marvel panels, she worked hard to make the characters' clothing on-screen as accessible as the personalities that captured their interest to begin with. "One of the things that really moved me about our fans was how the young girls related to Simmons and Daisy and felt, 'Oh I can dress like that? I can dress like Simmons and I love this character so much and I relate to this character and to her flaws,'" she said.

"I always tried to make what they were wearing accessible not only financially but visually. And I loved the fans reaching out to me saying how much it meant to them. To be able to have these characters to watch every week and then get their clothes and dress like them because it made them feel like they were sort of finding a part of themselves through these characters. That's powerful stuff."

"Marvel was really the first company that I felt that was accepting of cosplayers," said Yaya.

MARVEL WAS REALLY THE FIRST COMPANY THAT I FELT THAT WAS ACCEPTING OF COSPLAYERS.

Costume designer Ann Foley (right) with Elizabeth Henstridge, who played Agent Simmons on Marvel's *Agents of S.H.I.E.L.D.*

Marc agreed, spotlighting the Marvel staff, people like Judy Stephens, who not only understood fandom but were a part of it, and worked to hold the door open for others. "There is an up-and-coming generation of people who are working in creative industries, who are working in media, who are creating the content that we're all consuming, who are, or were, or understand the cosplay community. For example, there was a shift at Marvel where they started thinking about people building the costumes that they were designing."

"With Marvel, I could see repeatedly and continuously at every convention, [they] had cosplay events at their booth," said Yaya. "And it wasn't just the contests. You had photo ops on the stage, you gathered them up for photo shoots at the booths, and also organized the big, big, big photo shoots, where you can just come in and be in a photo and have it watermarked as Marvel and posted on the website. That is all we want as fans . . . to be accepted by the creators.

"We don't necessarily need to go on a stage and win an award to feel like we're accepted. Just being there is enough."

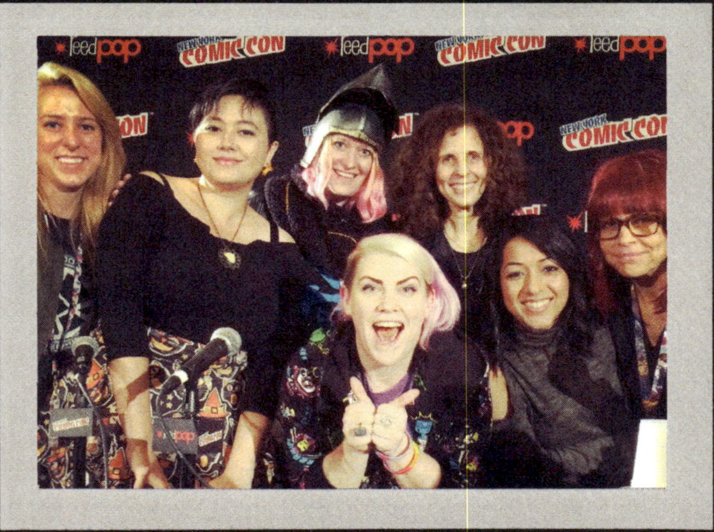
NEW YORK
COMIC CON

CHAPTER ELEVEN

SUNDAY MORNING

Rise of the Women of
Marvel Panels

A huge part of the Women of Marvel Initiative, launched in 2010, was a reimagining of the Women of Marvel panels, and then the conception of the *Women of Marvel* podcast, both of which have become two of the most consistent vehicles for outreach in the decade since.

The

panels were always scheduled for first thing Sunday morning, which, for anyone attending all three or four days of a con, is a rough time slot.

Typically, no matter the convention, the final panel Saturday night was usually the biggest, and the party would continue from there with creators and fans at the hotel bars, companies holding private events elsewhere in the cities. Most people would roll onto the convention floor on Sunday well after opening, around noon, which made that first panel slot on Sundays a tricky one for panelists, and most would see sparse numbers of fan attendance.

The first iteration took place at San Diego Comic-Con early on July 27, 2008. It was originally called the Women at Marvel panel, and was conceived on the fly when a previously organized panel was canceled.

Though very few photos exist, the descriptive copy calls out the power-houses of Marvel.

She-Hulk and Ms. Marvel are powerhouses in the Marvel U, now meet the real women powerhouses who work in Marvel Comics today! Writers Robin Furth (DARK TOWER) & Marjorie Liu (NYX), Jen Grünwald (Editor), colorist Christina Strain (RUNAWAYS), and Occasional Superheroine's Valerie D'Orazio are here to answer your question about their titles, announce new projects, and explain how more women are breaking into comics every day!

Jen Grünwald as the Marvel representative on the Women in Comics panel at San Diego Comic-Con in 2008.

These women were joined by writer Sherrilyn Kenyon, colorist Sonia Oback, cartoonist Colleen Coover, colorist Emily Warren, and artist Irene Flores, moderated by then Marvel marketing and publicity associate Jim McCann.

Comic Book Resources, one of the industry's leading news sites, did a write-up of the panel. It covered now-familiar ground.

> *A fan asked,* "Do you think there's a resistance [*from*] the male readers? I want to write X-Men, I'm not interested in writing romance stories. I've been told to my face girls can't write super heroes."
>
> *Colleen Coover:* "There's a lady named Gail Simone who's doing a pretty good job."

It was a success, and in 2009 it was submitted by Marvel in their first round of panel requests for the convention and renamed Women of Marvel. It was held on Sunday, July 31, and featured writer Marjorie Liu, colorists Christina Strain and Laura Martin, and then-editor of special projects Jen Grünwald.

That was then-producer Judy Stephen's first year attending San Diego Comic-Con as a Marvel representative, and she excitedly recalled attending each panel she could, including getting up early that fateful day.

"I still remember being in the room, seeing a stage full of women. The next year at SDCC, I made sure to ask to join as a panelist. I wanted to say, 'Okay, I don't touch comics. I'm never probably going to touch a comic, but I work at this company that you all want to work at, and you can do that, too.'"

In 2010, the Women of Marvel panel was first added to the lineup at New York Comic Con. With the inception of the Women of Marvel Initiative, the women inside the House of Ideas insisted that the panel have a showing at what was their "home" convention. It was the first year the convention moved to its permanent month of October, and was also when the show merged with the New York Anime Festival, bringing in a potential new audience, many of whom were women.

"I remember my first panel was at New York Comic Con in 2010," says Sana Amanat, who would go on to be co-moderator, cohost of the podcast, co-creator of *Ms. Marvel*, and, well, *the* Sana Amanat. "I had been working at [Marvel] for over a year by that point, and felt I was really integrated into the company. Before 2009, I had known Marvel people, but after starting, Jeanine Schaefer and I got really close. I remember Jeanine was moderating that panel, with a whole bunch of women, and we just had so much fun."

Also on the panel that year were editor Lauren Sankovitch, artist and writer Colleen Coover, editor Rachel Pinnelas, writer and colorist Christina Strain, writer Grace Randolph, and artist Stephanie Hans.

"I was surprised because there were so many more women than we expected!" says Sana. "I remember I showed up hungover. And it was the first thing that I said, and it became a tradition that Sana was showing up hungover because it was a Sunday panel. I believe everyone was surprised at my bluntness at that point. But once that happened, everyone was so much more relaxed. Anything goes on this panel."

It's the anything-goes atmosphere that made it *the* Sunday panel to attend; Andrew Wheeler, in his review of the 2012 panel for the beloved comics and pop culture news site ComicsAlliance, called it "the antidote to corporate comics buzz." Instead of using it for company promotion, the women on the stage were open for any question, and answered everything honestly and passionately.

After that year, the panel became a staple at both San Diego Comic-Con and New York Comic Con, and attendance grew as word of mouth spread that this was an honest peek behind the curtain. There were no announcements, no outward marketing. It was a true dialogue, one that could only happen when both sides of the discussion were treated as peers.

It was also a party—a joyous celebration of the women onstage and in the seats next to you. Said Sana, "I remember during [the] Q&A, an audience member stood up and said, 'This is really amazing because also I don't see many women in my industry, working in TV development. It's really nice to hear conversations like this, and I would love to see more.' From there, every panel grew more and more. Jeanine and I realized we had great chemistry together, and the panels became about having a good time."

New York Comic Con 2011 was the first year that saw Kelly Sue DeConnick as a panelist, nine months before the release of *Captain Marvel* #1 and six months before it would even be announced.

"She started my favorite tradition at the panel," said moderator Jeanine Schaefer. "The first year she was there, we had decided to open it up to questions right away. But before we started, Kelly Sue said, 'Wait, I want to know who here in the audience wants to make comics.' A few tentative hands went up, then more and more, and then she asked them to stand. She said, 'Look around, it's not impossible, these are the people you're going to make comics with—go say hello and get to work!' Then she asked for a big round of applause.

"I'm a crier to begin with, but I was a wreck. It was a really special, humbling, awe-inspiring moment."

The following year at San Diego (still three days before the release of *Captain Marvel* #1), there was a line—mostly women, and featuring a good number of Captain Marvel cosplayers—snaking around the conference room hallways starting two hours before the panel, waiting to get in.

"When we turned the corner to go to the panel and saw the line, I looked at Sana and said, 'Are we in the right place?'" Jeanine said, about the sheer spectacle in the hallway.

The room was packed to absolute capacity, with many people tweeting they had tried to get in but were turned away.

"That was also the year we sang 'Happy Birthday' to Kelly Sue!" said Judy Stephens. "It was such a fun party vibe every year."

And there was always something new to celebrate.

THAT SEEMED TO BE THE TIPPING POINT, AND THE FOLLOWING YEAR THEY CELEBRATED THE FACT THAT IN ALMOST FOUR YEARS, MARVEL HAD GONE FROM ZERO FEMALE-HEADLINED TITLES TO SEVENTEEN.

———

In 2013, Marvel relaunched their flagship X-book, *X-Men*, with an all-female team, and copies were set aside to be signed by series artist Olivier Coipel and specifically handed out for free at the Women of Marvel panel at San Diego Comic-Con, making it a must-attend for X-fans.

In 2014, with the introduction of Jane Foster as the new Thor, the topic was covered on NPR in "Where's Thor When You Need Her? Women in Comics Fight an Uphill Battle." When the numbers for San Diego's attendance were released and almost half were women, *Time* magazine published "The Rise of Fangirls at Comic-Con." And in October of that year, *Rolling Stone* picked the Women of Marvel panel as one of its "Top Ten Best Things We Saw and Heard at New York Comic Con."

That seemed to be the tipping point, and the following year they celebrated the fact that in almost four years, Marvel had gone from zero female-headlined titles to seventeen. In 2016, the women of TV's *Agents of S.H.I.E.L.D.* joined the panel.

By that point, the Women of Marvel panels had expanded to include a regular spot at not only San Diego Comic-Con and New York Comic Con, but also C2E2 in Chicago, with appearances at YALLWEST (in Los Angeles), Dragon Con (in Atlanta), and the Atlantic City Boardwalk Con. It was also the year it moved from its home in the "small room" to a room with an almost nine-hundred-person capacity.

OPPOSITE: The Women of Marvel panel at San Diego Comic-Con 2018 featured the cast and crew of *Marvel Rising*. From left to right: Writers G. Willow Wilson and Mairghread Scott, voice actors Kathreen Khavari and Milana Vayntrub, and director Kristi Reed.

"Every panel we had was so electric," said Sana. "I remember the year we announced Margaret Stohl was writing *Black Widow*. We had all these women piled up onstage, and the energy was rippling throughout the room—you could feel it. I've been on a lot of Marvel panels and I've never had as much fun as I do on those Women of Marvel panels."

"Sitting on that stage, with all those women, I had this moment, 'What is this community?!'" says Mackenzi Lee of her first appearance in 2019. "Seeing all of these people, with all this excitement, as this community. And of course it's not just women who go to these panels, but for me it was seeing the women and little girls, and talking with the fans. I had never gotten that feedback when I was there. I didn't have that female community. It was so thrilling."

X-Men writer Leah Williams says she will never forget her first Women of Marvel experience, at New York Comic Con in 2018. She had been nervous to say yes, and had reservations right up until walking out onstage. "I had kind of, I guess, mixed feelings about doing it, because I was worried that it 'othered' me? That it made me a target, basically, as not being a regular default-setting Marvel writer, but the lady-flavored one."

It's a valid concern, something the women at Marvel talked about among themselves then, and still do. Do we still need the Women of Marvel panel? Or "Women in Comics" panels in particular? Many women have a hard line, and will not appear on them, while many others will champion them until their voices give out. Still others take it convention by convention. But most are always wondering, *Is this the only place for me?*

Gail Simone is no stranger to this question. "I will say, a lot of us have a bit of fatigue about being on so many 'Women in Comics' panels—we all feel we have more to say than that. But it never fails that, at every single con, I have young women come up who say they attended one of those panels years before and it showed it was possible, it made them feel it could be done. So I think it's still an important topic. I know it's inspired a lot of new creators."

It's a question that has no clear-cut answer. But starting in 2013, it was a question that had penetrated the upper echelon of Marvel decision-makers, and there was a push at the company to make sure there were women on other panels, too. It takes a deliberate effort to make sure women, people of color, and other marginalized communities are adequately represented, an effort that the women of Marvel took on in genuine partnership with the literally thousands of fans who have attended for the past fourteen years and counting.

"It's not a coincidence that at the same time we're seeing this content we're having these conversations, because we felt like we were outsiders in this community," said Sana. "So we decided, we're going to take this by the horns, make something out of it, and talk about our experiences. From Carol to Kamala, then you get Squirrel Girl, America Chavez, Ironheart, Silk, and on and on. It's all connected. We were rallying and championing and cultivating a dialogue. And before the films were released. I truly believe it started with us. And I truly believe that it was a relationship that we built with the community and with the fans."

The Women of Marvel panel at New York Comic Con, 2018.

Leah remembered the panel she had been so anxious about starting, and the moment she felt *it*, the same "it" we all felt the first time we clicked into this community. "I don't remember what the question was," she said. "All I remember is listening to Margie [Stohl] explain the importance of this space and why it exists. And just, my eyes getting big and getting racked with chills because I realized, 'Oh God, yeah, she . . . she's right.'"

"Kelly Sue used to say that she was doing this work so her daughter wouldn't have to," said Jeanine Schaefer. "My daughter was there for my very last Women of Marvel panel, at New York Comic Con in 2014. She was nine months old, and dressed up like America Chavez, sitting in my mother's lap. Kelly Sue literally gave my mother her chair from the stage because it was standing room only by that point. It's something I think about a lot, that my daughter got to experience that. Like maybe I helped do something good here."

272 / SUPER VISIBLE

"These spaces are important because it shows us how many of us there are, and we carve out space for each other to . . . to tell these stories and to exist like this," Leah said. "But it's less about us and more about who's witnessing it. We do this because nobody is going to do it for us. And if we don't do this for ourselves and for each other, we will not be recognized, because our accomplishments are not held in the same regard because we are women. We do this for each other because no one else does. And I just sat there like, 'Yes, I get it now. I get it.'"

"A FEW years after we started the panels, in 2013 or 2014, Jeanine and I were talking about continuing the conversation as a podcast," said Sana Amanat. "I'd look forward to it every year, as each time the women in the audience would be so engaged. So we approached [VP for the Marvel Unscripted Group] John Cerilli and [VP and creative executive for Marvel New Media] Ryan Penagos with the idea, which is when they connected us to Judy [Stephens], and Adri [Cowan, executive director for Marvel Social Media]. We put two and two together, drafted a few ideas, and recorded our first podcast."

Launched on June 20, 2014, with a logo designed by Irene Lee, a prominent and indispensable production artist and designer in the Bullpen at the time, who has since gone on to create the character Lil' Deadpool, among her

KELLY SUE USED TO SAY THAT SHE WAS DOING THIS WORK SO HER DAUGHTER WOULDN'T HAVE TO.

original work, the podcast had four cohosts: Judy Stephens, Sana Amanat, Jeanine Schaefer, and Adri Cowan, and the women's vision for the project was that they wanted to stand out from the pack of other comics podcasts.

"When we started the podcast," Judy said, "we wanted to have more of a conversational show."

"Yes, conversational!" said Sana. "We tried to do different things than the other podcasts Marvel had. In the beginning, we'd just talk about highlighting women in the industry and the content that we have. With the success of *Captain Marvel*, it had proven there was a market, and the content featuring female characters and creators was growing."

But soon they wanted to expand, and they felt there was a place for a podcast that talked about Marvel—and comics in general—as women, not necessarily just about women. They had received feedback from fans of all genders that simply hearing a woman's point of view on comics, supported by the company itself, was revolutionary on its own.

"It came from a real place of us wanting to share the experience and energy that we had at these panels, and by the way, we were people that felt like we did not belong in this community. We not only embraced the community and embraced this content that we weren't necessarily traditionally allowed to be in, but the community eventually embraced us."

As the years went by and the reach of the podcast and the panels went further than anyone would have thought, the format was revised to prioritize intersectionality. Highlighting people of color, the queer community, and folks of all genders is truly revolutionary in the world of mainstream comics, and who better to take it on than those very people who were already working behind the scenes at one of the most popular entertainment companies in the world?

In 2016, the podcast introduced a segment called "Voices of Marvel," for which they interviewed bestselling author Ta-Nehisi Coates about his run on *Black Panther*. Two years later, that segment would go on to spin off its own podcast, *Marvel's Voices*, hosted by Angélique Roché, who would become a permanent host of the *Women of Marvel*. For Stonewall 50 and World Pride in 2019, the podcast had on as guests *X-Men* writers Vita Ayala, Tini Howard, and Leah Williams.

In 2019, the Women of Marvel panel celebrated the two hundredth

The evolution of the Women of Marvel logo throughout the years, including 2010, 2018, and 2022.

TOP: Frequent guest and friend Margaret Stohl with Judy and Sana after a *Women of Marvel* podcast recording. BOTTOM: The Women of Marvel panelists at San Diego Comic-Con 2022.

episode of the *Women of Marvel* podcast, under the guidance of Ellie Pyle, former executive director of audio content, who cut her teeth in the Spider-Man office at Marvel editorial and was able to bring the Women of Marvel baton across the country to the West Coast, where it flourished in new media, and it hasn't stopped there.

"What I always knew about the show and [its] potential was that everyone's story has power," says Angélique. "Creatives and creators, whether or not they want to admit it or not, are impacted by their own personal stories. How they grew up, their traditions, the way they see the world, the perspectives that develop, and whether they want to tell it from that perspective or if they want to reinvent what the world should look like or could look like. The possibilities are endless, but inherently unique.

"That's what it was always for me. What *Women of Marvel* is about, and what we wanted *Marvel's Voices* to be about, too. It gives our guests who are newer to the industry a platform to speak from, a place for them to tell their stories.

"And at the end of the day, you never know what's going to inspire another person."

IN 2022, the first year San Diego Comic-Con was back in person after two years of Comic-Con@Home during the Covid-19 pandemic lockdown, the Women of Marvel panel returned to where it started in 2008 . . . room 6A, a room with a capacity of almost 1,100.

Angélique Roché moderated, with panelists Lauren Bisom (Marvel senior editor), Nic Stone (writer of *Shuri: A Black Panther Novel*), Rebecca Roanhorse (writer of *Phoenix Song: Echo*), and Marvel Entertainment VP of marketing Jessica Malloy. It felt like the first time things were returning to normal, as a packed room brought the same raucous joy it always had to the panel . . . and a much-needed sense of connection.

"Creation," said Nic, when the panel was asked how to combat the loss of ground women and other marginalized groups who have suffered politically and socially that past year. "It's up to everyone in this room to create hope."

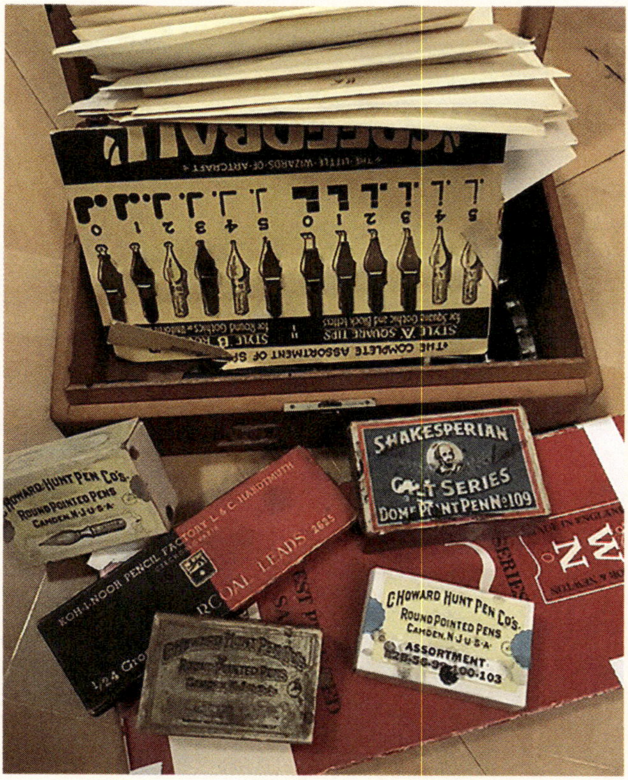
SHAKESPERIAN
SERIES
C.HOWARD HUNT PEN CO'S.
ROUND POINTED PENS
CAMDEN, N.J. U.S.A.
ASSORTMENT
KOH-I-NOOR PENCIL FACTORY

ORAL HISTORY

ORIGINS

In those first years of the Women of Marvel panel, there were always two standard questions to get the ball rolling: the first was "How did you start reading comics?" and the second was "How did you break into comics?"

"It started as a way to break the ice," said Jeanine Schaefer. "We wanted to demystify the ways that women came to comics, banish the idea that women who liked comics were akin to unicorns—for the sake of every gender in the audience!" She laughed. "Also, we weren't sure anyone would actually ask any decent questions or what the audience would be like, so we wanted to make sure we were ready to vamp a little."

After a few years, there were so many women on the panel that they started to skip those questions and go straight to a Q&A. But there is something to the idea of demonstrating that we all start our journey as comics fans—and as Marvel fans—in the same ways. No, women are not a monolith, but comics fans are all, deep down, cut from the same cloth, no matter your gender.

So: *How did you start reading comics?*

JEAN THOMAS: Oh, not super heroes. The things that I grew up reading were the newspaper comic strips, and I remember my dad reading me *Prince Valiant*.

JEANINE SCHAEFER: My very first sequential comics was *Brenda Starr*, every day in the newspaper—yes, every day! The era where it was drawn by Ramona Fradon. I was obsessed with her.

JEAN THOMAS: And then, of course, *Mad* magazine. I love *Mad* magazine. I mean, from the time I was old enough to reach it off the shelf, I loved *Mad* magazine.

AMANDA CONNER: Yes, I did grow up reading comics. When I lost my first baby tooth, the tooth fairy gave me a *Mad* magazine and a nickel. That's my first memory of comic reading. Then, every time I would get sick, my mom and dad would buy me *Archie* comics.

NANCI DAKESIAN: Growing up, I was an *Archie* girl. At that time, they didn't list the names of the artists on the books, but I could tell the different styles of art. One of my favorite artists at *Archie*, who I got to actually work with later on, was Dan DeCarlo. I remember thinking that as a child, "Wow, I love this," and then as an adult, "I can't believe I'm working with this person now." It was really a nice treat for me to come full circle, actually be able to ink some of this stuff, and work with him directly and his sons.

EVE L. EWING: I started reading comics when I was five years old. I started, probably like many people, reading *Archie* comics. It's funny, the novelist Walter Mosley, a very famous Black novelist, said this thing once: Whenever you interview authors and you're like, who were your early influences? They're always "T. S. Eliot and Toni Morrison." He's like, everybody lies. Because if you're telling the truth, people would say, "I grew up reading Nancy Drew and the Hardy Boys. Because that's what people read!" And so I

280 / SUPER VISIBLE

actually feel similarly about comics, because as women in any kind of nerd culture, we're always asked to prove that we really know things and that we really belong. And so it's only more recently that I can kind of come out as an *Archie* fan.

My mom brought home my first *Archie* comic book. I was five, and she got it from the grocery store rack.

PREETI CHHIBBER: So I grew up on *Archie* comics. My parents are immigrants from India. And my mom really loved *Archie* comics, so she would always have them in the house. So, then, I would always read them. It was just this really weird part of Americana that infiltrated our very Indian immigrant household.

ROXANE GAY: I found *Archie* in the grocery store at the cash register. I loved reading, and when I would wait for my mom to finish with groceries, I would just pick up a comic, read it, and she would let me get them.

I just loved the interpersonal dramas between Archie, Veronica, Betty, and Jughead. And the town of Riverdale, it was all really quite wholesome.

There were a lot of little melodramas, but they were always really good-hearted. And I mean, they're really just good, fun stories.

EVE L. EWING: It actually taught me a few really important things. Number one was that *Archie* had this recurring cast of characters. The idea that there's an ensemble of people that comes back, and that there's the continuity, which is a little iffy— that's something that makes comics different from other forms of pop culture that I at that point had previously consumed. . . . And another thing that was interesting is they would reprint strips adjacent to each other, some that were clearly from all different eras. I could tell the different art styles. And so as a kindergartner, this [was] a very interesting lesson.

ROXANE GAY: Looking back, what the hell was I so obsessed with? But at the time, I just thought that it was a lot of fun.

PREETI CHHIBBER: It never even occurred to me as being a strange thing until I was an adult and thinking back to it. I was writing something for Book Riot and realized, "Why did we have so many *Archie* comics in this household?"

Because it was a combination of *Archie* and then these Indian folklore-slash-religious mythology comics that told various stories from our culture and our religion. And so it was this bizarre mix of visual storytelling, but two very drastically different stories.

MING-NA WEN: I always loved comics, but the [ones] I was reading actually were a lot of Chinese comics when I was younger. Then that led into *Archie*, *Richie Rich*, *Peanuts*, and, of course, the Sunday comics. That was the first thing I always went to—the Sunday comics.

BOBBIE CHASE: Growing up, I read comics. I was aware of super hero comics, but I didn't necessarily read them. My brother and I would walk to our local drugstore in the summertime to buy comics. My favorites were *Archie* and *Richie Rich*.

LINDA FITE: Nothing was more pleasurable on a hot summer day than walking down to the drugstore near my grandmother's house and buying an ice cream or a Popsicle and a couple of comics, which were, like, a dime when I was a little kid.

IRENE VARTANOFF: One night, my father wanted cigars. We lived in the suburbs. My father did not drive. My mother did, which was unusual for her generation. She had started driving at the age of fourteen before they had driver's licenses in Illinois.

And she had her own car, and she taught a lot of girls how to drive.

So, okay, he wanted cigars. It was the evening, he's an old-fashioned kind of man. "Margaret, go get cigars. You. Go with your mother." Okay. I was eleven, I guess. Maybe twelve. The cigar store was only, I mean, we're in a suburb. There's nothing. It was maybe three miles from the house. I don't know. It wasn't a long trip.

While Mother was getting the cigars, I wandered around the little pharmacy, and I saw these comic books. And I guess my mother felt sorry for me because I asked her to buy these two comics for me. One was *Batman*, one was *Jimmy Olsen*.

And she did. So began an addiction.

IMAN VELLANI: My high school is right next to a comic book store, Hero's World. Every month, my parents gave me my allowance, and I would spend it on old sixties and seventies runs of *Iron Man* and Marvel comics.

VITA AYALA: So I grew up in New York City. I was born here, bred here, [raised by] a single mom. And so whenever she would go down to the bodega, she would take us with her. And back then, there was a spinner rack.

The spinner rack is almost like in a video game, where you choose your weapon. You've made your choice, you've chosen your personality. So on the spinner rack, I remember there were two comics that caught my eye immediately.

One of them was *X-Men*, and Storm and Bishop were on the cover. And I was like, "Yep, I would like that," and the other one was a *Wonder Woman* issue. I misidentified her as Puerto Rican, and I thought, "Oh, look at all the Brown people. I'll take those," even as a little kid.

And I'm Black and Puerto Rican myself. So I saw this woman who, to me, was clearly Puerto Rican. And we didn't really have a ton of money for extra stuff, but my mom said if it's books or reading, "Sure. You can have that."

JENNY LEE: In the eighties, when I grew up, my older brother and I would go down to the corner sweetshop with our allowance money. And there was a spinner rack, where he would buy comics, and I would spend all my money on candy. But after he read his books, I would get to read them.

He was mostly a Marvel kid. He read a lot of *Batman*, but also was really into *Spider-Man*. I remember reading a lot of *Cloak and Dagger*, *Moon Knight*, and, of course, *X-Men*. As things progressed in the eighties, and when Frank Miller did his run on *Elektra*, my brother was still buying comics. As a little girl growing up, I had gravitated toward female characters. But Elektra was not a character who was feminine in any of the traditional ways. She was not in pink—she was in blood red. She was a ninja. I was just floored by how mysterious, powerful, and completely unapologetic she was. I still remember when he came home with *Elektra Lives Again*—that oversized hardcover with the white dust jacket. That book really left an impression on me both in the elliptical storytelling and the art.

IRENE VARTANOFF: I don't recall ever seeing a comic book until a friend of my older brother brought one . . . when he came over to play with him. My brother was four years older than I am.

It was an issue of *Detective Comics*. I went to play with a girl in either fifth or sixth grade who had a pile of comics, just one afternoon, and I read a *Superman* comic [*Action Comics* #235, December 1957, "The Super-Prisoner of Amazon Island"].

TINI HOWARD: My opinion about comics being for boys changed while I was still in college, actually. It was my senior year, and I started rooming with a woman named Sandy Platycocyk.

I'm under the opinion that super hero stuff in general, and comics as a medium, is just boy stuff. I am not their target demographic. It is not made for me.

And Sandy starts going into this thing where she's describing Batman lore to me—she's talking to me about what the comics are like. And [I said], "That's insane. I didn't know any of that! That's crazy!"

She's putting nuance back into this mythology that I thought was solely about nipple suits and Catwoman's ass.

And fast-forward a few months later, we're thick as thieves, BFFs, and moving in together. I'm seeing these heavy boxes of trade paperbacks and omnibuses get unloaded for the very first time. "Wow, okay. I guess comics aren't for boys?"

CAROLE SEULING: First of all, I read comic books in the 1940s. In fact, that's how I learned how to read.

VITA AYALA: So I didn't learn to properly read until I was ten years old. I learned a little late, mostly because I can run my mouth. And so people assumed I knew what I was talking about and that I could read, which is great.

But I had already been into comics by then because they had pictures in them.

FRANÇOISE MOULY: I never saw any super hero comics, and I had no idea that [they] existed until I came to the US. When I arrived in New York in 1974, I couldn't speak English especially well. I sought out comics because I felt [they] would give me an experience of the language as it is spoken and . . . used, and a good point of entry into the culture. Through friends, I was enlightened to underground comix, such as *Arcade*, which was edited by Art Spiegelman and Bill Griffith. I was fascinated by Art's work specifically, and I got to meet him.

MING-NA WEN: I was learning English at the time, too, so that had something to do with it. Putting pictures to words. And I love art, I love drawing. So it was just a natural progression, something that I really liked, and then, of course, cartoons.

Megan Bradner at the premiere for Marvel's *Runaways* on Hulu.

MARGUERITE BENNETT: My gateway drug was *Batman: The Animated Series*. It came out when I was five years old, and I radically misunderstood what the whole premise was. I thought that Batman was a bad guy who felt really bad about the fact that he was a bad guy and now was turning in all of his ex-bad guy friends.

MEGAN BRADNER: I watched soap operas as a kid, and I watched the *X-Men* animated cartoon. It was a full soap opera. I loved the Wolverine/Scott/Jean triangle, and Rogue and Gambit—I loved all of that stuff. I'd been exposed to some comics earlier.

My sisters read some of the DC stuff in the seventies, and so I had those as hand-me-downs, but the stories that really pulled me in and would forever alter the course of my life was that [*X-Men*] animated show really. Maybe it was an access thing, and the societal expectations the girls were reading . . . but that cartoon was delivered straight to you at a time when you had four networks or whatever.

JUDY STEPHENS: Though an avid reader of the Sunday funnies and *Calvin and Hobbes*, it was Saturday morning cartoons that first introduced me to super heroes. The TV was in the basement, so I'd rush downstairs, sitting down on the pink carpet, and catch up on the latest episode of the *X-Men: The Animated Series*, or the Distinguished Competition.

I remember being enthralled by the countless female characters on-screen, and they weren't just sidekicks, but powerful, front-leading heroes. Or even villains!

NIA DACOSTA: When I was young, one of my uncles lived in my grandma's basement. He had all these Spider-Man and Fantastic Four tapes and comics. That was when I first got into Spider-Man, and really loved him. And then I discovered the X-Men, which of course, it's hard to explain or overestimate how important X-Men is for so many kids my age.

The X-Men show that everyone can find their place.

You're all welcome here, no matter who you are or how you are, how you feel about yourself.

Also, Storm was my favorite hero. It wasn't just that she was a Black woman, but that she was so cool being able to control the weather and fly. So amazing.

KATE HERRON: Yeah, honestly I love fantasy, and I loved big genre with heart. And I think that's something we've seen Marvel do so well.

X-Men was definitely my gateway. I think for me, I was just so wrapped up in the cartoon and I loved it. But I think I loved that they were outsiders, but that's what made them strong. And I always felt a bit like that, I suppose, growing up. So that really connected to me.

I remember somehow getting bleach and dying one of my doll's hair to make her look like Storm.

NIC STONE: My introduction to Marvel happened through after-school cartoons. I was super into Spider-Man and X-Men. And part of the reason I was into X-Men is because Storm did actually exist when I was a kid.

She was everything that I wanted to be as this powerful Brown-skinned woman who could control the weather.

And what you were saying earlier, about this idea of representation and not knowing you can be a thing because you don't see it—I got that coming from two directions because I am Black and female.

So not only did I not see Black characters, that compounded with not seeing female characters. I had this weird, gray space, this liminal space that I feel like I existed in, from birth through seventeen or eighteen, when I started reading Alice Walker.

I remember stuff in school that was required reading, and if there was a Black character, that character was male. And that character usually was in some kind of position where they did not get to be the hero of the story.

So I would always circle back to this idea of Storm as this woman who could do basically anything. And she kicked a lot of ass, and people were terrified of her.

And I liked that.

I liked the respect that that particular character seemed to receive.

LEAH WILLIAMS: I loved [*X-Men: The Animated Series*]. The show was definitely a formative part of my queer experience, and I hold it in such dear regard, both [that] and also *X-Men: Evolution*, and the cartoons that came after, too. Because once you fall in love with the character, you are going to follow them in [whatever] else they appear.

G. WILLOW WILSON: I'm trying to think of the first comic book I actually read. I can't remember, but in my head, I had a digest of some Chris Claremont-era *X-Men*. I was huge into the *X-Men* animated series on Fox Kids; that was, of course, so central to the childhoods of so many eighties and nineties kids. [*Laughs.*] That was sort of my jumping-off point. [Comics were] definitely part of my childhood, but I didn't get into comics as a community and as a platform for telling more and more varied types of stories until I was a teenager and got super into the British Invasion-era Vertigo. I ate that stuff up [*Laughs*], and that was the point, I think, at which I started thinking about telling stories in addition to reading them.

JEANINE SCHAEFER: The first super hero comic I ever bought was *Uncanny X-Men* #274. With Magneto and Rogue in the Savage Land, and Ka-Zar was there. I had no idea what was going on, but I loved it, and I kept buying random issues to try to piece it all together— Toys "R" Us used to sell these blind-bag multipacks. I ended up back in the Claremont stuff, because I recognized the storylines from the cartoon, which I never missed.

ORIGINS / 289

SOPHIA DI MARTINO: Before being cast [in *Loki*], I had a basic awareness of super heroes and Marvel.

For me, as a kid, Marvel and other comics did seem to be more geared toward boys, though I do remember loving She-Ra. Growing up in England in the 1980s, she was the closest to a female super hero that I had.

When I got a little bit older, I did read other comics that had more female characters, such as *Tank Girl* and the *Fables* series.

RAINBOW ROWELL: Yeah, I started reading when I was young—my dad read a lot of comics. And so he would buy [them] for me, but he definitely had ideas about what were kids' comics and what were girls' comics. And so I would read a lot of *Richie Rich* and *Casper the Friendly Ghost* . . . He read Marvel and *Heavy Metal*, so adult comics. I was really fascinated with super heroes for as long as I can remember. The television shows, *Super Friends* or the *Spider-Man* cartoon; just anything super heroes, I was really into. But as I got older, my dad really thought comics were for boys. Super hero comics. So he actually had comics that he saved for my brother.

AMANDA CONNER: My mother was a Wonder Woman fan when she was little, and my dad actually wanted to be a comic book artist when he was growing up. Unfortunately, like many kids in the fifties, his parents discouraged him from it—which is sad, because I think he would have been really good. His parents ended up telling him to get a "real job," so he went into advertising. Both my dad and mom are happy that I'm doing comics.

EVE L. EWING: My father is a cartoonist, and when I was a child, he had a syndicated weekly cartoon strip in our local paper. Actually, my parents met because my dad drew . . . a satirical comic book about Ronald Reagan. He was selling it at the Greyhound bus station for a dollar. And that's how he met my mom, because she bought [it] from him . . . and it was her first time taking the

Greyhound bus. So comics are actually part of my literal origin story, because my parents met over a comic book.

SAM MAGGS: Yeah. Growing up, my dad was a big comic book fan. He read Silver Age comics when he was a kid, and his favorite was always *Spider-Man*.

So I [had] a household that was really steeped in nerd culture, and I guess instead of rebelling and getting into football, I just went with it.

And before I was born, my dad had gotten my mom into a lot of nerd stuff. They're big *Star Wars* and *Star Trek* fans. So they just shared the things that they loved with me and never really made a big deal about me being a girl. Which is when I started to discover that it was difficult to find other girls to talk [with] about this stuff. Because girls don't often feel safe or able to talk about it.

I had thought, "Oh, this sucks."

I just didn't know. Because growing up, it was totally normal for my parents to take me out of school to go see *The Phantom Menace*.

That was just the thing that we would do.

TINI HOWARD: I have always been drawn to comics as a medium, from a really young kid, even reading newspaper comics. My dad wasn't really a super hero comic guy, but he always had a lot of collections of newspaper comics.

He had graphic novels like *The Cartoon History of the Universe* by Larry Gonik, which is the first graphic novel I ever fell in love with. And I still love it. I just reread it over the pandemic.

So he had a lot of really weird, interesting graphic novels. And I was really drawn to the medium.

JUDY STEPHENS: It was in high school that I was introduced to manga and graphic novels. But once I moved to NYC for college, and got

The women of Marvel celebrating the Women of Marvel's tenth anniversary at San Diego Comic-Con in 2019.

that first internship at Marvel, it would be my boss, Peter Olson, who would help me find my love for super hero comics. First with the Wildstorm Universe and Authority series, and then later *The Ultimates* and the *New X-Men*.

LINDA FITE: I read comics all along, then stopped, and when I was in college, I went down to Raleigh, North Carolina. And there was this cool dude who ran a place called the Sidewalk Cafe. Very ahead of his time . . . a lot of hippies. And he was into Marvel Comics. It was just the beginning, when Stan was starting to get very literary on one level and also lots of personality stuff.

So I started reading Marvel Comics, and I went into Lynchburg to the newsstand and bought [them]. I did that for about two years, just buying Marvel Comics.

IMAN VELLANI: I really wasn't into it till seventh grade. Something awoke inside of me, and I became super obsessed with the movies.

And I basically grew up with Marvel, as I was born in 2002, and remember when *Iron Man* came out in 2008. Later when I got to high school, that obsession just heightened.

I was the kid who did every single project I could on the MCU and watched the movies frame by frame to find all the Easter eggs and make theory boards. I would do my nails with a character on each nail.

And yeah, I have an Iron Man shrine. It's still a work in progress.

PART FIVE
THE WORLD OUTSIDE OUR WINDOWS

THE MARVEL UNIVERSE IS OUR UNIVERSE

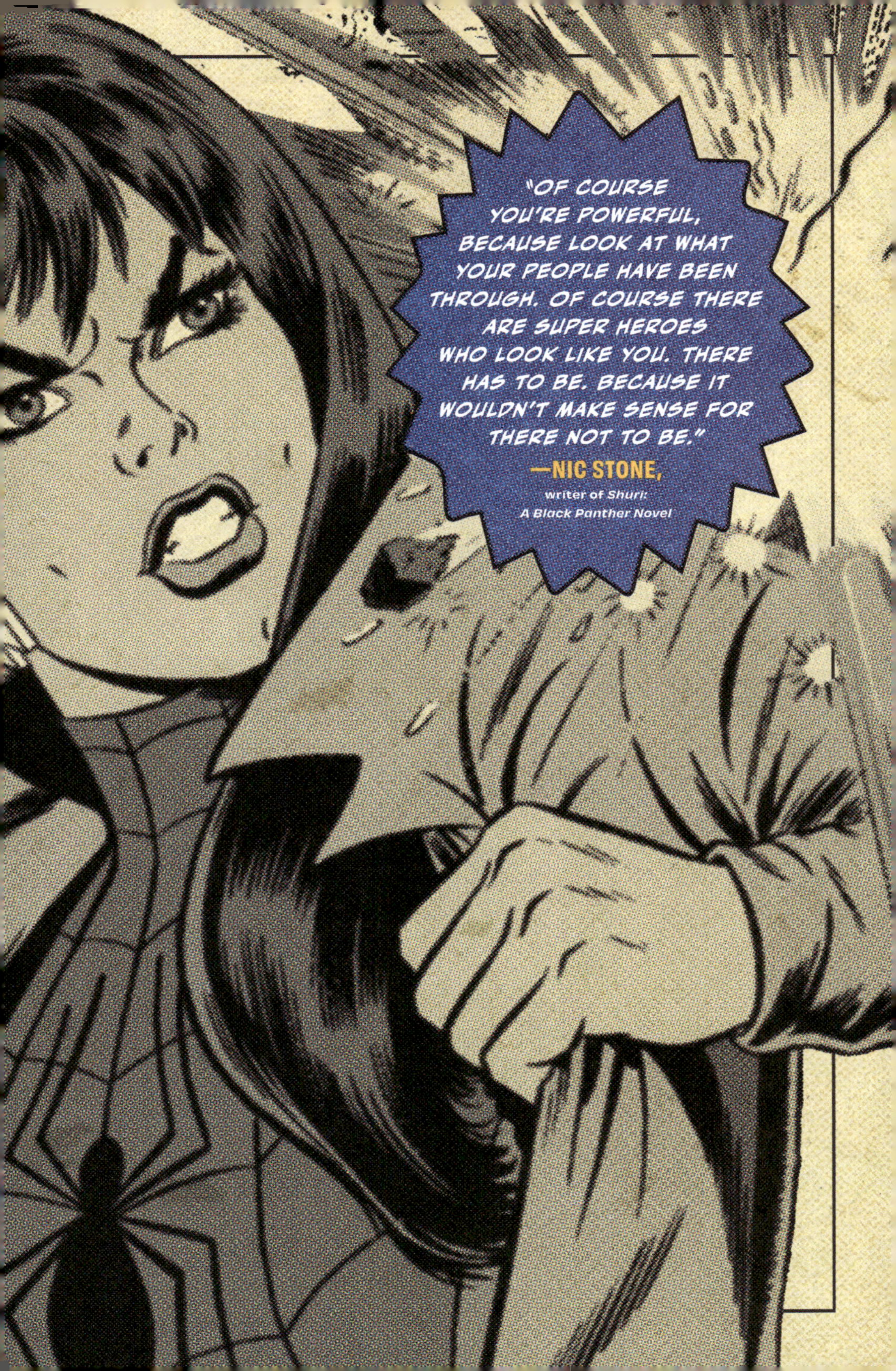
"OF COURSE YOU'RE POWERFUL, BECAUSE LOOK AT WHAT YOUR PEOPLE HAVE BEEN THROUGH. OF COURSE THERE ARE SUPER HEROES WHO LOOK LIKE YOU. THERE HAS TO BE. BECAUSE IT WOULDN'T MAKE SENSE FOR THERE NOT TO BE."
—NIC STONE,
writer of *Shuri: A Black Panther Novel*

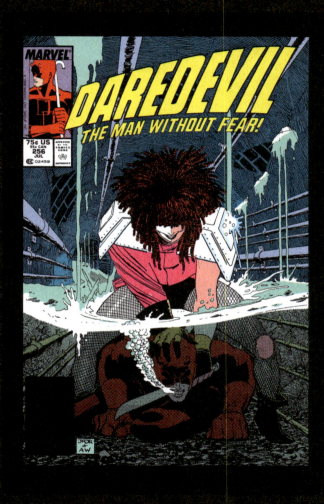

Typhoid Mary on the cover of *Daredevil* #256, 1988, cover art by John Romita Jr.

CHAPTER TWELVE

KNIGHTS, NOT DAMSELS

Marvel Knights, Feminist
Manifestos, and Finding
Catharsis Through Empowerment

Marvel's Typhoid Mary, the *Daredevil* villain created by Annie Nocenti and John Romita Jr. in 1988, was named after Mary Mallon, the first known asymptomatic carrier of typhoid in the United States during the early 1900s, who unknowingly infected over a hundred people with typhoid fever and was subsequently kept in solitary confinement for thirty years. Alternately Matt Murdock's lover and mortal enemy, Typhoid Mary is the answer to the question of what would happen if we turned the camera lens and followed the woman who was hurt in the process of advancing the male hero's story.

"Typhoid Mary certainly was my attempt at looking at the female stereotypes in comics," said Annie. "And even though she was, to a certain degree, satirical . . . because I saw that in comics men seemed to view women as 'she's the Virgin,' 'she's the Madonna,' 'she's the whore,' 'she's the feminist.' Typhoid had all those personalities, but they were very tongue-in-cheek."

It's analogous to the sort of compartmentalization we see marginalized groups doing on a regular basis in order to function day-to-day, the sort that, when given the opportunity, women will examine in the female characters on the page.

Jenny Lee had similar things to say about Elektra, probably one of the most historically misunderstood and divisive female characters in comics. Like Typhoid Mary, Elektra is Daredevil's sometimes lover, sometimes enemy, her fate tied to his, to both the betterment and detriment of her as an autonomous character. "I looked at Elektra and [thought,] she's a woman, and she was traumatized by seeing her father killed," said Jenny. "What kind of compartmentalization has she had to do in order to keep moving forward and to live with that? And then to become a killer herself?"

"I love Daredevil, Matt Murdock," said Annie. "He's a complicated guy, but [could be] sexist. I folded that into Typhoid Mary, to create a female villain who was empowered and unempowered at the same time."

It's a question many women interviewed for this book have asked themselves about this industry: Why am I doing this? The question lingers as Jen Grünwald describes having to insist she did read and would keep reading *X-Men* comics, even if she was a girl; as Sana Amanat remembers struggling with burnout after her experience at Virgin Comics and really weighing the cost of continuing; as writer Kelly Sue DeConnick gives interview after interview even in the face of repeated harassment.

"My heart was in this," said Irene Vartanoff, "and I could break my heart in this business because of it. Because it's human nature to clench to this thing, to make it part of you. To come into something that you care about is to leave yourself open to tremendous disillusionment."

"Sometimes it is difficult to see other people invited to the table," says Alitha E. Martinez. "But at the same time, it's also a testament to that—you were the first to walk in this door and challenge them. And now that [next] woman walked in easier because you did that. They can't say it's impossible, because they literally used to use that word. Now everything is possible.

"But, you know, the older I get, I don't want to labor and die in complete obscurity. Maybe in a few more years, let me get another decade or two under my belt. Maybe it would be lasting enough that they can't erase you, and I won't know about that. I'll be dead and gone. I don't care. But I definitely would not want to think that I spent my whole life, my whole childhood, everything that I ever thought or felt, dedicated to something that really didn't want me."

Christina Strain put it more bluntly: "Comics will never love you back."

The answer for many women is that they don't know how *not* to fight, and once you get inside, finding allies and working together to shut off the valve that is spewing toxic waste is the ultimate goal.

Sometimes literally.

"It was probably after hours, Marie and I sitting in the Bullpen talking, and we decided to write this story about Toxic Avenger's girlfriend [in 1992's *Toxic Crusaders #7*]," Annie Nocenti reminisced about her time working with Marie Severin. "We wanted to empower her, and so we came up with this

COMICS WILL NEVER LOVE YOU BACK.

story where she demanded to be the protagonist and the lead in the comic. . . . So she goes into her kitchen and she wants a super hero suit. And so she puts together an outfit based on some pots and pans. We're empowering Toxic's girlfriend, but we're not really taking her out of the kitchen because she's using her kitchen stuff to make her outfit. And we proceeded to have her be the super hero for one issue. . . ."

Elektra was also only supposed to be a super hero (or villain) for one issue, but the response to her as complicated and grounded spawned some of the most iconic books headlining a female character, including *Elektra and Wolverine: The Redeemer*, the first illustrated prose novel Marvel ever published, edited by Jenny Lee.

"That book was completely done outside of the conventional editorial system at Marvel. I remember when I would go to the editorial meetings, I was the only woman there, and one of the only people of color besides [editor in chief] Joe Quesada and [senior editor] Axel Alonso. I would always take a seat with my back to the wall. I felt I wasn't necessarily seen as part of editorial, because even though I was editing books, I was doing it completely in this splinter cell by myself."

Around the same time, another splinter cell was getting off the ground: Marvel Knights.

"Marvel Knights was run by women," says Joe Quesada, who, in 1998— two years before being named Marvel's editor in chief—was working exclusively for Event Comics, the independent comics company he cofounded with friend and inker Jimmy Palmiotti, when Marvel contracted with them to outsource some of their more mature titles. "It wasn't just [lead editor] Nanci [Dakesian], but also Kelly Lamy, who Nanci brought over from Archie. They were a two-person wrecking ball."

"Starting off at Archie Comics, I got a good grounding of what it was really like working in a male-dominated world," said Nanci. "Women were treated as if they were secondary, with no voice, and I fought [that] every step of the way. This was not something I was taught as a child, but it was definitely something that I learned there. I had to stick up for myself because nobody else would."

The overly simplified history of the imprint lists Joe and Jimmy as the overseers of the project, but anyone who was there at the time, including Joe, vehemently corrects the oversight. "As we were a Marvel imprint, we had to manage all the elements: trafficking, voucher, getting freelancers paid, scheduling, conventions, and more," said Joe. "We had to do all of this on our own, and with Jimmy and I feverishly working on *Daredevil*, Nanci and Kelly kept it all together. They edited every book under the imprint, and babysat a lot of our creators. There are many Nanci stories, as she was famous for always making deadlines. From driving down to Jae Lee's home to collect pages to locking Mark Texeira on the roof when he snuck out to avoid working. She kept the crew in line, which is why when Jimmy and I were hired by Marvel, we wanted Nanci to run the show."

This setting straight of the record is another theme we heard of from many women, who used their position as the current caretakers of these characters to inject agency back into their stories . . . or give it to them for the first time, as when Jenny reached out to Richard K. Morgan, the award-winning author of the cyberpunk noir *Altered Carbon*, regarding Black Widow. "This Natasha he pitched to me was older, out of the super hero game. It was this totally unapologetic hard-core feminist treatise," said Jenny.

That treatise was the Marvel Knights limited series *Black Widow: Homecoming*, with interiors by Goran Parlov and Bill Sienkiewicz. One scene stands out for Jenny the most: "In that first issue, there is this scene where Natasha takes down these two greasy truck drivers who are about to sexually assault this young woman. It's a double-page spread of her dispatching them as she drops her coffee cup outside a gas station. That scene was so memorable to me because it shows a woman being really comfortable with her own power and just being—and this is an incredibly feminine quality—really pragmatic about getting [stuff] done. And having no time and no interest and pity for men who don't show that for women. That was, for me, such an iconic moment with that character. I bought the original artwork for that spread from Bill; it's hanging in my office right now."

Sometimes the splinter cell is even further embedded, as it was with Hildy Mesnik and her self-described powerhouse team working on the Barbie line.

"It was a magical time in that working with these talented people was fabulous," said Hildy. "On the other side of it was that these were licensed products and I had to satisfy some tough licensors. And it also added a lot of time into the comic production, getting approvals from the licensors. Luckily Mattel rarely had any comments. They pretty much loved everything we did. We really pushed the envelope. I don't know if you're aware, but one of our philosophies was that girls can do anything. And we made sure that Barbie and her friends could do anything and go anywhere."

Barbara Slate was one of Hildy's writers, and she would spend her days touring around New York City to find a way to reflect the lived experiences of the women and girls who she met in the book. She told us a story about meeting a guitarist for a well-known band who asked if he could pitch a story, because his daughter would be excited. But when his pitch came in, he had Barbie as a backup singer. "I said Barbie is just not the backup—Barbie is the lead!" They argued, and she eventually won. A small win, but to the girls who would line up to see the Barbie creators at conventions, it was everything. "And the older women, when they come in," said Barbara, "they're practically in tears because that book was so important to them every month."

Canon is really interesting when it comes to women and diverse creators taking over the authenticity of a character. Because for all the women who historically have worked incredibly hard, they generally were not given the latitude to create a character. So it becomes re-creating it in a way.

When a woman is writing—or has agency of the performance of—a female character from a female point of view, some things become incredibly different.

Guardians of the Galaxy actor Zoe Saldaña holds that agency, that re-creation of how women have been allowed to be seen, as a crucial part of how

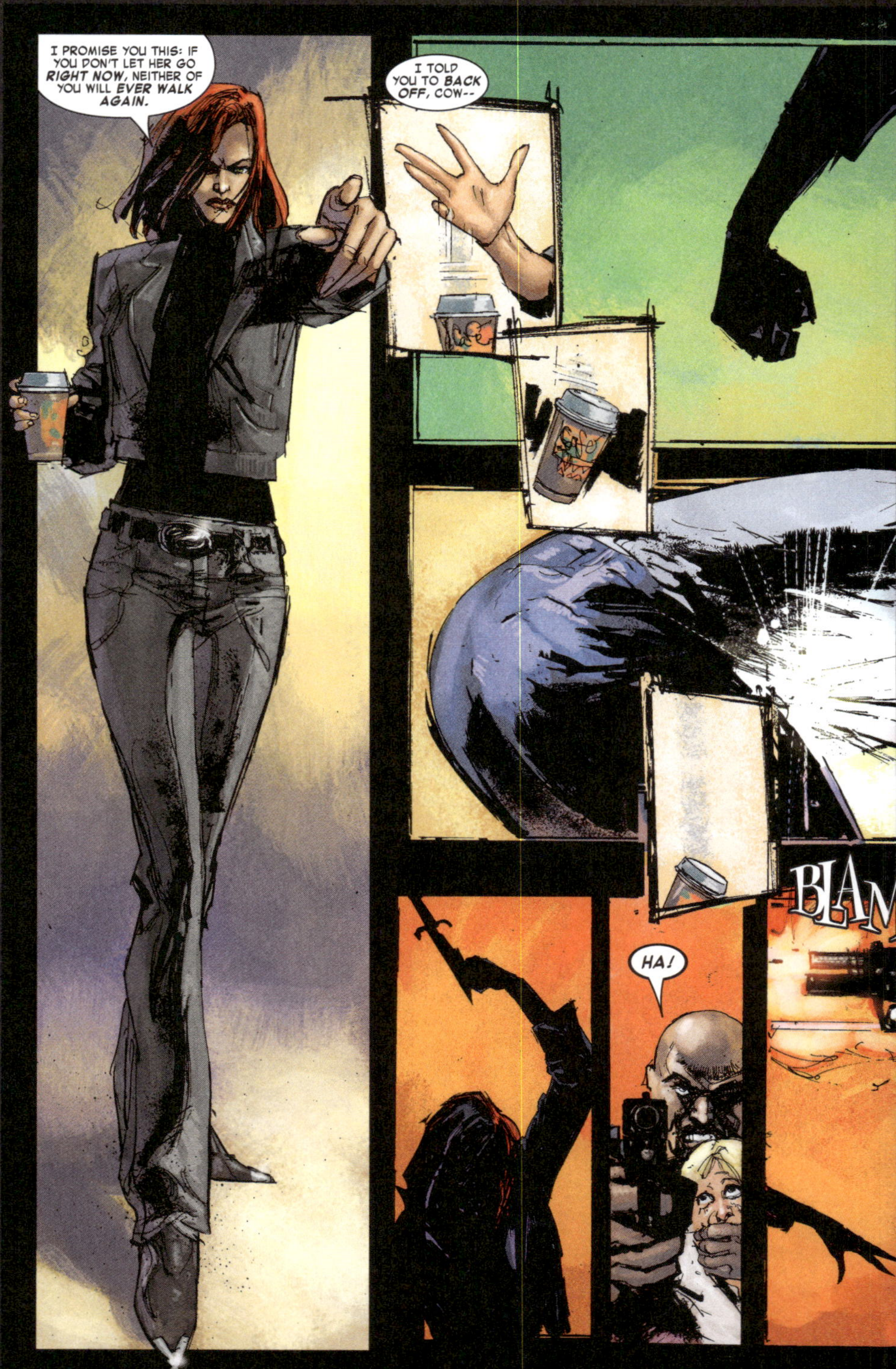

I PROMISE YOU THIS: IF YOU DON'T LET HER GO RIGHT NOW, NEITHER OF YOU WILL EVER WALK AGAIN.
I TOLD YOU TO BACK OFF, COW--
HA!

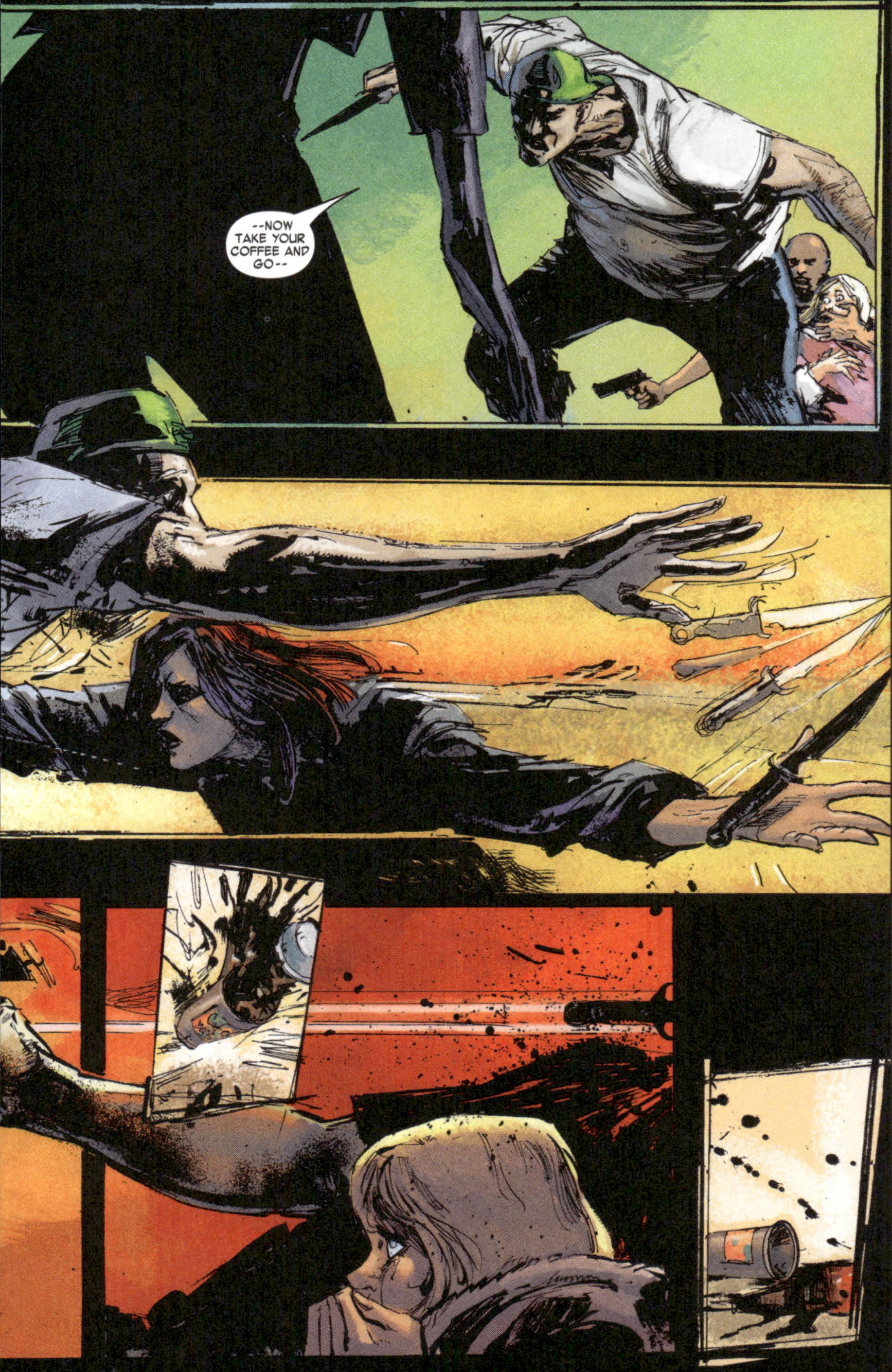
--NOW TAKE YOUR COFFEE AND GO--

Editor Hildy Mesnik and assistant editor Lia Pelosi star in 1994's *Barbie Fashion* #41, written, drawn, lettered, and colored by an all-star team of women.

NAME A WOMAN, [AND] YOU WILL GET A MAN TO YELL AT YOU ABOUT HER ON THE INTERNET.

---

she chooses roles. "When people go, 'You like to play these strong women,' I say, 'All my life I thought I was playing real women that carried their trauma and wore them on their sleeves. I'm carrying the pain that this person has.'"

"I heard, I think it's Geena Davis, say once that if you want to see women in crowds, in movies, you have to literally say, 'Half of the people in this crowd are women,' because otherwise there's this bias, always toward men, that if you say it's a room full of people, some people will think of that as a room full of men," said renowned YA author and *Runaways* writer Rainbow Rowell. "So I think of that a lot when I write, that if I want the crowds to be diverse, then I need to specifically say half of these people are women. And [*Runaways*] takes place in Los Angeles. So it's going to be racially diverse, too. . . . The scripts for *Runaways* were really explicit about what these kids looked like, especially the girls. That Molly was thirteen. And so what does a thirteen-year-old look like?"

When Leah Williams was hired at Marvel, she was almost shocked at the difference in the ways women and men, even online, interfaced with the characters, especially men who had only ever been exposed to mainstream fandom, having been the target audience for everything they liked for so long. "Especially when it comes to really complex characters like Betsy Braddock or Emma Frost or Jean Grey," she said. "Name a woman, [and] you will get a man to yell at you about her on the internet, because when I start talking about things, that makes them real and complex, flawed, but fleshed-out and developed characters, [and] it kind of takes away the fantasy that men have been projecting onto the lesser-developed version of this pretty girl character. It takes away the fantasy when you talk about the fact that Betsy Braddock has body image issues, and she has [for] her entire canon."

"That first comic I wrote was a ten-page *Star Trek* comic for IDW called 'Legacy,' and it was about the only female redshirt in *Star Trek: The Original Series*," said writer Sam Maggs. "I was able to give her a backstory. It was my first experience contributing to a canon of an IP that I was really passionate about, and so I felt it would be a good experience for me. And it was the first! My writing all has themes of women, [whether] teaming up, female friendships, strong women. From the start, that was what I wanted to write about, and that's what I write about in all my comics now. Teams of women/squads are really important to me because I only ever saw that in *Sailor Moon*, and that's all I want to see now. Or just queer characters. I didn't come out till super late because I never saw queer characters in media, so I didn't know what that was. And if I had, maybe that would have made my life very different."

"I think comic fans, men specifically, are learning that when female characters get commended into the hands of women, women are going to put their experiences in there in ways that will make them unfamiliar to men," said Tini Howard, *Excalibur* and *Knights of X* writer. "And I think the same can absolutely be said of Black characters, of queer characters, of disabled characters. If you are creating a character in a shared world that has something about them that you want to represent on the page, but maybe aren't personally, isn't part of your life personally, you have to accept that when other people get a hold of that, they're going to explore that."

"I always assume a female readership," said Kelly Sue DeConnick. "I write for a woman reader. And the same way that there have been a million comics that were written assuming a male audience that I was welcome to read, too, I assume a female readership, but welcome anyone who may be interested."

She told us a story about a now-famous passage from *Captain Marvel #1*, and the first time she realized that they were making headway. "I had written this line 'Have you ever seen a little girl run so fast she falls down?' And I got a note back saying could we change it to '"Have you ever seen a little kid run so fast they fall?" We don't want to alienate the male reader.'

"And I'm like, 'Here we go!' I'm cracking my knuckles, pushing my sleeves up, we're going to throw down, right? I'm ready to quit the book over this, take my name off it and everything . . . and I say, 'No. I have every faith the male reader can cross identify,' and they were just like, 'Okay, cool—stet.'

"Have you ever seen a little girl run so fast she falls down?" From *Captain Marvel* #1, written by Kelly Sue DeConnick, art by David López.

"And that was it! I thought this was going to be this big fight, and I gently pushed back and they were like, 'Oh, okay.'"

It's the rejection of the idea that one subsection of the audience's comfort should be prioritized over another that has driven other creators like author and host of the podcast *History of Marvel: Black Panther*, Nic Stone. "I never have felt comfortable, getting to lean into the resilience I've had to exhibit just as a Black woman walking around in this super [messed-up] world. If I can survive some of the [stuff] that I've been through, I can definitely write a super hero. I remember coming to the point where I realized that being descended from slavery was not a shameful thing. There's this ability to frame history in a way where somebody can look me in my face and go, 'You should just get over slavery. It happened a long time ago.' And it took me a while to realize that, wait a minute, if I'm here, that means the people who were brought over here against their will survived long enough to procreate, and then they survived, and then they survived, and then they survived.

"So now I get to do things that those people who were picking cotton—I literally have ancestors who picked cotton and tobacco in fields here in Georgia—they managed to survive. And now I get to be beyond their wildest dreams."

"For me, the reason why we put up with all this is because there's nowhere else to do this kind of creative work," says MacKenzie Cadenhead. "There's just not anything compared to comics for me because nothing is as collaborative."

She grinned. "One last story to leave you with: One of my passion projects are these *Marvel Adventures* chapter books, because I really wanted quality young reader content. At the time, I was pregnant with my third child. So the day we got the composite for the book, I was in the hospital, as I had gone into preterm labor at twenty-seven weeks. And my cowriter, Sean [Ryan], was in Ireland for his wedding. While I'm sitting there hooked up to all these machines, going through the composite, I discovered that an entire chapter was missing. As none of our editors could find it, I pulled up my laptop and began sending notes. I decided, 'I care so much about this particular project that I'll manage it while trying to keep a baby in.' And I would have done that with any project. 'This is it. This is my reality.' I don't know if it's a partial or huge victory, or 'Well, this is what we do.' To me, it's sort of all those things at once."

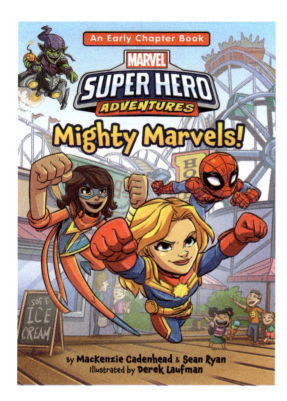

The cover of *Marvel Super Hero Adventures: Mighty Marvels!*, written by MacKenzie Cadenhead and Sean Ryan, illustrated by Derek Laufman.

That reality is where so many women have found themselves—both literally and figuratively.

"I just completely fell in love with the type of films that Marvel was doing," said Marvel executive producer Trinh Tran. "I was like, 'You know what? I want to stay. This is amazing. This group of people is amazing to work with. How can I leave this place?' Since then, I've seen the growth of the company, how we've all grown individually and together. I think that's been one of the most rewarding things. To be here to witness what we've gone through."

"I can give you a million reasons why I should, but I want you to just give me one where I shouldn't," said Zoe Saldaña. "There's no reason why I shouldn't. Because I want to. Because I like it. Because it's a challenge. Because I'm curious. Because I mean, everything. Every shade of the rainbow of reasons.

"Why shouldn't I do anything?"

ORAL HISTORY

REIGN OF X

The editorial offices of the X-Men line of books, or the X-Office, as it's affectionately known inside the House of Ideas, have been pushing boundaries since its inception in 1963, when they served as an allegory for the civil rights movement. In the sixty years since, they've continued to serve as parables for marginalized communities, a mirror held up so underrepresented groups could see themselves, giving us many Marvel—and comics—firsts.

Thunderbird was the first Apache super hero, in 1975. Mutant Jessie Drake was Marvel's first openly transgender character, debuting in 1994. Canadian mutant Northstar became Marvel's first openly gay super hero when he came out in 1991, in *Alpha Flight* #102. He would go on to another milestone in 2012 when he married his longtime boyfriend in *Astonishing X-Men* #51, marking the first such occasion in Marvel's history. In 2009, Marvel published its first on-panel same-sex kiss between X-Force team members Shatterstar and Rictor, after years of "will they/won't they" subtext.

There are three creators at the heart of that office who take their task of carrying that legacy into the next chapter very seriously, pushing boundaries and welcoming new fans into the X-Men fold: *Reign of X* writers Vita Ayala, Tini Howard, and Leah Williams.

"Leah and Vita and I are very close friends," said Tini. "And we have Judy [Stephens] to thank for a lot of that because she saw in us this little coalition forming, and invited us on the [*Women of Marvel*] podcast for Pride Month, which was super exciting. And it was also a trip to Marvel that we all got to do together. So we formed this little squad. And literally one of the best things about it is that we support each other in the room."

VITA AYALA: I would not learn until I was, like, sixteen that Wonder Woman was not Puerto Rican, which is heartbreaking. She just looked like one of my cousins. And I think proximity to the X-Men, who had two Black people on the cover, I was like, "Comics are Brown people like us." And she's from an island of very powerful women.

To me, comics were just predominantly women and a lot of Brown people. Growing up, being where I'm from, I was surrounded by, like, 95 percent BIPOC people. And I think that really shaped my idea of what could be. They were a place where I could exist in the same way that I saw on TV, as I'm a big TV fan, sci-fi, just anything fantasy, and my mom's a big *Star Trek* fan. Clearly there are women and Brown people and even queer people all over that.

So we have a place there.

TINI HOWARD: I started going to the library to look for books, because I was a young girl in the nineties. And even though I watched the Batman animated series and *X-Men: The Animated Series*, there wasn't really a lot of access beyond that, as comics had stopped being sold at newsstands.

I think the first super hero comic I ever bought was probably a Harley Quinn [single-issue] floppy off of a rack that was at a Borders. And by then I had been reading and buying graphic novels. I'd read all of *Sandman*. I'd read *Watchmen* because it was on the shelf at the library. The comics that had the prestige to be on the shelf at the library were the kind of things I read. So I ended up reading things like *Fun Home* before I ever read *Spider-Man*. But I didn't really feel like I was welcome in comic shops.

And then, my cousin Nick introduced me to *X-Men* comics. We lived together when I was a kid, when he and his family lived with my family. And he was a big X-Men, Marvel fan. So that was kind of my first exposure to actual super hero comics; I was living in a house with an older boy who had *X-Men* comics he'd gotten from the place that I wasn't allowed to go.

LEAH WILLIAMS: I grew up in Oxford, Mississippi, and we did not have a comic book shop. But what we did have were these tiny spinner racks of *Archie* and *Jughead* digests at the grocery store. I would always beg my parents to let me get one of those, wherever I saw them. And that was it for the longest time.

[*X-Men: The Animated Series*] was part of my childhood. But I didn't make the connection of the source material until years and years later, when I was starting to get into comics.

VITA: I have a theory on manga and anime and being a Black kid, is that you just wake up and realize, "There it is, it's already in my veins. I already speak the language."

In terms of the fan stuff, it's just so wild.

But yeah, I loved anime, like *Sailor Moon*. And I was really lucky to grow up in New York City, as St. Mark's Comics was right there.

Rough place to be. Very rough place to be as a Black person. Very not good.

But they just had manga and indie comics, so I discovered *Ghost in the Shell*. *Flame of Recca*. All that kind of stuff. And I read manga for years, only dipping into mainstream comics here and there.

Also, I did love Storm in the X-Men animated show.

LEAH: And from there, I started working in a comic book shop. So once again, comics became my haven, my outlet. The comic book shop that I worked in, it's called Mega City One now, is right on Melrose Avenue.

But it was insane because I was the first girl they had hired in fifteen years to work there, which was enough of an upset [for] some longtime customers. "How dare you bring a girl into the clubhouse?" But meanwhile, I was just having the time of my life because all I did was sit at this counter and sell comics and talk about comics and read comics all day.

And it was just the best. I loved it.

VITA: And then working at a comic book shop, what you do [in order] to not go absolutely bananas, get space madness, is to just talk about character and talk about, not just what you would do with them, but a lot of really in-depth character analysis and story analysis.

All on the floor of a comic book shop, because that's all you have. It's just you and your colleagues standing there trying to explain to someone why it's *Watchmen* and not *Clockman*.

Literally happened. Multiple times. [*Laughter.*]

TINI: The book that I read that really, really caused me to fall head over heels in love with the idea of writing comics was *Invincible Iron Man*, which was mostly a Matt Fraction run.

I loved it. And I remember reading it and being like, "Not only is this a really great take on my favorite character. It's a take that I can relate to so strongly. I felt that's a version, that's a super hero I could write."

And to me, that understanding of Iron Man unlocked my greater understanding of super heroes as a writer. That was the moment where I stopped thinking about them as just a fan and started thinking about them as . . . a mythology I wanted to be a part of.

I've always been a brainstorming person. I've always been the kind of creator I am now. "Give me a prompt. Any prompt, I'll backflip off of it." I just love thinking *around* the thing I love.

VITA: I went to college for philosophy, psychology, and then later, for creative writing. And I think that the philosophy and psychology degrees [have] really shaped the way that I think about storytelling in a real way, the way that I think about why I want to tell stories as well as how I want to tell stories. And the way that I think about character.

Psychology in particular, but also philosophy makes it really easy to empathize with other people. That you truly get an understanding the other beings that are walking around that you interact

Inside the *Reign of X* writer's room, with (clockwise from left) Jonathan Hickman, Jordan White, Chris Robinson, Leah Williams, Vita Ayala, Tini Howard, Ben Percy, and Ed Brisson.

with have internal lives. And then there's philosophy, which is just the history of all of our existential dread. And that is also very humanizing.

And so I got a lot more nuts-and-bolts craft from the creative writing stuff, but I really couldn't immerse myself.

But philosophy and psychology really kind of changed the way that I interacted with stories, not just [the ones] that I wanted to tell, but [those] that I would read or watch or hear as well.

TINI: So not only was [there] the appeal of writing comics because I love to read the medium, but I started to realize that in order to be a writer in this world, you were part of a collaborative. I knew for such a long time that the writers of a lot of my favorite comics weren't always drawing them. But for some reason to me, that's an exception that doesn't apply to me. "I don't draw, so I can't make comics."

VITA: I really liked comics. I wanted a discount and I was in high school and I spent stupid amounts of money at that store [they worked at]. And if I got a job, I could not go to school.

I was hired because I knew all about anime and manga, but working there, you have to know the product, right? So I got into more super hero stuff just because I had access.

I was poor. I couldn't afford it all. But working there, I got to read more and more stuff.

And that's when I started reading credits.

I realized that was a viable job option for someone. But it wasn't for a bit till I actually thought I could do it.

TINI: Once I fell in love with some Marvel comics, I started looking at how they were made. And I've always been a writer, but mostly just for fun. I was a fanfic writer. My mom still has these little books I would write about falling into Super Mario Land and stuff.

My journey to writing comics was first really falling in love with super hero comics, but realizing that I'm a Scorpio. I can't just simply like something—I have to get into it and eat its guts and wear its skin.

So here I am at Marvel Comics, eating its guts and wearing its skin.

VITA: It's weird because part of my queer journey was to be the opposite of what anyone would expect of me at any time. *Sailor Moon* spoke to this place to me where I thought, "Oh, every single one of these girls is wildly different and they're all friends. I like that."

I've always liked team stories. I like when you have weird and complicated dynamics, but you all seem to work like a weird found family, which is why I love *X-Men*. And it was really interesting to me that the lens for storytelling in *Sailor Moon* was relationships between people and sacrifice, and how that gives you strength.

To look at what kind of storytellers, especially cartoonists, that lens—and I don't think there's anything necessarily intrinsic to a woman's perspective nature-wise that makes someone concentrate on these things—but what I do find is that people in general who have had to survive in certain ways tend to then convey [a] story in a certain way.

TINI: [My first Marvel work] was *Captain America*. [Editor] Alanna [Smith] reached out to me for a year of annuals. I believe it was 2018. I think Alanna and I had talked about *Band of Brothers* before on Twitter, because we both really like war stories.

But it was a great opportunity. And the most exciting thing about it was that Alanna reached out to me. There's something really exciting about having a woman reach out to you and also having it not for girlie stuff. "Hey, do you want to write a *Captain America* war story in the forties, because I know we both like that [stuff]."

And yes, we do, thank you. Yes!

So I wrote this Cap and Bucky classic war story and I'm still so, so proud of it.

VITA: It was through Donny Cates and [Matt] Rosenberg. Donny had reached out to me and asked, "Hey, we're doing *Marvel Knights 20th*. Do you want to do one of these?" I was like, "Yeah, sure, who is it?" And he told me it was for Black Panther. Which for my first Marvel work, big guns immediately. All right.

TINI: And it was so perfect for me because that's exactly what I want to do, what I'm going to do. And it also felt good because it [was] an editor setting me up to succeed. Instead of being set up as the woman to take the blame, to take the fall.

It felt really good to be set up for success and to feel as if they told me, "We trust you. Knock it out of the park."

And before the issue had even come out, I'd gotten other offers for Marvel work. I've just overall had a really positive

320 / SUPER VISIBLE

experience—I mean, work is work. We all have to go to the mat sometimes, but I feel really respected.

Which is crazy because I don't think of myself as being terribly deserving of respect.

LEAH: Before I had found [Tini and Vita], who've now both become my best friends and my peer group at work, I was still operating under this [assumption]: "I'm the impostor. And all I can do is just run with this opportunity while I still can, because obviously they're going to figure me out and know that I don't belong here."

I remember when I started working on the script for that very first Marvel short, it was a backup story in *Totally Awesome Hulk* #1. I still had that day job working for an ad agency, and I would come home from work to my two-hundred-year-old cabin and start scripting and just kind of dissociate. "This doesn't feel real—I am waiting for the rug to get yanked out from underneath me."

VITA: This was early 2018. After that, I was offered *Prisoner X* through Darren Shan. I picked up a couple issues of *Shuri*, and [was] then asked, "Do you want to write *Morbius*?" And why, yes, I like vampires, so I can make this work.

TINI: And I think some people were saying that I was the first woman to write *Captain America*, maybe since the Bullpen [days], as there were women working in the Bullpen before there were names on books.

But I think I was the first credited woman on the mainline *Captain America* comic, even though it was an annual.

Wild, right?

VITA: I had no idea that I was the first Black nonbinary person to work both at Marvel and DC. I'm the first person. And it is 2021.

I think about all of the uncredited anchors that were women or even people like line artists, colorists, letterers, all of that, just completely uncredited.

And it bums me right the hell out. But it is good to know the work to start giving credit has [begun].

LEAH: I had self-published a YA fantasy novel and I'd had some articles and essays published. It was after an article I wrote for the *Atlantic* about how Hollywood whitewashed stories of the Old West and what cowboys looked like when I heard from Chris Robinson and he asked me, "Hey, have you ever thought about writing comics?"

When I opened this email, I was sitting on my little Walmart couch in this two-hundred-year-old cabin in Leadville, Colorado, populated with all my long boxes, nerd [stuff] that I had been amassing over the past few years. And there was a giant vinyl poster of the X-Men behind me.

VITA: I was asked by Chris Robinson if I wanted to work on *Children of the Atom*, but then it got delayed a bunch. And then in 2020 at C2E2, we had a mini-creative retreat after the show.

LEAH: So it was just this surreal experience to see that email from him. I had to take twenty-four hours to calm down enough to reply. And the answer is no, I have never once considered writing comics. That is not a door I knew was possible to be opened to me, ever. But of course what I told Chris was "Yeah, sure! I've thought about it before."

He actually talked about [it] in this *Vice* article from a few years ago. It was the *Atlantic* article, but he also said, "I recognized the author from back when she was working in a comic book shop and blogging about her experiences on Tumblr." It's insane. And he knows the way that he has transformed my life for the better forever. He held a door open that I didn't even know existed.

VITA: After Chicago, I was offered *New Mutants*, but I asked [*X-Men* head writer] Jonathan Hickman, "Why? Why am I on this book? I really think it could be anyone. I'm glad that it's me, but why?"

ORAL HISTORY

Jonathan Hickman (right) would kick the doors wide open for fresh voices like Leah Williams, Vita Ayala, and Tini Howard.

He told me, "Well, I read *Prisoner X* and, you know, you can write *X-Men*." Which, fair. And I told him, "That's high praise from you."

I'm sure he regrets it now, because I give him sh*t every day. [*Laughter.*]

TINI: The person who offered me their hand across the table for it was Jonathan. That was him as a creator saying, "I want you to write this with me because I want to work with you. And I think you are ready."

It was really exciting because it was him saying, "You and I both wrote this story, we've built it up together, so let's tell it together." And that was huge.

And that's a huge part of my experience in the X-Room—that I've not been told to go write the *girl* book. Everyone in the room genuinely wants my best ideas. And when I give them my best ideas, they're like, "Those were great. Do you have any more?" It's such a good feeling.

LEAH: Okay, so all of the X-Office dudes are the good ones, they're the good eggs. And it's become one of the recurring themes of my friendship with Tini and Vita—that we're constantly checking in with each other.

I won't list all of the ways that they make room for us—Tini and I as women and Vita as a nonbinary creator, and Vita is Puerto Rican. The way that they elbow space for us specifically to tell different kinds of stories and add our voices to the conversation and feel like we matter and also feel safe around them.

But there's nobody [who] we are more obsessed with advocating [for] than Hickman himself, because he was wholly unexpected from anything that we would have anticipated him to actually be like as our mentor and leader in this. He's on a different planet, is the thing.

When he advocates for us, as diverse creators, it's more in an effort to make sure that we can tell the best possible stories that we are capable of telling and that we want to put out there.

And when he sees that we face different obstacles because we are different, he does not let up in ensuring that we are protected as creators, [that] we are not treated differently because we are accommodated differently in ways we can't always see happening, but we definitely know the effects of when we have difficult conversations about queer representation in comics and the ways that it needs to be improved.

TINI: Well, working in the X-Men Office, and writing within this era of Krakoa has been really therapeutic. We have the baked-in homosexual relationships, but also Krakoa is a very utopian, open, welcoming, come-as-you-are place as a sort of reprieve from some of the nastier parts of the mutant metaphor.

And writing those comics, but also being a part of that community, was really an important and powerful part of my year.

We both know how incredible the X-Men community can be, especially online. 2020 was supposed to be my first Marvel event coming out. And I wanted to be able to go to cons and see fans and see everyone and take pictures and go out to dinner and drinks and go to karaoke and celebrate all the hard work I did with my friends to make this amazing thing. And it's been hard to celebrate it from my apartment.

But I have, and I felt very celebrated.

And I've been really, really lucky that X-Men fans are so vocal and into the community right now.

So definitely, we created a fictional place where it was okay to be a lot of things and, among them, queer. And *Excalibur* has a lot of very rare elements from having a bisexual lead, to having Richter and his journey through finding himself and feeling like he could go to Krakoa, which was really nakedly writing a metaphor for feeling like all the other gays are allowed to go to the gay party, but you're bad and evil for some reason.

I think every queer person I know has, at some point, tried to convince themselves that the community wasn't for them, for

TOP: Bonded by their love of writing and the X-Men, Tini Howard, Leah Williams, and Vita Ayala would become fast friends. Here they're meeting in person for the first time at C2E2 2020.
BOTTOM: Leah Williams on the Women of Marvel panel in 2019.

some reason. And so I got to write about that experience for Richter.

But I also, I wrote a lot this year about the death of distance and the rise of community. And it was definitely sad to write it during [pandemic lockdown] and not actually get to have those things. But maybe that's just what made it more potent on the page—because I was really missing it.

LEAH: I think . . . It's like night and day, my experiences before this, before Hickman's X-Office specifically, and the way that things are different now. Hickman has opened our eyes to the possibility of, "Oh, we can collaborate in the Slack and bounce ideas off each other."

This is an environment that he endeavored to create for us, one where there's not a diva who's going to be really territorial about a character and refuse to play in the same sandbox with the rest of us.

We're all super collaborative and there's no ego in the room. And the fact that Tini and Vita and I feel like writers. We don't feel like a woman writer or a nonbinary writer or a Black writer— we feel like *X-Men* writers. And it's been the most liberating experience of our careers. And as a result, we are also doing the best writing of our careers.

It directly impacted the quality of our writing.

TINI: I remember exactly what I wore on my first day of the first Marvel room I had to be in. What's funny now is it was the X-Men room, [and] I'm now supercomfortable with all those people.

But yeah, that first time. I remember deciding I had to wear a skirt and tights, but I also had to wear a turtleneck because I can't look like I'm trying to look, like . . . sexy, you know? So I had this turtleneck and earrings and my hair combed a certain way. I was so thoughtful about it.

And then I went into the Marvel office and everyone was in jeans and Captain America jackets. What was I doing? [*Laughter.*]

LEAH: Me, Tini, and Vita in particular, [we're] the Trash Queer Squad, TQS. That's the shorthand we use to describe the three of us because we have made our lives run parallel and interlocked with each other ever since the podcast.

And one of the most life-changing aspects of being friends with them is seeing that they're both in disbelief about how good this all is, too.

Alone, none of us are very good at advocating for ourselves or believing in ourselves, believing that we belong in the room and we deserve to speak up. But together, it is so easy for me to advocate on Vita's or Tini's behalf.

If we're spitballing and brainstorming, and somebody starts kind of getting close to connecting an idea that I know Tini and Vita have already had some really great thoughts for, and they could contribute to that—that's the first thing out of my mouth.

And I have pitched books for Tini and Vita just because I'm excited about it. I have had the privilege of being friends with them and hearing about these ideas as they have them.

We can't believe in ourselves, but we believe in each other so much that it makes up for it. It is so hard to believe in myself and not feel like an impostor, but if I'm friends with those two and they're hyping me up, then obviously I'm not *that* worthless because they're so amazing to me. I feel taller by proximity. I feel like I belong.

TINI: There's a type of power you're afforded when you are not the only person in the room. And also that's something we try to do. Leah and I are white women. There are times where we try to speak up for a Vita as a Black person or a nonbinary person or a Hispanic person, [and] there are times where we know that we can use the power we have all together for something that, maybe Vita is the only person in the room and doesn't have to be.

We can be that voice in the room with them.

And functionally, we use it, too. We usually talk before we

go into the room together. So, when [there], I'll chicken out and not want to talk about it. Vita or Leah will support me and say, "Tini had a good idea for that," or I'll do the same for them, too.

It's *scary* to advocate for yourself—so we don't have to advocate for ourselves, but it trains us to because we *should* advocate for ourselves.

And it's really special because people see it and respect it and understand what it is.

On one level, I'm happy that people see it and recognize that we're just here for each other. And on the other, it's nice that people can't pit Leah and I against each other.

We've already had this talk, and we're not going to let you do that.

LEAH: As creative freelancers, especially as, like . . . not straight dudes, you do feel like you're on an island at times, but it was becoming friends with those two and the X-Office experience in general that eliminated that feeling for me.

VITA: You know, it just wasn't intimidating, really, because the thing that is valued the most in the room, besides being respectful human beings, is the story. And it is a more diverse room than most rooms that I've seen, but it's still, I am *the* Brown. But besides being literally at the center of this stuff, all that we care about is story. That's it.

So nothing is sacred. There's no ego, which is wild to me. If something works in my book, then they'll be like, "Here you go."

When we built *X of Swords*—it is a Tini Howard–Jonathan Hickman event, but we are all part of it. That's fundamental that everyone contributed to [it], even if they didn't necessarily write. [Hickman's] like a showrunner and he's running a series. You write your own book, but everything is from this pool of creativity.

TINI: And, of course, we're not a monolith—like, we disagree.

Everyone in the room agrees and disagrees sometimes, but there's a really, really good sense of understanding of the fact that we're not just telling cool stories, but that we need to tell stories that we're proud of and that we can stand behind.

And I think a really good way to make people feel less alone in those rooms is not only to welcome them in, but to welcome them in numbers, and say you're allowed to have unique and safe spaces where you discuss things that make you uncomfortable.

VITA: That's honestly how I want to work in comics, forever, not necessarily just in this room. But you don't get into comics if you don't like working with other people—you shouldn't, anyway. This is a group project.

And I don't know if I would have stayed to find out necessarily if Tini and Leah weren't in the room, and that's really important, right? Because it gets very exhausting, translating your entire existence. So the idea of just these two other people with this shorthand who will also support me . . . and it's not that I *need* it in this room. But knowing that I have people who will protect me, and I will protect them.

And if not for them, I don't think I would be in the room.

LEAH: Literally life-changing. I'm going to start, like, getting weepy, but yeah, literally life-changing.

VITA: Let me be honest. My job is awesome. I get to write *X-Men*. I just created a bunch of trans and nonbinary mutants that I got put into my book, and a bunch of Brown kids and all this stuff. I get to do that [stuff] because I'm writing *New Mutants* right now. And especially going back to [Chris] Claremont's run, which literally changed my brain. It just rewired how [things] worked in there, and now I'm getting to write the same characters.

TINI: Now that we're here, we're going to take over. Get ready.

As part of the *Dawn of X* relaunch of the X-Men publishing line, Tini Howard would take on *Excalibur* (LEFT, cover art by Mahmud Asrar), and Leah Williams would helm *X-Factor* (RIGHT, cover art by Ivan Shavrin).

ORAL HISTORY

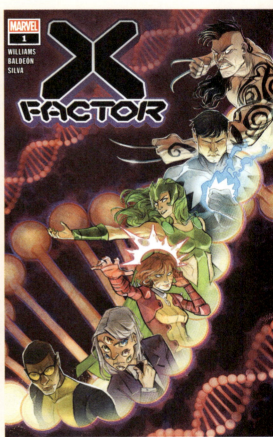

REIGN OF X / 331

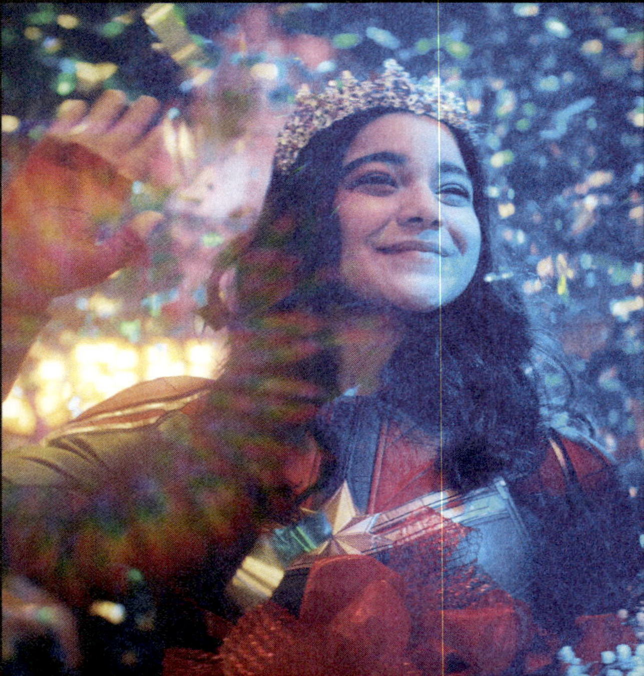

CHAPTER THIRTEEN

EMBIGGEN!

Ms. Marvel,
Kamala Khan, and
the Advent of
the Disney+ Era

Iman Vellani, the *Ms. Marvel* writer who also portrays her on the big screen, laughs when she's asked how she found out about the casting call for Ms. Marvel. "The Brownest way possible: WhatsApp. My aunt was in a group where another person had posted the casting call. It was so fated, by the way, as she usually keeps the chat muted, but then one day she decided to open the group. She forwarded it my way, as she knew how much I loved Kamala [Khan]. She had seen me in my Ms. Marvel costume for Halloween. In the beginning, I wasn't sure it was a real thing, but I sent in a photo anyway." She grins. "And clearly it was real."

When she got the message from her aunt, Iman was an ordinary high school senior, just like any other high school senior. Just like Kamala. She went to class. She went to rehearsal for her school play. She went to mosque with her family. She went to her local comic book shop to dig through the back issues. She applied to colleges. But on her last day of high school, a few months after she auditioned for the role of Kamala Khan—a fact she didn't even tell her friends, in case she didn't get it—and hadn't heard back, something extraordinary happened.

"On the last day of school, I was hanging out with my friends, when [casting director] Sarah [Finn] texted me to join a Zoom call. I had to get out of my friend's car—we were parked in a driveway—with my friends watching from the car, and join the call. Which was very weird.

"I open the call and the first face I see is Kevin Feige, and then it was Sarah and the producers. *Oh my God.* They were arguing over who's going to tell me, but Kevin did the honor. 'The decision was unanimous. We want you to play Ms. Marvel.'"

She laughed, almost still in disbelief. "And then we hung up, and I had to go back in the car and explain to my friends what just happened to me. It was crazy. And the best graduation present, as I didn't get one because of Covid."

Then, like any other high schoolers would do to celebrate good news, they went to get burritos.

Iman, who was born in Karachi, Pakistan, and immigrated to Canada with her parents when she was a year old, is a huge Avengers fangirl—right down to her Arc Reactor phone case—and has been ever since she saw the first *Iron Man* film . . . though she was only six when it premiered in theaters.

It has since become her comfort movie.

"Whenever I was sad, I'd watch it," she told Marvel.com in June 2022. "Whenever I was happy, I'd watch it. The first thing I did when I got cast was watch the movie. Every big moment in my life also includes *Iron Man*. Because I have that attachment to it, it means a lot to me, even though, you know, it's not, like, the greatest movie ever created, but to me it is."

She would spend her off periods at school at the comics shop across the street, buying every back issue of *The Invincible Iron Man* that her weekly allowance would provide. And it was in one of those issues that she met Kamala Khan for the first time.

"As I mostly read only *Iron Man*, I picked up an issue with Riri Williams, and Kamala was on the cover. I immediately thought, 'Who is she? She looks like me!' and then that started everything. The first issue I got of *Ms. Marvel* was #19, and the title was "Mecca." Right off the bat it was about Eid, and I was like, 'No way. I'm Muslim. My family celebrates Eid.'"

Sana Amanat saw Kamala in Iman immediately upon meeting her at her second screen test, which was over Zoom. In April 2022, Sana told *Empire* magazine, "[Iman] showed me every corner of her room, and it was covered with Avengers. Then she said, 'Oh wait, I'm not done,' opened up her closet, and there was more Marvel everywhere.

"For me, there's two representations of Kamala," Sana said. "There's the Kamala of the comics, with her very specific voice and a point of view that is really coming from [G. Willow Wilson], and elements of my upbringing and my experience. And now there's this modern-day Kamala, which is more akin to my nephews, nieces, and today's youth. And I believe Iman encapsulates the essence of those Kamalas. It's really incredible. Even just from her first audition tape, I knew she was the one."

She smiled. "Willow has always said that Kamala is her daughter, and for me, Kamala is my little sister. And I do feel that with Iman."

Previously *Ms. Marvel*'s editor, Marvel executive Sana Amanat would move to Los Angeles and embark on bringing *Ms. Marvel* to the silver screen, seen here with Iman Vellani, who has said how important it was for her to have Sana on set, building a sisterly bond through filming.

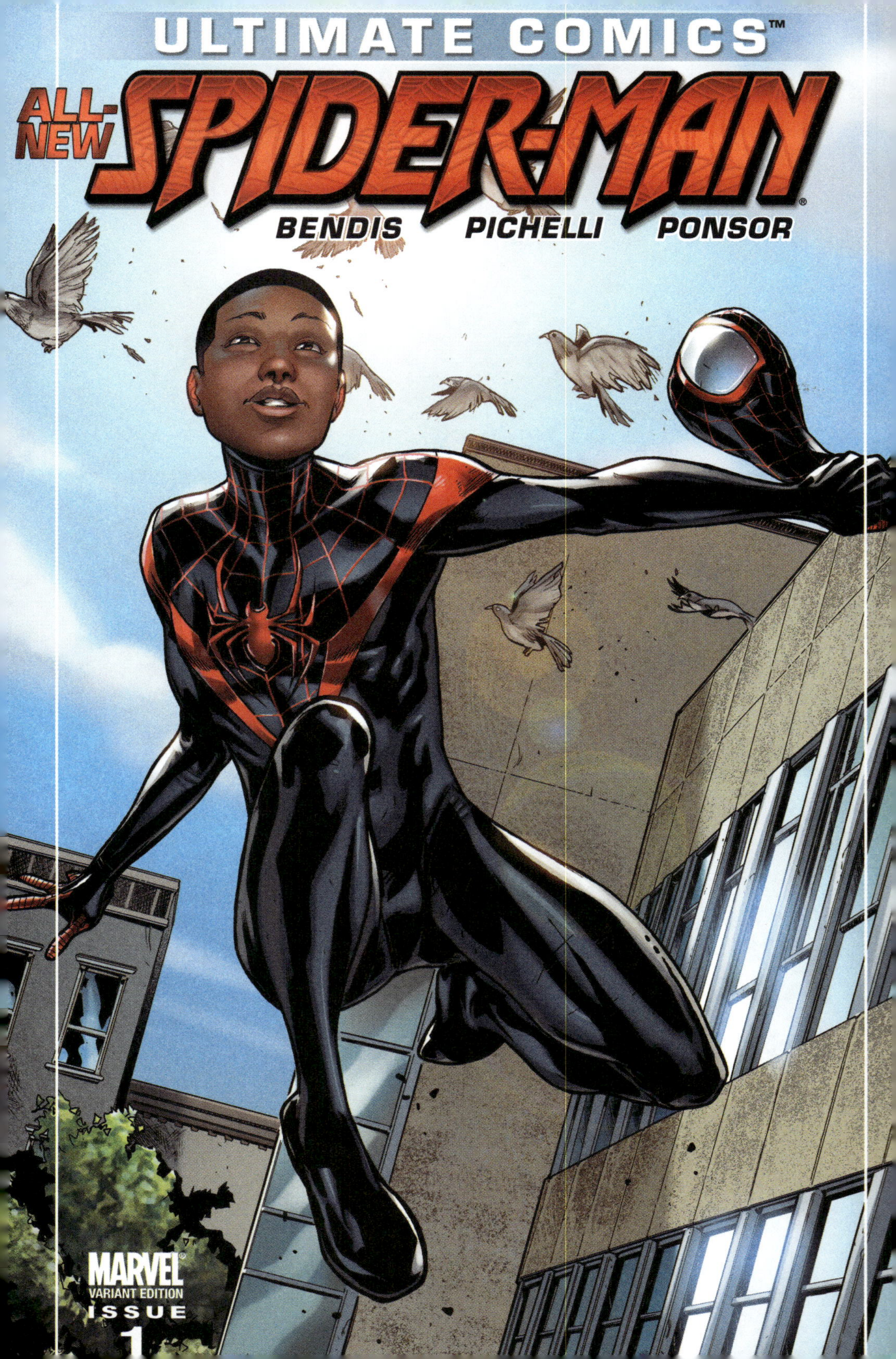
ULTIMATE COMICS™
ALL-NEW SPIDER-MAN®
BENDIS
PICHELLI
PONSOR
MARVEL
VARIANT EDITION
ISSUE
1

OPPOSITE: The debut of Miles Morales in *Ultimate Comics: All-New Spider-Man* #1, cover art by Sara Pichelli.

"I've found that after reading so many issues of *Ms. Marvel*, I've embraced myself more in my culture," said Iman. "The first arc is called *No Normal*, and to me, it was my normal, going to mosque and having to pray. That is my normal. It really awakened something in me. I've become proud of my culture after that."

That reflection, that pride, was exactly what Sana, herself a Muslim Pakistani American, was after when she and writer G. Willow Wilson conceived of the character back in 2014. Before she got her powers, Kamala was an Avengers fangirl, just like Iman, and looked up to Captain Marvel . . . simply because there was no one who looked like Kamala.

"For a person of color," Sana told *The New York Times* in June 2022, "you look outside and who are the people that you're worshipping and want to be like? They look nothing like you. Captain Marvel is really emblematic of that—she's blond, blue-eyed, and tall. And so the story spun from there."

Iman echoed this sentiment when she spoke with *NME* in July 2022. "For some reason, every time we see Muslims and South Asians [on-screen], especially teenagers, they're never proud of their culture. It's always something that's dragging them down. That's so not true. Kamala's story has always been about using her cultural identity as something that motivates her and guides her. That was really important to us [when making *Ms. Marvel*]."

Because Kamala *is* just like every other teenager. Her religion doesn't define her, but it is a part of her. And showing, as Sana put it to *The New York Times*, "some of the tribulations of being an awkward Brown teenager—going to prom by myself, fasting, and playing basketball or lacrosse, wearing tights underneath my shorts in 90-degree weather" in a comic book, the same way we depict Peter Parker's struggles with making rent or getting literally anywhere on time, shows other Muslim teenagers that they're normal, too.

In fact, Peter Parker was the exact analogy Joe Quesada used when he first heard the idea. "I remember pitching it in the room," Sana said, "and Joe saying, 'This is a classic Marvel comic. We should do it. This is *Spider-Man*.' He got it from the jump and was supportive of the project, including giving us feedback as we went."

There was another character that Sana looked to: Miles Morales.

Sana started her career at Marvel in the Ultimates office and was on the editorial team that helped facilitate Miles's creation. "In the Ultimate universe, you're rebooting characters all the time and we're trying different versions of them. So, I was comfortable, at least, with taking new stabs. I worked on Miles Morales—that was a really big one for me. Being an editor on the team that helped create Miles Morales was actually a big thing that was transformative for me, seeing what we did with [him] and applying that to Kamala."

She also spoke at length with Miles's creator and writer, Brian Michael Bendis, on how to best position a character like Miles, or like Kamala, at the early stages, and how to lay the right foundation for her to last. "His advice was mostly to first understand what her everyday life was before thinking about the big-picture stuff. He told me, 'You have to be able to channel that experience, what's true to it, and make sure that you're understanding the details of that life experience and putting that first.' Which was very helpful for Ms. Marvel, as that's really where we started figuring out: Who is the Khan family? Who are the friends? And how do we make sure we have the right kinds of friends, and what are their roles in Kamala's larger arc and story?"

Keeping in mind what was true, and not compromising on her original vision of a Muslim character told with an authentic Muslim voice, Sana knew she wanted to collaborate with a Muslim creator. She found that partnership with writer—and fellow Muslim—G. Willow Wilson.

"The first work I did with Marvel was actually another DC connection," Willow told us. "It was Jeanine Schaefer. She had come over to Marvel and was interested in doing more YA-focused stuff for girls. And so she gave me a call. My first work was *Mystic: The Tenth Apprentice* at Marvel. And, you know, it was a really good book. It was fun.

"But it was through Jeanine that I met Sana briefly in passing while she was working at Virgin [Comics]. . . . We were connected being women in comics who were also Muslim in comics, which made us a club of two. But then when she came over to Marvel and after I had done *Mystic* with Jeanine, and that picked up some good press, that's when she called me and was like, 'Hey, we're in this tiny little club, why don't we do a book?'"

The co-creators of Kamala Khan,
aka Ms. Marvel, Sana Amanat and
G. Willow Wilson.

KIDS ARE JUST SMARTER, AND CAN TEACH US MANY THINGS. I FEEL LIKE KAMALA IS PART OF THAT ZEITGEIST.

———

"[Willow] converted to Islam when she was nineteen, so although she did not grow up in the Muslim community, she was able to bring her own life experiences, as the Muslim community is quite diverse," said Sana. "She was able to rely on her Pakistani friends, who gave her terms and phrases that I hadn't heard before. She'd put pen to paper and then tell me, 'My friend's aunt says that all the time.'"

Willow also came up with Kamala's name. "We went back and forth, with so many different names, but we decided to match the theme of Marvel names, with alliteration," said Sana. "She came back with Kamala, and initially I actually disagreed, as 'Kamala is a Hindu name. That might be problematic.' But she pushed back, 'Kamala is a feminine version of Kemal, which means "perfect,"' and we decided that yes, she'd be named Kamala, and that we'd build the meaning into her story. That's a really important turning point for Kamala, understanding the significance of her name and drawing strength from that. And Willow wrote a beautiful scene, one of my favorite scenes in the book, of Kamala talking to her father about the name, of the meaning of her name."

Former *Ms. Marvel* writer Samira Ahmed likens Kamala to a "Revolutionary Girl" who is claiming her space and not apologizing about it.

"I grew up at a time where it was said, 'Girls don't like reading comics. Super hero comics [are] not a girl thing,'" she said. "And now so much has changed with Gen Z kids. They have this understanding about gender. Kids are just smarter, and can teach us many things. I feel like Kamala is part of that zeitgeist."

And maybe knowing they had that understanding helped Kamala's Muslim creators to feel freer in telling an authentic story.

"As she is a part of just a very small group [of] South Asian and Muslim characters than we have in comics, she is forced to have these giant shoulders and to carry the weight and expectations of over a billion people on top of them, and no character can do that," said Samira. "So I feel like when you are from those same sort of intersections as that character, you feel that weight on your shoulders. And I definitely feel that for writing [*Ms. Marvel*], because not only do I want to do right by her, and how she means so much to so many people, and so many kids, and how she is such an important character, because of her uniqueness in sort of the Marvel family of characters.

"But also South Asian culture is huge, right? There's so many countries. We have so many varied cultural things—I was born in India, but half my family is in Pakistan, because of the Partition. My great-aunt is actually the first woman appointed to a superior court in Pakistan. I was thinking about her so much as I was writing *Ms. Marvel*, because Majida Auntie is this Revolutionary Girl in Pakistan. So, no single character can bear that burden for everyone, because she is also just her own person, too. She is just her."

"I never envisioned that I would end up in a place where I was doing legacy planning for a character that I helped create—that never entered my mind, plans, ambitions, scope," said Willow. "So that's been absolutely wild. Obviously, anytime you do something new, you hope that it's well remembered. It's very rare to do something and know that it will outlive you, which is a very different kettle of fish. And that's been an amazing experience.

"It [was] time for me to step away because that character had opened so many doors that created possibilities for storytelling, for employment, for all kinds of stuff, for people who had never had a chance to work in comics before. . . . I reached a point where I felt like it was time for me to step back, that this character was going to have a life beyond what me and Sana had imagined for her at the beginning. And it was time to step away and let her have that life."

"I think back to when Willow told me she was ready to let go of Kamala," said Sana. "She called me up and said, 'I'm not going to be continuing to write this story anymore.' That was also the same time where I decided, if Willow's off, then I'm going to start cycling off myself. I remember Willow said to me,

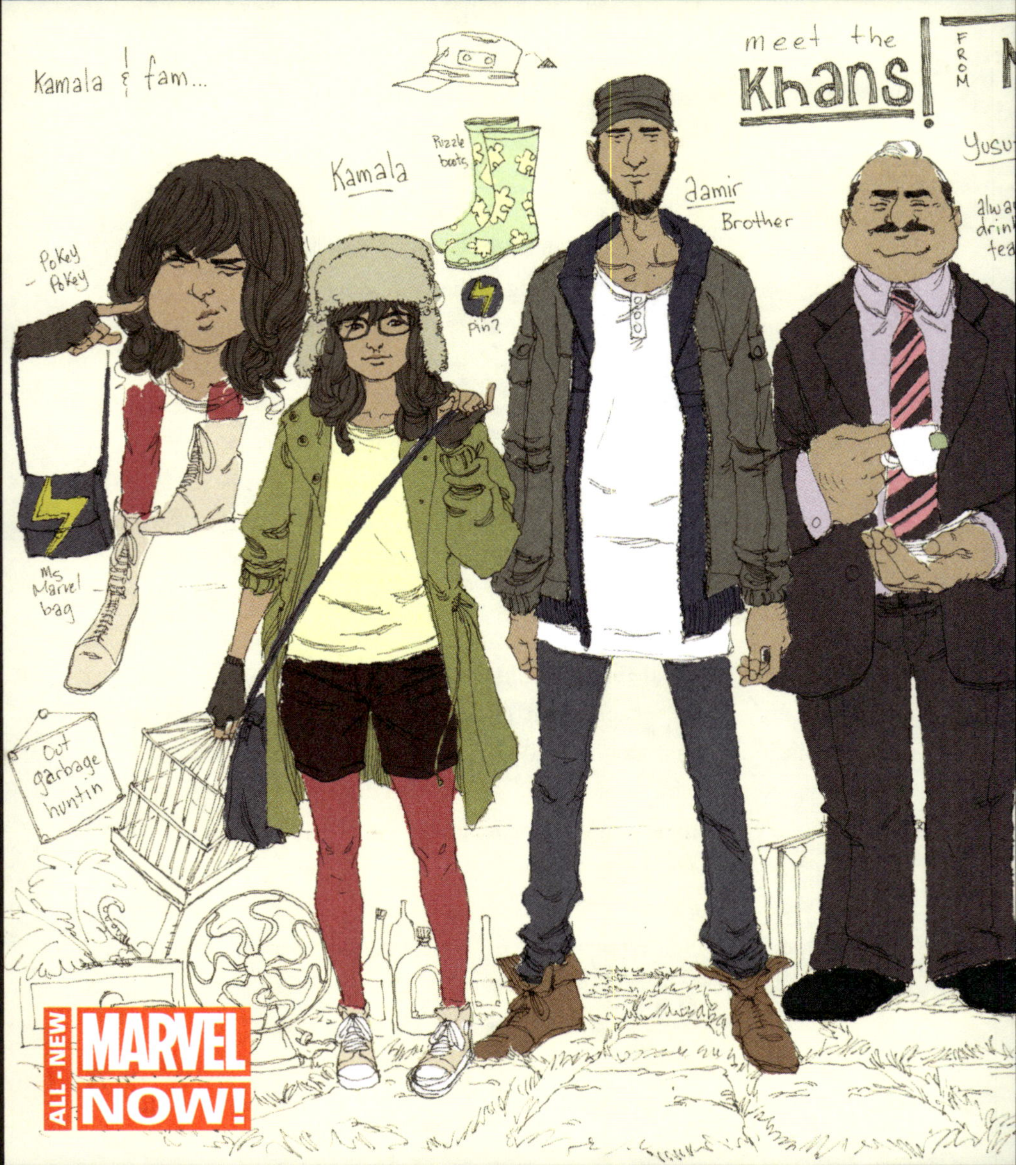

Kamala & fam...
meet the
Khans!
FROM
Kamala
Puzzle boots
aamir
Brother
Yusu
Pokey - Pokey
pin?
Ms Marvel bag
Out garbage huntin
ALL-NEW
MARVEL
NOW!

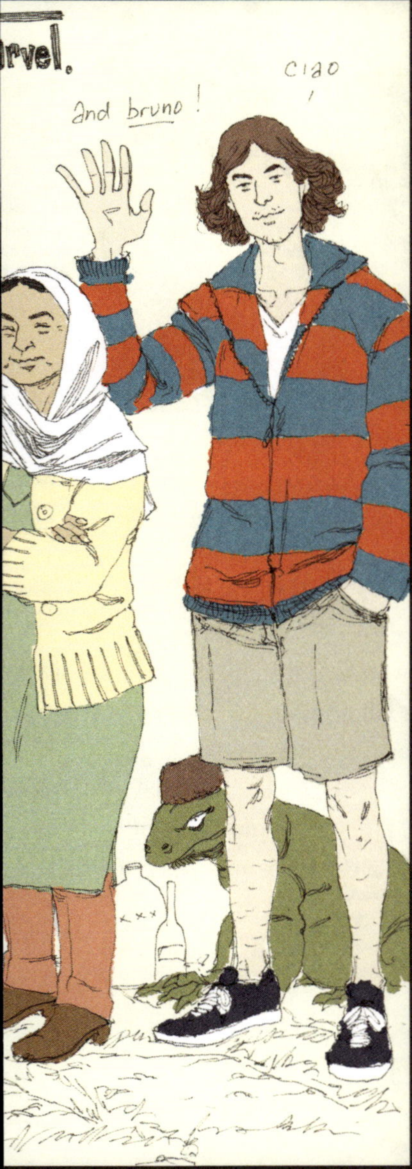
rvel.
ciao
and bruno!

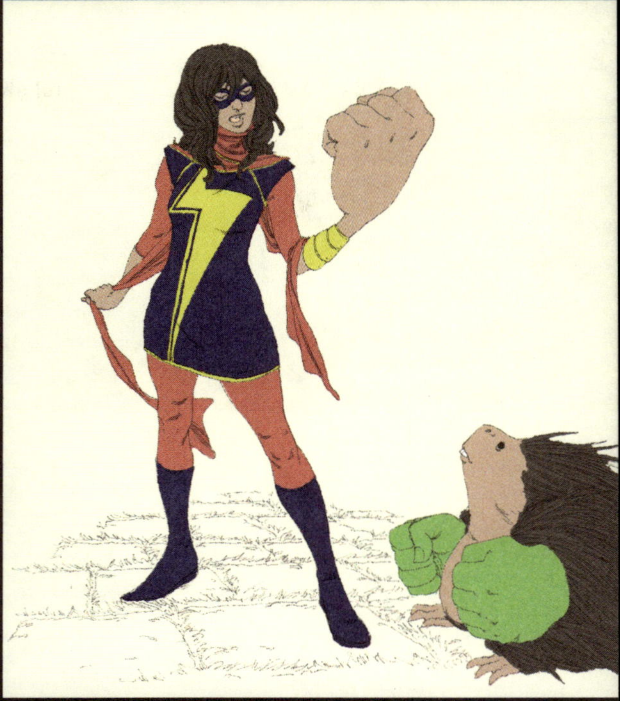

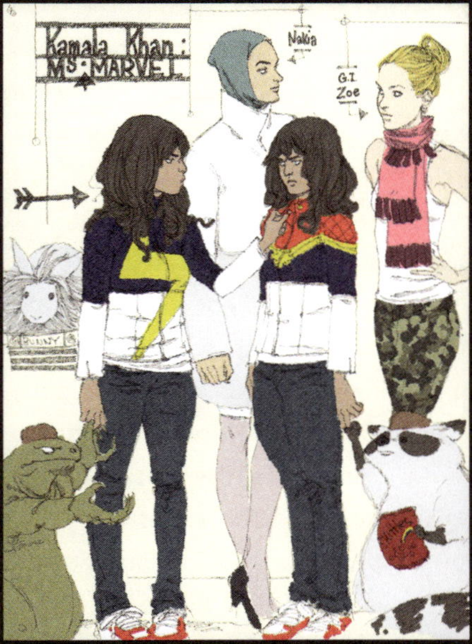
Kamala Khan:
Ms. MARVEL
Nakia
G.I. Zoe

LEFT: Next to take on the task of writing *Ms. Marvel*, Samira Ahmed at New York Comic Con in 2022.
RIGHT: Writer Maurene Goo poses with *Silk* #1.

'I feel at this point, Kamala kind of belongs to the people. And now real success is someone else coming in wanting to tell her story. I've told the stories I wanted to tell about Kamala. And now I'm excited to become a fan.'

"It's different now, being now a producer on the show, and being heavily involved in the development and production of the show. Thinking back to how Willow stepped back has allowed me to follow in her example and allow the writers on the show to tell her story, as they have their own perspective to tell, and my job is to make that happen."

"I have two kids—my daughter is a sixth grader and my son, a third grader," said Samira. "The process for signing on to the book took some time, and I had to wait till I knew it was a done deal to tell them. I finally told them, and they both literally screamed. They were jumping up and down, and my son was almost in tears. He said, 'This is the greatest day of my life, because my mom is writing one of my favorite super heroes.'

"And so, this is why it's also important to me, because alongside those kids, the strangers, the passersby . . . who tell me I better do a good job, I also know I have to do a good job for my own kids, because they see this hero. They see a bit of themselves in this hero."

MS. MARVEL'S success—by 2018 it had sold half a million copies of the collected trade paperbacks—kicked the door open on what young adult comics could look like at Marvel . . . and what audiences they hadn't been reaching.

"On books like *Ms. Marvel*, there's a lot of pressure on it to be successful," said Sana. "You can't look to experiment without feeling the weight and the responsibility of that genre on your shoulders to have continued success. We were very lucky because we tapped into a market that was hungry for the content at the time *Ms. Marvel* came out. Especially the conversations about representation that had not been happening before at Marvel, and then started happening. For characters that were representative of minority groups being told by those very minority groups."

Over the next few years, the team curated books about characters who better reflected their audience, created by members of that audience and their deliberate allies, as well as giving those authentic voices the opportunity to take characters who looked like them or had backgrounds like them on a more personal journey from an experiential point of view. Books like *Squirrel Girl*, *America*, *Silk*, *Spider-Gwen*, *The West Coast Avengers*, and *Hawkeye*, as well as franchising Miles Morales the same way they did with Peter Parker.

"I got *Silk* and I knew that Robbie Thompson wrote this before me," said Maurene Goo, award-winning YA novelist and writer of the 2021 *Silk* limited series. "And he did a great job, as seen in how passionate the Silk fanbase is. When I read them, I realized there was no specificity to her culture in the stories. And that's okay. I'm glad, rather than him trying to attempt to put [in] weird Korean stuff he wasn't familiar with, he just was the approach

I ALSO KNOW I HAVE TO DO A GOOD JOB
FOR MY OWN KIDS, BECAUSE THEY SEE THIS HERO.
THEY SEE A BIT OF THEMSELVES IN THIS HERO.

of 'She's a Korean American character, but first she's this super hero that I know how to write with all these issues.' But her issues, to me . . . it's, like, ten times more interesting if you have the context of her being raised as a Korean American woman."

Silk is about Cindy Moon, a Korean American science student who gets bitten by the same radioactive spider as Peter Parker. She got her own series in 2015, written by Robbie Thompson and drawn by Stacey Lee. Maurene Goo collaborated with artist Takeshi Miyazawa for their 2021 run.

"So [Silk's] got all these anger issues, right, because she was stuck in a bunker for ten years," said Maurene. "And anger and Korean people is a big thing. We have a word for it in our culture. It's called *han*. It's this idea that you inherited trauma and then, with that, rage. Rage that is impotent because we have been colonized and really abused throughout history, and it's this feeling of never getting revenge. That's such super hero gold. And Silk has that in the way Robbie wrote her, and I didn't go into it with this version of Silk. . . . She's been in therapy for however many years now, so she's now kind of evolved from dealing with anger and dealing with trusting people again. And instead of being close to people [as] a vulnerability—like it is with every freaking super hero, it's the big thing, right? You can't get close to people because the people you love will get hurt—I wanted her to draw power from her relationships.

"So I don't know if that's a female thing or what, but that's important to me in all my books I've written. Literally, it's the through line of every single book I've written. Vulnerability is actually good. Comics usually imply that people in your life make you weak. And I'm like, 'Man, I want to reframe that, as it can make you strong.'"

Another reframing many of these women did was how women were allowed to look.

"We love the way Erica Henderson designed Squirrel Girl in this latest iteration," says Shannon Hale, cowriter of the *Squirrel Girl* prose novels, "that she does not conform to that comic book standard of what a woman should look like. That she was really thinking: If she has that powerful of a kick, what do her thighs look like? What kind of butt would be able to support that big of a tail? And she drew that way and I love it. She's got short hair, and big strong thighs.

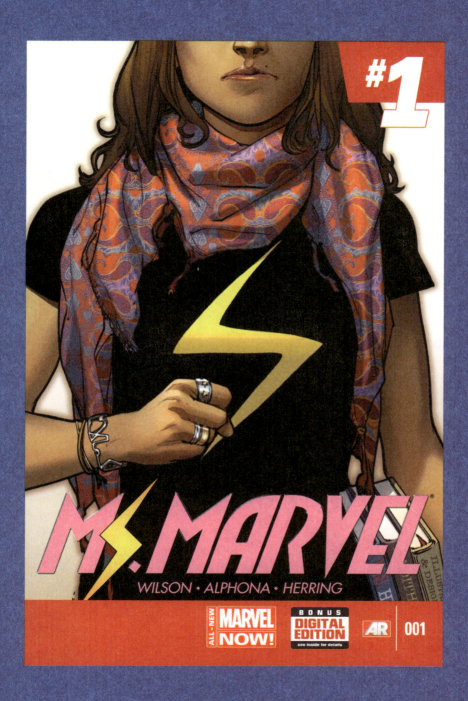

The now-iconic, bestselling cover of *Ms. Marvel* #1, cover art by Sara Pichelli.

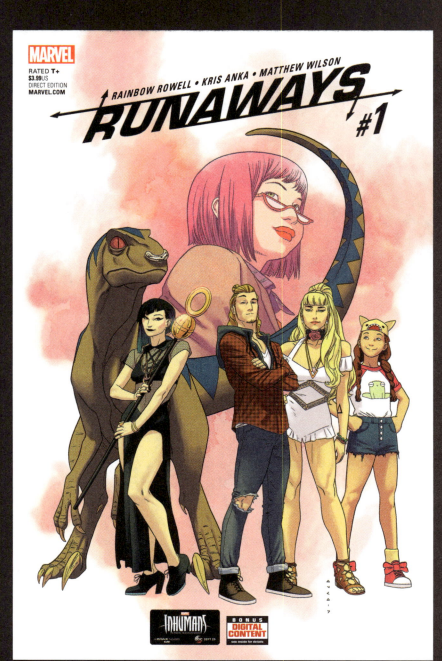

ABOVE: Rainbow Rowell would bring back the Runaways, almost a decade after they were last a team, with a modern outlook; cover art by Kris Anka. OPPOSITE: *Ironheart* #1, 2018, cover art by Amy Reeder.

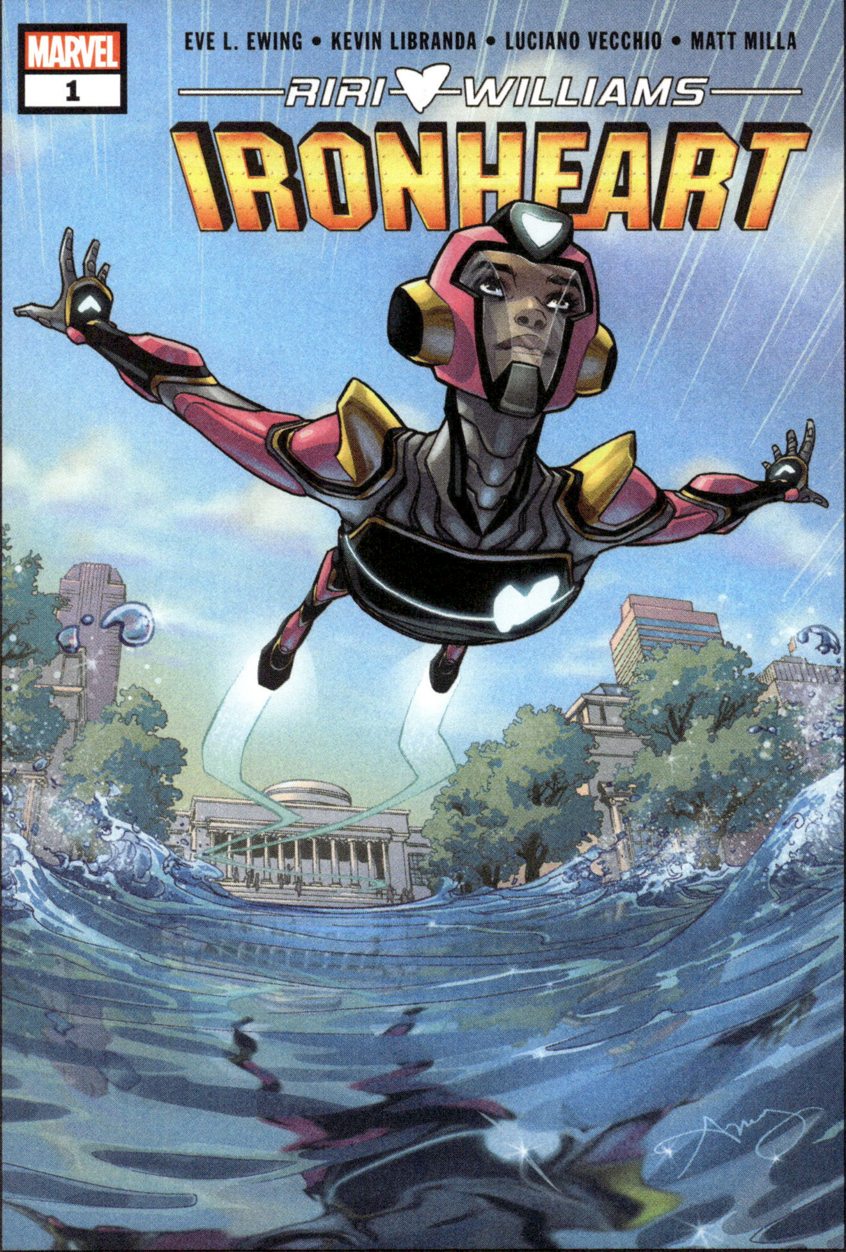
MARVEL
1
EVE L. EWING • KEVIN LIBRANDA • LUCIANO VECCHIO • MATT MILLA
RIRI WILLIAMS
IRONHEART

Eve L. Ewing signs a comic for a fan at New York Comic Con.

"And we tried to make sure that was reflected in our book, that the girls are not defined by their bodies and that their bodies are unique and powerful however they came, and there's lots of different ways to be powerful."

"We connect more with the female characters that look like us that we see on the page," says Tini Howard. "I am super tall. I'm five foot ten, I've got broad shoulders, I've never been petite. And I often cling to very tall female characters because I've always been looked at a certain way for my height. And I love Spider-Woman because she is mouthy, but also because she has a big butt. As this girl with a beautiful butt and dark hair, I was like, 'Well, hell, that's me.'

"This is a backwards thing where it was not intended to become empowering, but because women have such complex feelings about our own bodies, sometimes that can feel empowering to you when it's not meant to. You know, we find representation anywhere."

"What I found is there were a lot of girls like me, women who kind of latched on to Gert because they saw themselves in her," said Rainbow Rowell of her work on *Runaways*, in particular the deliberate way she centered Gert. "And if you are fat—especially if you're fat and you're over thirty—you didn't see yourself anywhere in mainstream entertainment. Anywhere.

"I've now met a lot of people in their thirties and forties who love the Runaways and who loved Gert because they were like, 'Wait a minute, what's happening? That's a fat girl. Did she just kiss a boy?' It brings me such pleasure to know that she is just unquestionably fat. . . . And there's no pushback. None.

"And it's just wonderful that [executive editor] Nick Lowe from the beginning has always been, 'Yeah, of course.' And then both of the artists that I've worked with, Kris Anka and Andrés Genolet—he draws the most beautiful fat girl, you know what I mean? And then you think, 'God, why did this have to be so hard?' Because I just had to say, 'This has to be this way.' Nick agrees. Kris is on board, Andrés is on board, it's just been so lovely. How did it get to be so lovely, this experience?"

Even if there's no pushback from inside the House of Ideas, it still hasn't been an easy road for many women working to open the doors for a broader audience.

"I'm just laughing because it's still so controversial and absurd," said Eve L. Ewing, the Chicago-based sociologist, professor, poet, and writer of *Ironheart*. "When Brian Michael Bendis was leaving Marvel—on a podcast, fans were talking about who would pick up different titles. A stranger said Eve Ewing should write *Ironheart*. And I was like, 'Wow, that's cool.'"

Afterward, there was a petition started by Tirhakah Love, a senior writer at *New York* magazine, that picked up steam and was shared by thousands of fans, which all culminated in a text from *Black Panther* writer Ta-Nehisi Coates. "He was like, 'I've been talking with people at Marvel about you, and you're a really good writer. Is this something you're really interested in?' And I was . . . 'Yeah, it is something I'm really interested in.'

"He told me, 'If you do this, it's going to be the most racism and sexism you'll ever experience in your entire life,' which is saying a lot."

She thought of everything she had done—how could writing for Marvel be controversial? "Writing for Marvel seemed to me to be about the least political thing I had ever done," Eve wrote for *The New York Times* in April 2021, for a piece titled "Flying While Black." "To me, this was about fun. It was the stuff of youthful miracles, a shiny new bike and unlimited arcade tokens rolled into one.

"And then [executive editor] Tom Brevoort sent me an email," she said. "I've received thousands of emails in my life, and I don't think I could tell you the subject line of any of them except for this one. And the subject was 'Marvel Calling.'

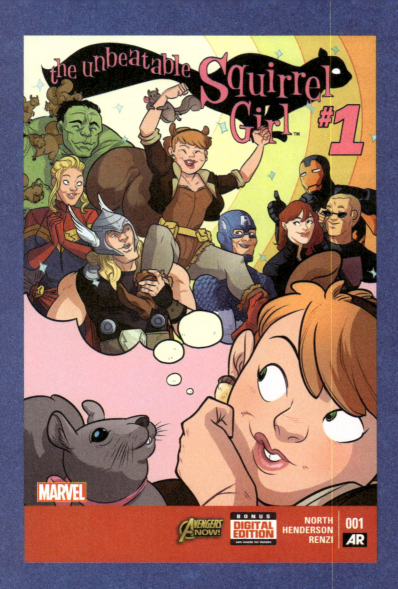

For a new generation of comics fans, characters like Squirrel Girl showed that there is space for those who don't conform to the standard of women in comics; cover art by Erica Henderson.

"We had this in-person meeting and it was just very general. It was Tom and [editor] Alanna [Smith], and I just talked to them about what I think makes a good story. I remember mentioning the harassment element. And on the way out, Alanna stopped me and was like, 'Hey, by the way, don't let those people stop you from writing.'"

It was advice she held close to her heart as she wrote. "I was so terrified, but I had no choice. It was like, at this point, all these people really want me to fail. And I had been successful as a writer in other arenas. And it was bizarre being a beginner again, on the one hand, and on the other hand, having the highest stakes of anything I'd ever written in my life, both in terms of the level of the platform and in terms of people's genuine desire for me to do a bad job and to prove them right. And so I *had* to write it."

And she did, to such huge success that Riri Williams is a major part of the *Black Panther* sequel, *Wakanda Forever*, and will be getting her own solo Disney+ series.

"I wanted to show the unbridled joy Black kids from Chicago would feel if they got to meet Ironheart and experience flying for the first time," Eve wrote in *The New York Times* for the article "Flying While Black." "It's important to me to push against the adultification of Black children, and show them being silly and having fun."

That's exactly the absolute elation that viewers feel when they see Riri Williams take flight for the first time in her homemade Iron Man suit during *Black Panther: Wakanda Forever*, played in a star turn by Dominique Thorne. "To be young, Black, and gifted, right?" Riri says to Shuri with a grin in the film, and Shuri smiles back, the two of them luxuriating in seeing each other and being seen. "I hope that when Black girls see Riri Williams, they see someone who is reaching for their dreams, which means that they can reach for their dreams, who's doing so fully in herself, fully in her truth, unapologetically and that means they can as well," Dominique told ABC7 Chicago just a few days after the premiere of *Wakanda Forever*. "I hope they feel encouraged and inspired to reach for whatever they want to reach to, how they want to reach for it."

"It's still true that some people are pretty angry about the future of comics, but it doesn't bother me," Eve wrote for *The New York Times*. "I'm on the best super hero team. And as you may have heard, we are mighty."

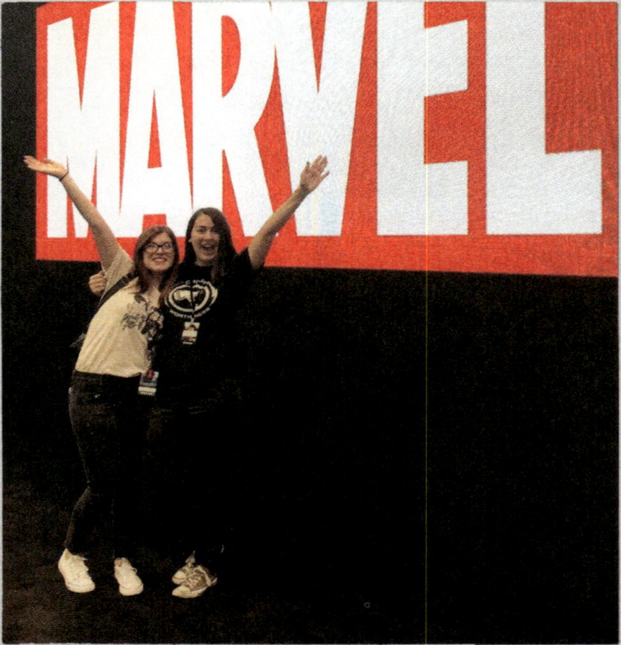
MARVEL

CHAPTER FOURTEEN

GENERATION M

The Next Generation of Heroes . . . and Readers

"Hero stories go back to the origins of storytelling; however, with a few exceptions, these stories were centered around male heroes, while women were largely either used as property or as representations of temptation," said Elizabeth Olsen, who portrays Scarlet Witch, another lightning-rod female Marvel character in both the films and Disney+ series. "It is important for us to show the many facets of the modern woman: one who is free, autonomous, and in control of her destiny. We can honor the classics while still honoring modernity and embracing a new kind of female hero story."

And

make no mistake, many classics—or rather, our modern accounting of them—have done women wrong for many years. Joseph Campbell, author of *The Hero with a Thousand Faces*, considered by many to be *the* expert on mythological storytelling, wrote extensively about the monomyth, the idea that all epic narratives derive from a single template. In the decades since his work became popularized, the pattern of "the hero's journey," as he called it, has become the shorthand for telling modern myths . . . but it might be difficult for half the world's population to see themselves in his work. "It's not like there are *no* women in *The Hero with a Thousand Faces*," wrote James Parker in his 2021 piece for the *Atlantic* titled "Joseph Campbell's Woman Problem." "Look, there she is in the index: *woman*, right between *wolf image* and *womb-image*. The problem is, of the hero's 1,000 faces, 999 are male."

Marvel is where popular culture so often finds our parables and our lessons. Marvel is at the forefront of teaching our young people how to *be*.

Ruth E. Carter, the Academy Award–winning costume designer on the *Black Panther* films, holds very close to her heart the words from her mentor: her drama professor, Linda Bolton Smith. "She would say, 'You know, think of the people that you admire. You are side by side with them. You're not competing with the student who's sitting next to you in this classroom. You are side by side with the great artists that you admire. Think of yourself like them and that one day you'll be inspiring someone else who's sitting in a classroom.'"

"I taught English as a second language for twenty-five years," said Carole Seuling, "but I worked part-time, like all teachers, in a bookstore, and they used to sell comics. And I would just clip the corners off and bring them in and, during homeroom to keep my students quiet, I would just pass out comic books. I had the quietest homeroom in the building.

"When the principal came in and saw all these kids busy reading, she said, 'Oh my God, they're reading, this is amazing. This is incredible,' and then she said, 'But they're reading comic books,' and I said, 'Well, they're reading, aren't they?'"

Jean Thomas reflected on her life at Marvel and how it influenced the rest of it, even though she's moved on. "I've concluded that chapter in my life. Unlike some people who've had a fifty-year career in this industry and have repeated their story time and time again at conventions and in fanzines and interviews, I haven't done that. Once I went on to another line of work, I didn't look back.

"But I was very into their stories, absolutely. I mean, how could you not be? Let me put it to you this way. Just a few years ago, when I was still working and I was with some IT guys and they were saying something about 'this is so much responsibility,' I just looked at one of them sagely and said, 'With great power comes great responsibility.'"

"We have seen a significant shift that happened in the industry— I'm talking from the children's perspective—when we had diverse books launched," said Preeti Chhibber. "It pulled the conversation that happened behind closed doors into the mainstream. I worked in publishing for a little over a decade, and I went from sitting in a room where someone would be like, "We cannot put a Black person on the cover of this book"—out loud, in front of people, like it was a totally okay thing to say—to now, where you look at the *New York Times* bestseller list, and it is a majority of people of color on that list. There was a significant shift that happened, and it bled over into every aspect of entertainment, period. And some industries are slower than others, but the conversation is happening on multiple levels."

MARVEL IS WHERE POPULAR CULTURE SO OFTEN FINDS OUR PARABLES AND OUR LESSONS. MARVEL IS AT THE FOREFRONT OF TEACHING OUR YOUNG PEOPLE HOW TO BE.

———

Said Sam Maggs, "Just because I'm advocating for *Captain Marvel* does not mean I'm advocating to get rid of *Captain America*. It means that there is room for both of those stories to be told, as well as *Black Panther*, as well as *Silk*, as well as all these other stories that we haven't had the opportunity to read or watch or play before because of the people who are allowed to tell their story. For me, as a consumer, I have seen every iteration of white man with a light dusting of stubble get superpowers that maybe there is to be told. And you know what? I loved all of them. They were all so great and so much fun. But I think the reason that people get excited about a movie like *Black Panther* or *Wonder Woman* is that's a new story from a new perspective that we have not seen before."

"I have been playing empowered, strong women on-screen for sixteen years, and I have been living as empowered and strong as I possibly can," said Evangeline Lilly, the actor who portrays Hope Van Dyne, aka the Wasp, in the *Avengers* and *Ant-Man* films. "That's always been a huge part of who I was. And now I think there's room for those stories. I want to tell those stories where compromise and sacrifice is heroic. There's another side to this female story that has not been told that we're now starting to tell.

"I have two sons and I get really excited when I watch how, when they see an empowered, really incredible woman on-screen, they don't blink an eye. They're not like, 'Oh, wow, girls can do that?' They're like, 'I want to be her.' There's no sort of distinction of 'I can't because I'm a guy.' It's more 'She's really cool, so why wouldn't I want to be her?'"

IF I CAN DO THIS, THEN OTHER GIRLS WILL LOOK AT ME AND GO, OH, THIS IS SOMETHING THAT GIRLS DO.

———

Game designer Paige Pettoruto had a similar reaction when we asked them about what it took to make that choice. "Growing up, I never loved being in women-centric spaces; I felt like an impostor in those spaces. I felt like an outsider. So anything that was, like, a program for women in computer science or women who liked games, it really irked me. I just didn't want to be involved. I just want to be me. I wanted to be good at what I did for my own merits, not because I was a member of a particular gender class.

"As I got older, my thinking changed on this a bit. I still don't feel super comfortable in an all-female space; I don't feel like I'm a woman a lot of the time. But I realized that, from my perspective, it was important to expand people's understanding of gender representation and to be counted among women, just if only to normalize the diversity of what women are and who women are."

"I knew there weren't many women in the industry, but I loved Wendy Pini and *Elfquest*," said Amanda Conner, one of the most well-known women working in comics today, and one of the most generous with her time and enthusiasm. "Plus [artist] Jan Duursema had graduated from the Kubert School, and I saw she was working and living the life. I knew I could do this! And when I started working, I wasn't discouraged at all, as most people, men, were friendly and supportive. I knew I had a shot, and I thought, 'If I can do this, then other girls will look at me and go, oh, this is something that girls do.' Now there are so many more women in the comic book industry than there were when I first started. It's great. It was what I was hoping would eventually happen, and it finally did. 'Yes, it works!'"

"I think we have to understand as the core, the ground level in this particular fight, while there have always been women in comics, there's a certain acceptance of certain roles and areas," said Alitha E. Martinez. "And they've been invisible. That's the other part of it. And that's why they seem like they weren't there before."

"I think looking at the women and queer people I know in comics now that are kicking ass, everyone from people at Marvel like Annalise Bissa, who I think is genius, and Sarah Brunstad and Lauren Amaro and all of the amazing women editors I work with," said Tini Howard. "And then people outside of Marvel, people like Spike Chapman and Shelly Bond, who've been around forever, and people that are creating their own publishing empires. And then women like Raina Telgemeier, who blows away any book I've ever written in numbers. . . .

"I think in ten years, we're going to be the ones running [things]. I frankly, really do."

"We really have to help each other out," said Trinh Tran. "Push for more doors to be open. There are so many smart women, and all they need is just one little door to be open for them. The writer currently on set with me today is one of the junior ones from the writers' room. But you see potential in a lot of these great women, who have great perspectives, and a point of view that is so important to make a difference in these types of movies and shows. They just don't otherwise have the opportunity."

"As a general policy, I never turn down a job without also suggesting at least three more artists that they could reach out to," said artist Jen Bartel. "It takes a little bit of extra time, but I've found that a lot of the time, if I suggest just two or three people, oftentimes those art directors or editors will either reach out to them for a future project or might even actually consider them as a replacement for the project that I had to pass on. I think it takes a certain amount of conscious effort to get through a door and not let it shut behind you."

Or, as Cate Shortland puts it in her straightforward way, "We all have to carve out more space for the generations coming up. And that's not just women. That's people of color, gay and lesbian, transgender people. It's just too long. I think everyone's exhausted by the act that we all have to put on, and that we're playing by these rules that we don't believe in. And it's about time it shifts, because we don't want the next generation coming up and having to deal with stuff that's really a waste of time, and it's a waste of energy."

Tini calls back to the creators of the first wave of mass-produced super hero comics, Marvel's founders, who did it for the same reason we're all still doing it today, to be seen and heard. "Comics have always been a weird haven for the Other. From the very first Jewish kids writing super heroes to nerds growing up, to when comics shops were havens for nerds to now, because comics have such a low barrier to creation, they're kind of a hotbed of new and exciting things."

"I remember one of the first people who we met when we were doing research [for *Captain Marvel*] was literally the first female fighter pilot in the air force," says director Anna Boden. "General Jeannie Leavitt. And this was in 1993. It was really eye-opening to me, as that really wasn't that long ago. I believe so much of why Captain Marvel, and that part of her history, is so powerful is because it is such the epitome of a space where it's challenging to be a woman and to really allow yourself to *be* yourself without hiding behind that armor."

"You know, when I went to the Society of Illustrators, I found out I was the first woman of color to draw for Marvel flagship titles, for both Marvel and DC," said Alitha. "That's a sad commentary on this industry. I'm not that old. And I just want to work and be respected as an artist one day, not be labeled as a Black artist, Hispanic artist, Latinx artist."

"I think about resilience," said Nic Stone. "I think about the resilience required to live in a space like this one, where you are fully aware that when you walk around on the street, there are definitely people who are looking at you and thinking that you are inferior simply because of the body that you exist in.

"I didn't realize how internally oppressed I was. How I had internalized so much oppression that I didn't even recognize my own power. Of course you're powerful, because look at what your people have been through. Of course there are super heroes who look like you. There has to be. Because it wouldn't make sense for there not to be."

"We're the first ones that they're starting to go, 'We're here to fight,'" said Alitha. "We're making the *war*. So the ones that come after us can create. They'll be the creatives. They'll be the ones who can express themselves and do all of this."

"The most important thing to me is that I am creating reflections," said Nic. "I'm creating people in these stories. I'm getting to tell these stories, and I'm getting to expand on kind of canonical comic stuff for the sake of

BECAUSE COMICS HAVE SUCH A LOW BARRIER TO CREATION, THEY'RE KIND OF A HOTBED OF NEW AND EXCITING THINGS.

the reader who looks like the character, not for the people out there . . . and coming to realize that empowerment is the way, and empowerment in numbers. Empowerment on a large scale, empowering people who look like me on a large scale, that's the way that we actually make progress.

"And making sure, instead of latching on to the idea that there's only one space at the table for somebody who looks like me—no, I'm going to create more spaces."

"I'M ONE of the few since the beginning, just to sort of see the journey," said Marvel Studios executive producer Trinh Tran. "How our Marvel family has grown. It's amazing that we're about to do what we do today, tell these stories. Inspire little kids. Give a perspective that hasn't been there as much in the past. To be able to be involved in that process. I just get super giddy knowing that there are little kids watching and hopefully being impacted by the story we are telling . . . that anyone can be a super hero."

"I think about that line in *Captain Marvel* by Kelly Sue [DeConnick]," said former *Ms. Marvel* writer Samira Ahmed. "'Have you ever seen a little girl run so fast she falls down? In that one moment, every little girl flies.' That, to me, really embodies so much of the women of Marvel, because it's been a bumpy road."

She pauses, and smiles. "But we are making those characters fly."

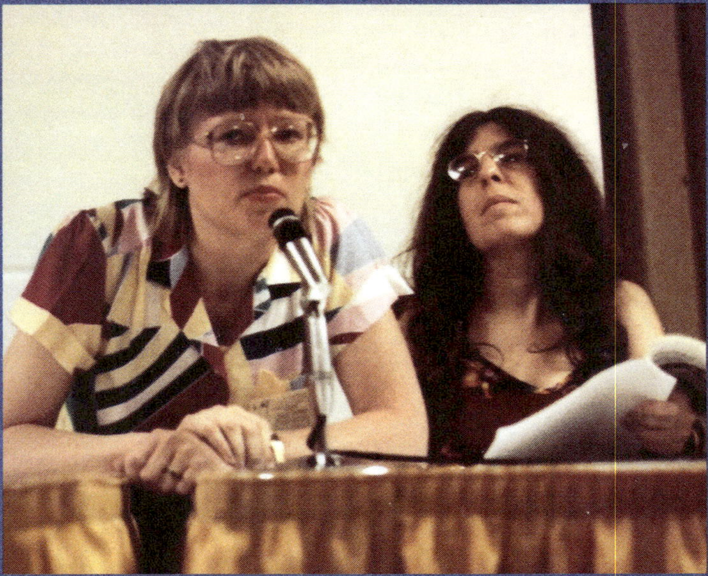

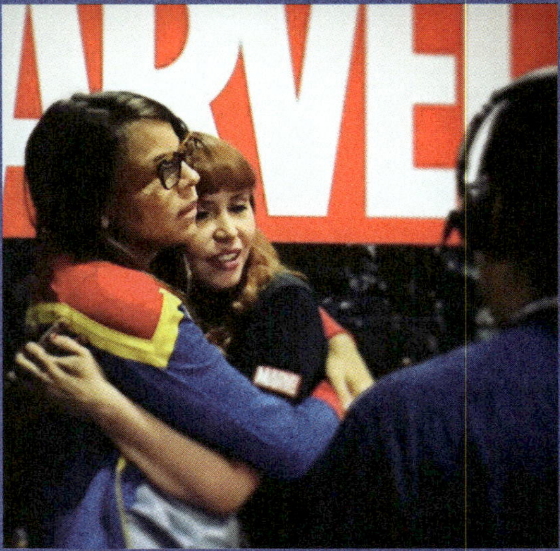

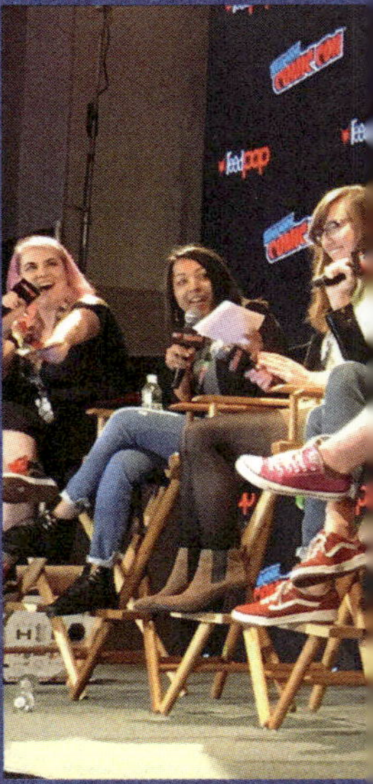

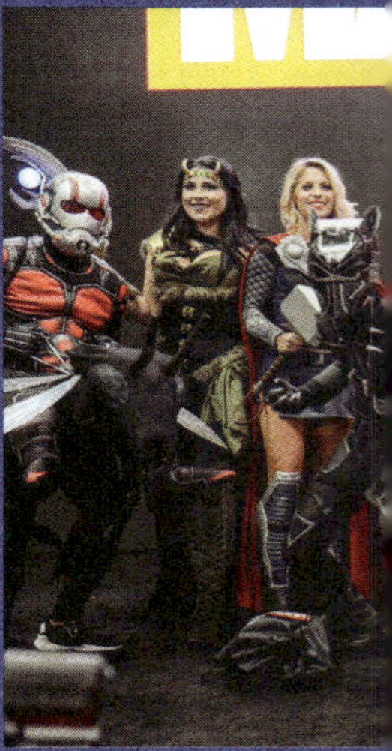

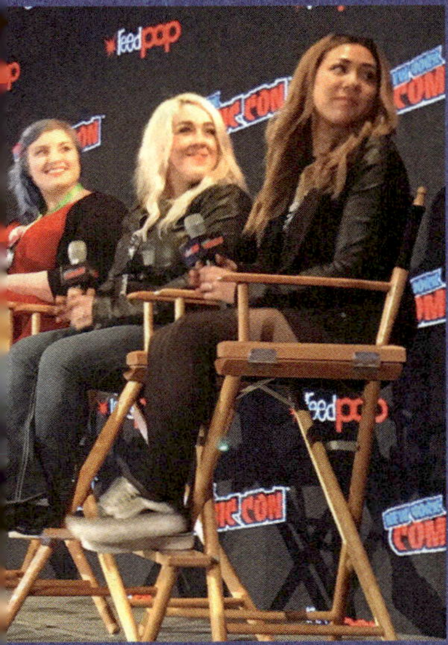
feedpop

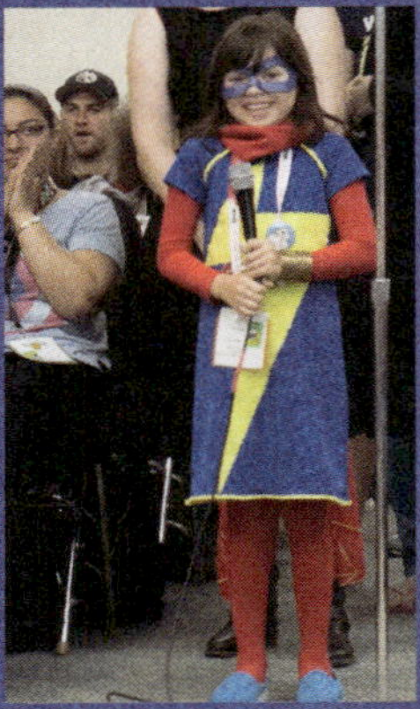

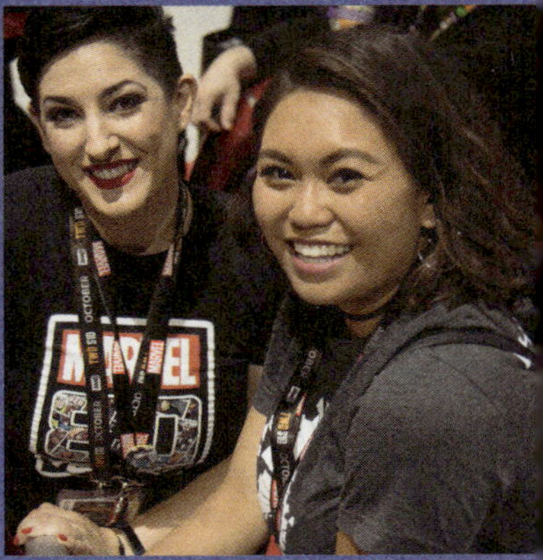

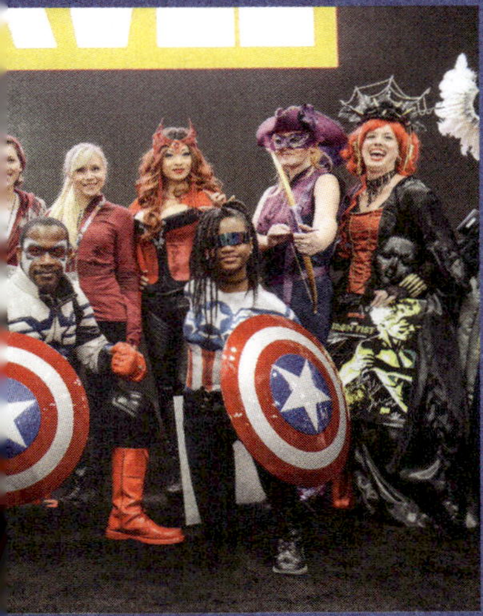

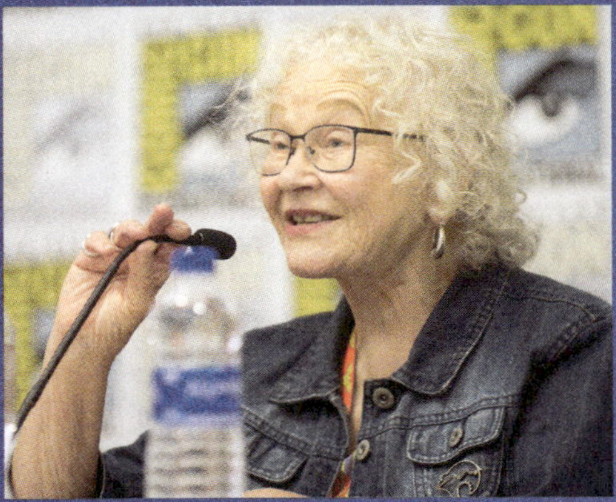

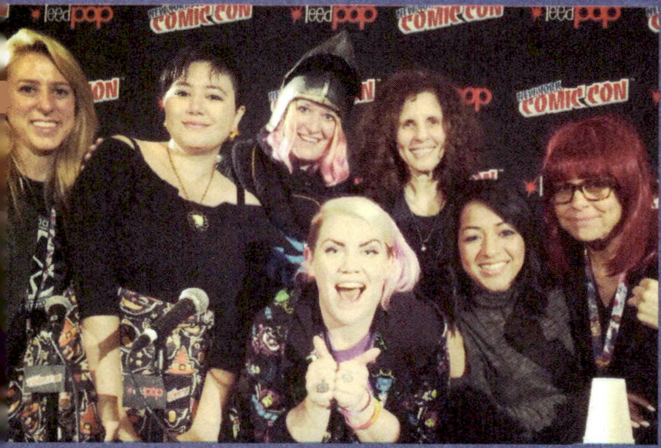
COMIC CON
feedpop
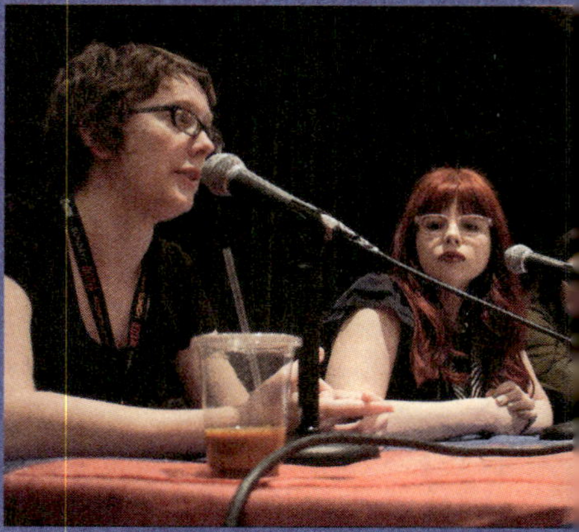
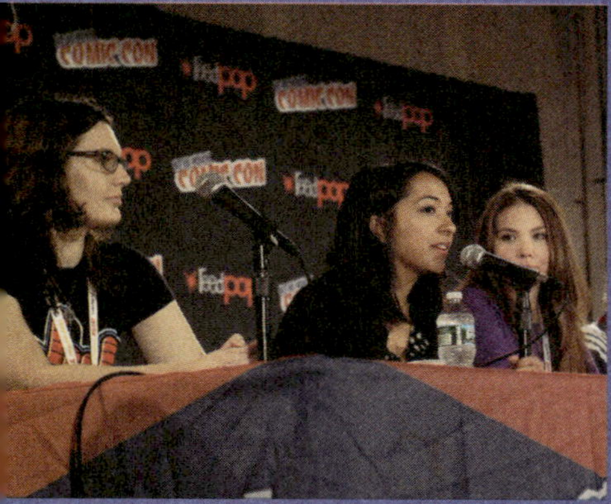
COMIC CON
feedpop
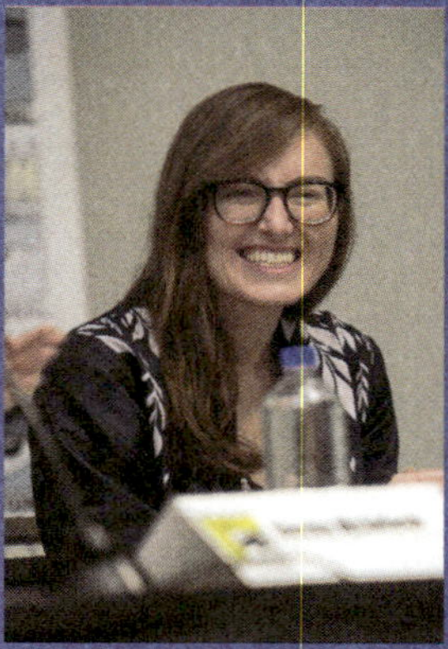
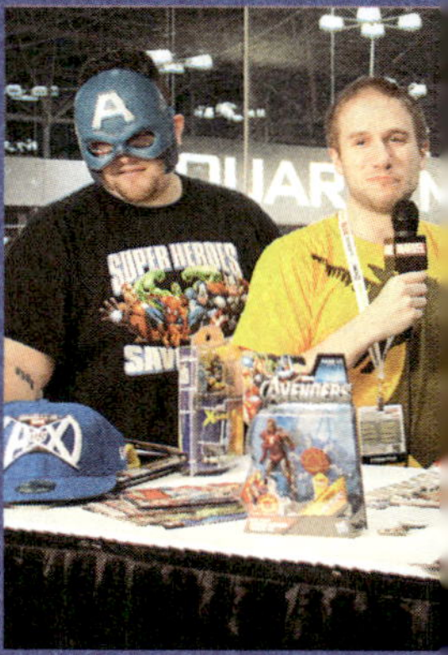
SUPER HEROES
AVENGERS
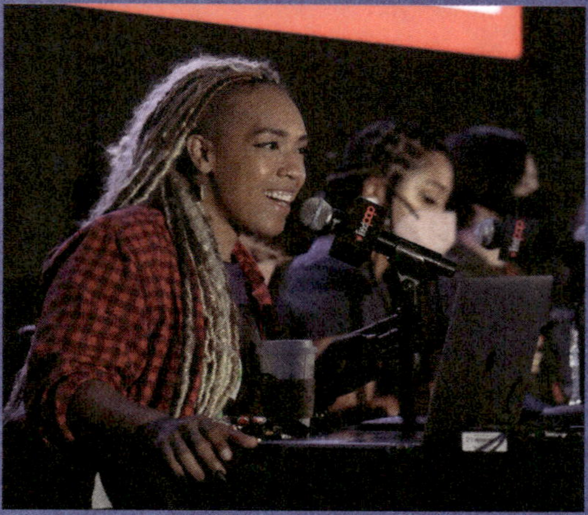
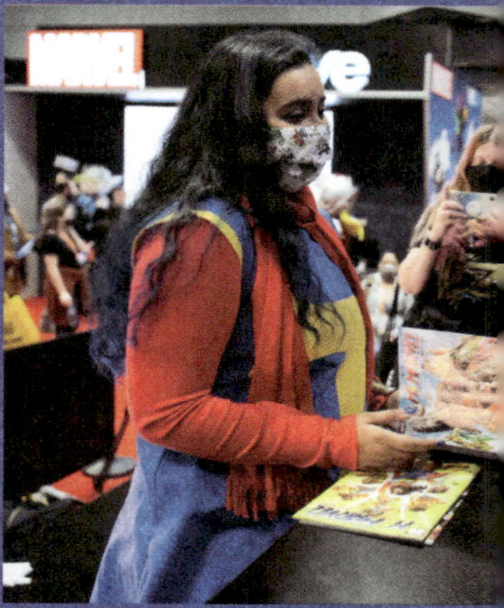
MARVEL

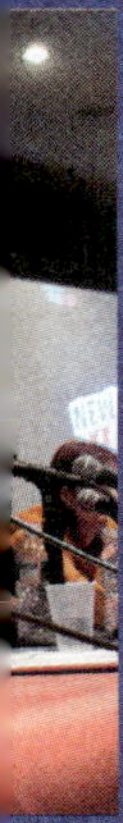

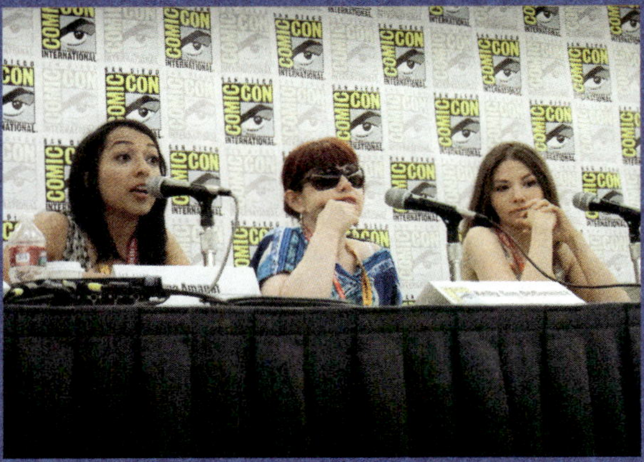
COMIC CON INTERNATIONAL

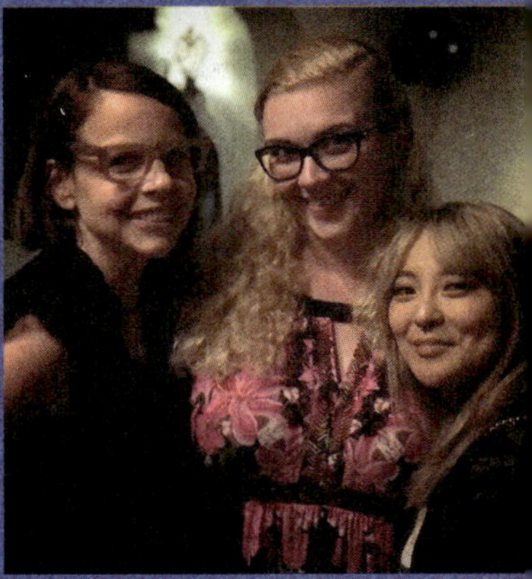

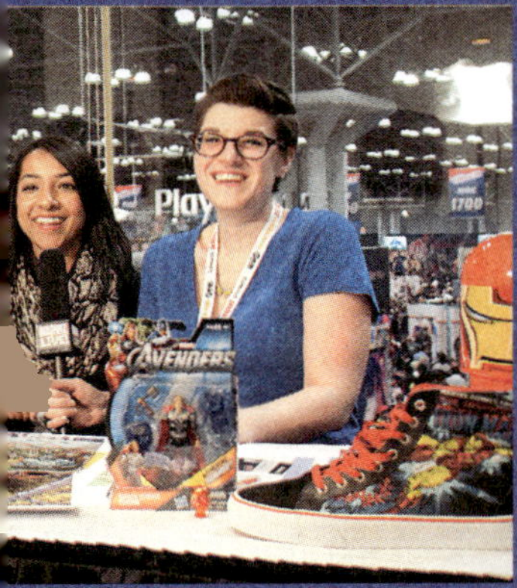
AVENGERS

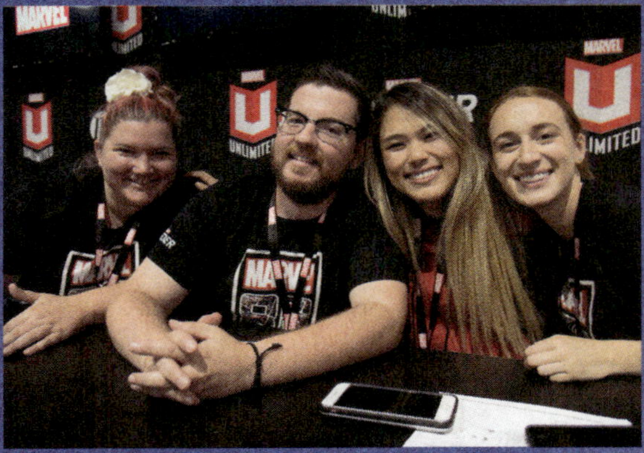
MARVEL
UNLIMITED

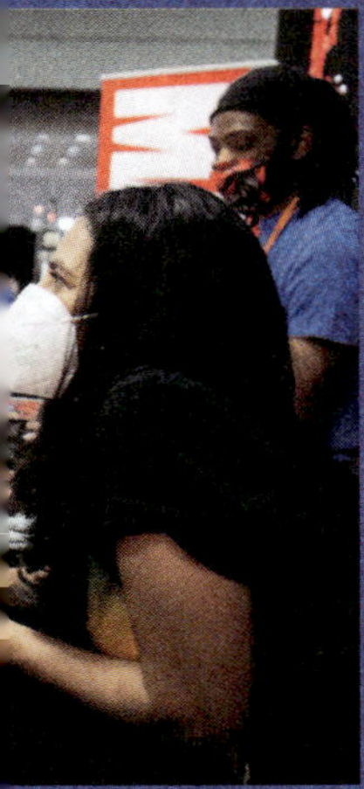

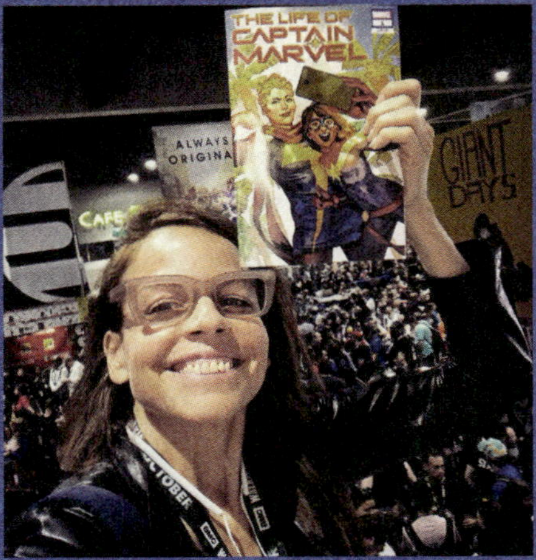
THE LIFE OF CAPTAIN MARVEL
GIANT DAYS

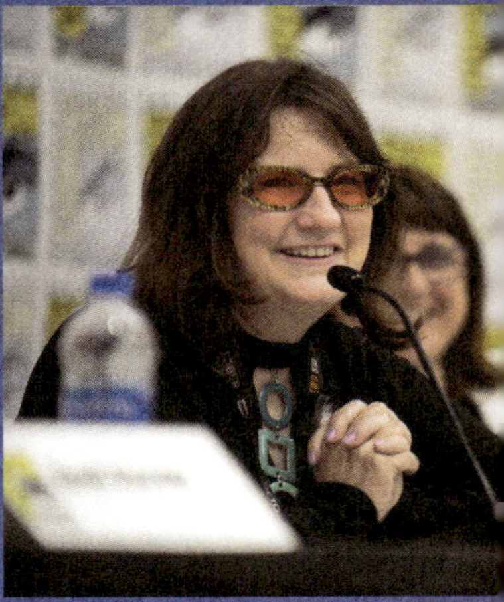

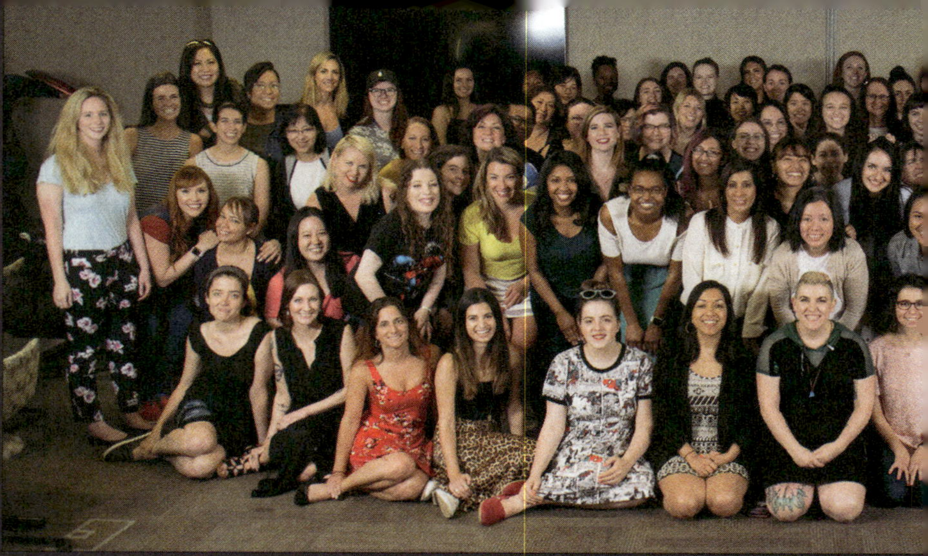

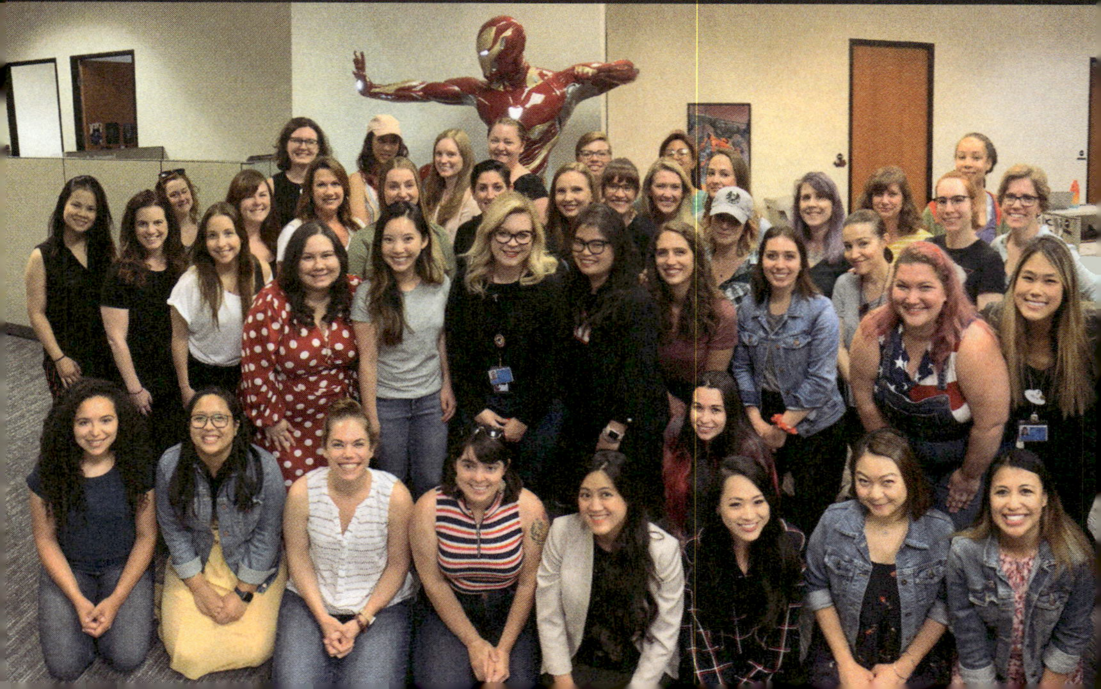

The women of all three Marvel offices, on the tenth anniversary of the *Women of Marvel* podcast. COUNTERCLOCKWISE: New York City; Glendale, Los Angeles; Prospect Studios, Los Angeles.

EPILOGUE

THIS BOOK is, at its heart, the story of a career that is hard to have but, for the women we spoke to, harder not to have, arguably not unlike getting bitten by a radioactive spider. The same industry that can launch a female hero–led blockbuster movie that made $1.28 billion worldwide also depends on local comics shops, where women are routinely asked if they are looking for something for their boyfriend. Many of our conversations centered on the conflicted experience of loving so deeply a career and an industry that felt, at times, like it could not love you back.

But however it felt, they were there, and we still are. And the comics industry, including Marvel, was and is a different place because of it.

Because the most successful super hero comics franchise of all time has been built not just by eighty years of high-profile men but also by eighty years of low-to-no-profile women, who crawled in the windows of the House of Ideas when they did not see an open front door. These "heifers in the Bullpen" are, to us, the very best of heroes, the sort whose hero's journey is the journey to being able to see yourself as a hero at all. For female characters in comics, that journey has been the journey from side character to protagonist. For female creators in comics, the journey has been the journey from uncredited or noncreative work to seeing female names on front covers.

Journeys change, which is, of course, what makes them journeys. There is progress. There are setbacks. Either way, for women in comics, it's a struggle and a journey toward visibility. We want to be seen for who we are and what we do. If you're reading this, we suspect you might understand that feeling, too.

Knowing that a journey is hard can also sometimes be freeing. For many of our female contributors, knowing they could never truly "fit in" was both a problem, and a power. Not being able to expect mainstream acceptance excused them from feeling like they needed to achieve it. Regardless, working in comics became, for most women of Marvel, an identity more than a job.

That's the story we wanted to capture here, while we could. As we said from page one, we undertook this project to help make visible a group of women whose role in the history of comics has largely gone unseen. To that end, over the course of writing and compiling this book, we've spoken to hundreds of women, for hundreds of hours, over many months or, in some cases, years. Some no longer work at the company; others are no longer with us at all. While every conversation taught us something remarkable, for every voice that made it into this project, there are many others that did not. Near the end of our drafting process, we had no choice but to narrow our focus to the women of Marvel *comics* in particular.

This decision meant that many excellent conversations did not make it into these pages, including the memorable hours we spent with Jason Aaron, Victoria Alonso, Charlie Jane Anders, Amanda Avila, Natacha Bustos, Nia DaCosta, Mary Demarle, Colleen Doran, Gerry Duggan, Sarah Finn, Laura Hathaway, Karen Green, Juliette Eisner, Isabel Hsu, Gillian Jacobs, Callie Jenkins, Scarlett Johansson, Mary Kenney, Vanessa Marshall, Laura Martin, Nicole Martinez, Christine Thompson, Bryanna Lindsey, Ryan North, Teyonah Parris, Jess Reed, Kristina Rogers, Bill Rosemann, Muntsa Vicente, Chloé Zhao, and Guoying Zhao.

This project would not be the same without them.

ACKNOWLEDGMENTS

IT TRULY TOOK A VILLAGE TO CREATE THIS BOOK.

Thanks to Sana Amanat at Marvel for conceiving of the project and of our doing it. Thanks to our team at Gernert Company: Margaret's longtime agent and friend Sarah Burnes, as well as Jonathan Lyons and Sophie Pugh-Sellers. Thanks as well to our team at Simon & Schuster: editors Ed Schlesinger and Kimberly Laws; Caroline Pallotta, Jamie Selzer, and Jaime Putorti for keeping us on track; Emma Van Deun for the beautiful cover; Jennifer Bergstrom and Aimée Bell for seeing the value in this; and Lucy Nalen, Sydney Morris, and Fallon McKnight. And to our interior designer, Laura Palese, who brought this book to life and made it real.

And to the Marvel crew: Sven Larsen, Jeremy West, Jeff Youngquist, Brian Overton, David Gabriel, C. B. Cebulski, and our champion Sarah Singer—this is important work, and having you there was extremely meaningful to us both as authors of this book and as women who worked at Marvel.

Thank you for the countless people who not only agreed to speak with us, but to those who dug through old memories for photos, memorabilia, and proof that they were there, and for sharing those things with us. To the crew who painstakingly transcribed literally hundreds of hours of recorded Zoom calls, phone calls, and interviews: Sophia Lee, Dani Lyle, and Sam Roach. Thank you to Lewis Peterson for the transcription software assist.

Jeanine Schaefer: I would like to thank my mother, Janet, for instilling in me from an early age a love of art and literature, for teaching me the value of creation, and for introducing me to the joy of fandom with yearly all-night *Star Trek* marathons; I thank my husband, Mark, for the endless late-night editing sessions followed by endless cups of perfect coffee; Kristin Baker, Shana Naomi Krochmal, and Jessica Maxwell, my found fandom family two decades strong, for always having my back; and my children, Margot and Henry, for sharing the way they look at the world with pure enthusiasm, boundless creativity, and unapologetic silliness.

I thank the women whose names don't fit under the Marvel umbrella but who changed not only the face of the industry but my life in it: Angela Rufino, Joan Hilty, Liz Marsham, Jann Jones, Rachel Gluckstern, Christine

Napolitano, Alison Gill, Sierra Hahn, Dafna Pleban, Shannon Watters, Sophie Philips-Roberts, Kate Henning, and Maggie Howell. There were many more, and I'm so grateful to them. To Sana, Stephen Wacker, Nick Lowe, and my entire Marvel family: there aren't enough words. You are in my heart always.

And last but not least, to my cohorts, Margie and Judy. Thank you, Margie, for trusting me with something so important and for helping me see my own strength. I would not have traded any of this for anything, not a single second.

Judith Stephens: I would like to thank my mother, Carol, for being an inspiration, as a woman in STEM (decades before that was even a term), to believe that I belonged in the room, too. Thank you to my namesake, Aunt Jub, who taught me there was a world outside Michigan, a place for me in the big city with loving friends, and to my father for driving me to every sports event, photo class, and even the Big Apple.

To the many, many faces who crossed my path at Marvel, who pushed me to be more, and who shared a drink or two after a long week. Plus to the incredible community of friends, many thanks to cosplay, who have been there throughout all the years and many more to come.

Margaret Stohl: I would like to thank Eric Konigsberg for his sage editorial expertise, and Marilyn and Harvey Konigsberg for sheltering and feeding me in the final writing days. I also thank my children, Emma, Havi, and May Peterson: May for getting her PhD in medieval art history and, along the way, reframing our approach to the invisible work of women. More thanks to David, Sara, Jake, Charlie, John, Burton, and Marilyn Stohl, along with Frankie Smith, Alex Kamenetzky, Eunice Lee, Susanna Hoffs, Raphael Simon, and Melissa de la Cruz for listening to the stories of this project for five years (talk about heroic!).

This book was a true labor of love and dedication to an industry that may not have always loved us back, but in which we've found best friends, partners, soulmates, and ourselves. Thank you to everyone who believes that comics should and can do right by the next generation. Thank you for never giving up the fight.

The story continues.

PHOTO AND ART CREDITS

Adri Cowan: 245 (top)
Alan Light: III, 250 (top)
Allison Baker: 117
Amanda Conner: 232
Ann Foley: 261
Annie Nocenti: 58, 64 (upper left)
Barbara Slate: 158
Bill Nation: 109 (bottom)
Bobbie Chase: 115
Christine Dinh: 210, 242 (top)
Colleen Doran: 278
Damon Jones: 352
Dawn Guzzo: 63 (top)
Dewey Cassell: 27, 28–29
Eliot R. Brown: XIXI, 32, 38, 53, 62 (bottom), 63 (bottom), 65
Emily Newcomen: 356
Gerry Duggan: 318, 323
Heather Antonelli: I
Jackie Estrada: 237
Jason Laboy: 292
Jen Grünwald: 176, 197, 198–199, 266
Jenny Lee: 165
JaxonPhotogroup: 153 (bottom)
Judith Stephens: 154–155, 245 (bottom), 262, 276 (top), 312, 326 (top), 368
June Brigman: 71, 72
Larry Hama: 49
Larry Houston: 109 (top)
Lauren Amaro: 201 (bottom)

Lauren Sankovitch: 190
Linda Fite: 24
Louise Simonson: 66, 75
Leigh A. Willis: 258–259
Margaret Stohl: 366, 369
Marguerite Bennett: 226 (left)
Marvel: 150, 187, 206, 209, 216, 241, 252, 255 (top), 271, 272, 276 (bottom), 326 (bottom), 347 (left), 366–367, 368–369, 370–371
Marvel Studios: 144, 153 (top), 167 (bottom), 332
Mary Wilshire: 44, 250 (bottom), 366
Maurene Goo: 346 (right)
Megan Bradner: 286
Michel Maillot: 220
Nicole Ciaramella: 133 (bottom), 341
Paige Pettoruto: 226 (right)
Pat Scanlon: 64 (bottom left)
Patrick Sun: 256
Preeti Chhibber: 242 (bottom right)
Sam Maggs: 181
Sana Amanat: 202, 337
Stephanie Graziano: 91
Stephanie Maslansky: 229
Trina Robbins: 2, 7, 8–9, 11, 19, 34, 43, 62 (top)
Van Eaton Galleries: 94–95, 96, 108

ABOUT THE AUTHORS

MARGARET STOHL is a #1 *New York Times*, USA Today, and internationally bestselling novelist, comics writer, and game writer. Best known for the Beautiful Creatures novels, Margaret has published fifteen novels in fifty countries and thirty-five languages; her books have sold more than ten million copies worldwide. For Marvel, she has written the *Black Widow: Forever Red* and *Black Widow: Red Vengeance* prose novels, as well as the *Mighty Captain Marvel* ongoing comic, *The Life of Captain Marvel*, and the *Spider-Man Noir* miniseries.

JEANINE SCHAEFER has been an editor, project manager, and world-builder for more than twenty years, at publishers and studios including Marvel, DC, BOOM! Studios, Riot Games, and Stone Kite, shepherding numerous dream projects, from *Buffy the Vampire Slayer* to *X-Men*. She lives in Los Angeles with her husband and two children.

JUDITH STEPHENS is a producer and author with ever-changing rainbow-colored hair. During her more than fifteen years at Marvel, she was at the forefront of production of video, audio, and photos for Marvel.com and Marvel's social media. She co-created the *Women of Marvel* podcast and is the author of the book *Cosplay the Marvel Way*. She lives in Queens, New York, with her two cats.